Robin Haines's books include *Charles Trevelyan and the Great Irish Famine* (2004), *Bound for South Australia: Births and deaths on government-assisted immigrant ships 1848–1885* (2004), and *Emigration and the Labouring Poor: Australian recruitment in Britain and Ireland 1831–1860* (1997).

For John

Robin Haines

Life and Death
in the
Age of Sail

The passage to Australia

NATIONAL
MARITIME
MUSEUM

First published in the UK in 2006 by the National Maritime
Museum, Greenwich, London, SE10 9NF
www.nmm.ac.uk/publishing

ISBN 0 948065 70 2

© Robin Haines 2003
First published by UNSW Press in 2003

1 2 3 4 5 6 7 8 9

A CIP catalogue record for this book is available
from the British Library.

Design Di Quick
Cover JC Dollman, 1851–1934, Great Britain, *The immigrants'
ship*, 1884, London, oil on canvas, 111.0 x 162.5 cm. Art
Gallery of South Australia, Adelaide. Transferred from the office
of the Agent-General of South Australia, London 1979.
Printer Everbest Printing, China

Contents

Acknowledgments

My primary debt is to the Australian Research Council, whose generous support, via a Research Fellowship at Flinders University and a large grant, enabled the research that made the writing of this book possible. One individual whom I wish to single out for special acknowledgment is my co-author of many articles on maritime mortality and other migration topics, Ralph Shlomowitz. Supported by ARC grants during the past 13 years, we have enjoyed a rewarding research partnership, while simultaneously pursuing interests in other fields. To him I am deeply grateful for his encouragement, his extraordinary numeracy and his warm and continuing friendship. I am indebted, too, to Eric Richards — who convenes, as it were, an unofficial migration studies centre at Flinders University — for his collegiality and intellectual stimulation over many years. I thank Eva Åker for excellent computer analysis over the past five years. To Greg Slattery, Judith Jeffery and Margrette Kleinig I am indebted for outstanding research assistance. I am also grateful to Nada Lucia for reasons too numerous to mention. I wish also to acknowledge the librarians at Flinders University, and especially the document delivery service. I also thank Phillipa McGuinness and Angela Handley of UNSW Press, my copyeditor Stephen Roche, and my indexer Barry Howarth.

Charlotte Erickson — the doyen and pioneer of migration studies, has been a constant source of encouragement and inspiration over many years, and I thank her sincerely for her continuing enthusiasm. Likewise, I am grateful to Anne Crowther at the University of Glasgow and Joanna Bourke at Birkbeck College. Also in the United Kingdom I extend, as always, sincere thanks to Deirdre Toomey and Warwick Gould for expert advice. I am grateful to the Cambridge Group for the Study of Population, Economy, and Society in Past Time, whose response to a paper upon which this book is based encouraged me to think laterally. I would especially like to thank members of the group, Simon Szreter, Eilidh Garrett and Alice Reid, for responses to various papers. Similarly, in the United States, my thanks go to Stephen Kunitz at the University of Rochester. I thank the Wellcome Trust for the History of Medicine in London, for hosting a summer spent working on draft chapters there. I also pay tribute to David Fitzpatrick, of Trinity College, Dublin who, over many years, has earned my profound respect for his incomparable analysis of emigrant letters, and for much more.

I also extend thanks to Barry Smith at the Australian National University for his comments and challenges over many years, and likewise to Deborah Oxley at the University of New South Wales. I wish also to acknowledge the assistance of the custodians of the original diaries, memoirs, letters and official papers explored in this book — the librarians, curators and archivists at the following libraries — the Public Record Office, Kew, the Merseyside Maritime Museum, the Cheshire County Record Office, the Trustees of the Ely Museum, State Records (SA), the State Library of South Australia's Mortlock Library of South Australiana, the State Library of Tasmania's Crowther Collection of Tasmaniana, the Archives Office of Tasmania, the Mitchell Library, Sydney, the La Trobe Collection of the State Library of Victoria, the Oxley Library, at the State Library of Queensland.

Individuals who have given me access to original or transcribed correspondence include Andrea Alexander, Joyce Bailey, Elizabeth Britton, Esma Cardinal, Henry Howell, Ruth Moffatt, Kate Shepherd and Pat Tedmanson. I thank them all warmly. Owing to the difficulties of tracing the descendants of correspondents and diarists whose papers have long been housed in various archives, the author would be particularly grateful to hear from any relatives of the writers quoted in the text who believe they are owed individual acknowledgment in a future edition. Meanwhile, I thank, collectively, the families whose representatives, possibly long deceased, lodged their ancestors' papers in archives in the United Kingdom and Australia.

No superlatives will suffice to acknowledge the diarists and letter writers themselves, whose correspondence meant so much to their descendants that they bequeathed them to libraries, where they would endure for generations. By recording their thoughts, actions and observations of the voyage and settlement, their commentaries open a window on the past that mere official recording can never hope to do. To these pioneers, who faced up to four months on the briny ocean and an unknown future, I extend my warmest appreciation. I only hope that I have done them justice.

In spite of my debt to those acknowledged above, I could not have proceeded were it not for the devotion, superb culinary skills, and critical judgment of John Harwood to whom, as always, this book is dedicated.

Further acknowledgments to paperback reprint

I would like to thank the many readers who wrote to me following the publication of this book in 2003. I have been truly warmed by its reception. I particularly thank Christopher Colyer, Ruth Hill and Joy Macdonald, for additional material and insights garnered from their own family archives.

Abbreviations

ADM	Admiralty
AJCP	Australian Joint Copying Project
AOT	Archives Office of Tasmania
BLFES	British Ladies' Female Emigrant Society
BPP	*British Parliamentary Proceedings*
CLEC	Colonial Land and Emigration Commission
CO	Colonial Office
GLCRO	Greater London County Record Office
MLSA	Mortlock Library of South Australiana
NSWPP	*New South Wales Parliamentary Papers*
PRG	Public Record Group (SRSA)
PRO	Public Record Office, Kew
SAGG	*South Australian Government Gazette*
SAPP	*South Australian Parliamentary Papers*
SC	Select Committee
SPCK	Society for the Promotion of Christian Knowledge
SPG	Society for the Propagation of the Gospel
SRSA	State Records (SA)
V&P	*Votes and Proceedings*

Preface

'A t ten minutes past seven in the morning our dear boy breathed his last on my lap. Oh! how can I proceed! My heart is almost ready to burst. Soon after four his body was consigned to the deep about 90 miles from Oporto'.

So wrote Sarah Brunskill, a pioneering emigrant en route to South Australia in 1838, within two years of the colony's formal European settlement. Having described the death of her young son from convulsions and dehydration following a severe attack of diarrhoea, Sarah broke the news to her parents that tragedy had struck again on the same day, when her daughter died from an acute attack of measles just a fortnight into the voyage:

> For her we prayed that she might be saved, but no, God in his good time thought fit to take her also to Himself, about 1/2 past twelve her dear spirit flew to that mansion from which no traveller returns, so you see in less than 24 hours our darlings were both in the bosom of God. Time, the soother of all things, will I hope reconcile us, but to say how we now feel I cannot, away from all our friends, bereaved of our darlings, our cup is indeed full! 'Tis said all is for good, and that I hope we shall find, but the stroke is most severe. What great sin have we committed to be so severely punished? Did we think too much of our darlings to do our duty to our God, or what?[1]

Was this tragic and heart-rending experience of a family travelling in the late 1830s to one of Australia's newest colonies typical of voyages to the Antipodes in the age of sail? How many other couples arrived having buried one or more of their children at sea? How many widows or widowers were left to face the vicissitudes of life as single parents in an alien environment? Did the experience of sea travel change over time? If so, why? These are the central questions with which this book is concerned. Statistical analyses of immigration records concerning government-assisted emigrants — about whom official information was collected assiduously throughout the 19th century — show that for adults the voyage from the United Kingdom to Australia in the 19th century was remarkably successful in terms of health and well-being. By the 1850s, adult mortality on government-assisted emigrant ships bound for Australia had enjoyed a remarkable decline to match death rates in Britain. And the mortality of older children was similar to that of their cousins at home. For infants, however (that is, babies under the age of one year), and children under the age of six, this was an era when the virulent infectious diseases of infancy and childhood — mainly measles, whooping cough, scarlatina and diarrhoea — swept mercilessly through the most vulnerable age groups among populations at sea as on land.

For all age groups, including infants, whose death rates were alarmingly high, their chances of survival on the long ocean voyage to Australia travelling under the auspices of the State, housed in steerage — in the belly of the ship between decks — were, however, far greater than those of their peers who sailed the much shorter, less-regulated, Atlantic crossing to North America. To be sure, some voyages on the Australian run suffered tragedies of monumental proportions. Pathogens such as measles, scarlet fever, smallpox, typhus, typhoid fever or, less often, cholera, picked up at the port of departure, irrupted far from shore — creating epidemic conditions within the contained populations on board. Although catastrophic in terms of wasted human life and dashed dreams, such disasters were rare after the mid-19th century. Yet voyages suffering high mortality, and the surprisingly few ships that ended in shipwreck have, in the past, attracted disproportionate attention, serving to characterise Australia's immigrants in the age of sail as victims of perilous voyages.

Some emigrants did experience a terrifying passage, enduring endless gales on a fully rigged ship with wind shrieking through the canvas while its hull, encasing the emigrants battened below in steerage, was pounded by heavy seas. But many emigrants enjoyed fair weather passages, encountering very little rough weather, never experiencing the terrible din, shuddering and lurching as giant waves washed over the decks and into every crevice. Nevertheless, life at sea, as on land, was appallingly hazardous for infants and toddlers, even on fair-weather voyages.

When listening to the grief-stricken voices of deeply distressed parents, we need to bear in mind that numerous ships carrying large numbers of children suffered no deaths on board, or very few. Yet, while the large statistical picture endows us with a view of gradual and sustained improvement of the conditions and outcomes of the passage, the individual experiences of parents like the Brunskills are a grim and evocative reminder of the tragic costs of emigration for many parents with young children.

This book develops the context for examining health and death in the maritime sphere. It draws upon my previous analyses — and those of my colleagues Ralph Shlomowitz and John McDonald — of the aggregate statistical picture of mortality at sea, and my own analysis of deaths and their causes on ships funded by Australia's colonial legislatures, which are published elsewhere. It explores the testimony of the emigrants themselves, as they voyaged to, and then settled in, the Australian colonies. My focus is upon the working-class emigrants, those who sought and gained a government-assisted passage in the expectation of finding full-time work and a prosperous future for themselves and their children in the Antipodes. With one or two exceptions, this book does not follow the cabin passengers — the well-to-do — who could afford an unassisted fare and whose reminiscences have been well broadcast. My interest here is in the systematic movement of families, travelling in sometimes crowded steerage quarters, emulating, as it were, the conditions of workers in the crowded dwellings and tenements of the United Kingdom's town-dwelling and rural poor.

Privately funded passengers, those better off travellers who sought no government subsidies to fund their passage, were not required to negotiate any bureaucratic turnstiles before embarking on their voyage to Australia. Consequently, they are almost invisible in the official record, unlike those who travelled on passages provided by each of the colonial governments. Those assisted by government from 1831 were scrutinised before departure by authorities in the United Kingdom and, on arrival, by colonial immigration agents. These migrants left in their wake a vast archive of information concerning their ages, occupations, religious persuasion, literacy, origins and family status. During the voyage, they were superintended by officially appointed, fully qualified, medical practitioners — known as surgeon superintendents — who kept formal records on births and deaths, and on the management routines that had been adapted from regimes introduced on convict voyages from 1815. These procedures had proven outstandingly successful for the transportation of Australia's convict workers, who were predominantly single adults. Like those on convict ships, the regulations governing assisted emigrant vessels were designed to lower mortality and to promote the comfort and well-being of families travelling in steerage. So successful were these regimes that private ships carrying fare-paying emigrants in steerage also adopted the regulations voluntarily.

The movement of government-assisted emigrants to Australia in the 19th century has left in its wake more information about the quantifiable characteristics of the United Kingdom's workers over a long period — almost exactly the span of Queen Victoria's reign (1837–1901) — than any other source, allowing us to investigate many aspects of their lives before departure. Victorian enthusiasm for collecting information left both a vast amount of accessible individual-level information in surviving passenger lists, and a great body of manuscript and published reports assembled by emigration authorities on both sides of the world. Although only a handful of surgeons' logs survive, for some colonies we have the surgeon superintendents' reports of the voyage, allowing access to important information, not only on births and deaths, but causes of death, epidemics and the success or otherwise of his supervision of the emigrants. These reports offer unique insights into the management of the public and private hygiene routines on board and draw an evocative picture of the emigrants' health experience. They convey, both individually and collectively, stark images of the rhythms of births and deaths and, significantly, the causes of those deaths along with the names and ages of those, overwhelmingly children, whose bodies were committed to the deep.

Equally important, and rare in terms of historical evidence, are the eyewitness records bequeathed us by the assisted emigrants themselves. Their letters and diaries confirm modern statistical analyses of the remarkable literacy of these working-class migrants. Fortunately for Australian, British and Irish history, many of these letters and diaries have survived, having been donated by descendants to Australia's state libraries. Does their correspondence, though, speak for the majority of emigrants? Do surviving letters represent those handed down by proud descendants mainly because the correspondence reverberates with the optimism and success that so infected its recipients that they followed the senders? Having brought the letters with them as the kernel of their own family archive in a new land, were they entrusted to successive generations as symbols of that hard-won success? Were the more pessimistic or dispirited letters, those sent by people who failed to reap the benefits of the momentous migration, thrown in the dustbin of history by their recipients in the United Kingdom?

These are unanswerable questions. But my reading of hundreds of letters suggests that the epic nature of a momentous three- to four-month journey to the other side of the globe — a far less reversible journey in terms of time and expense than, say, an emigration across the 'Atlantic lake' to North America — seems to have imbued the emigrants with an enduring sense of optimism and determination to build a new life in the colonies. Their stoicism, in the face of the innumerable obstacles that fate and the elements threw at them, mirrored the advice proffered by numerous emigrant handbooks. These guides to colonial emigration (examined in my earlier book, *Emigration and the Labouring Poor*) were packed with information and were designed specifically by empire-minded promoters of emigration to propel the United Kingdom's rural workers to the Antipodes. In Australasia their labour was not only in demand but, according to the promotional arguments, their skills were poised to fuel the development of primary industry essential for colonial and imperial development. In return, argued the pamphleteers, higher antipodean wages were primed to create a thriving proletariat eager to consume British-made goods.

Hence, the movement of their labour from the United Kingdom to Australia — their human capital, as an economist might put it — was worth far more to the British Empire than had they migrated to the United States. There, the products of their labour and their buying power were largely lost to the imperial economy. Judging by the number of times they spontaneously burst into 'Rule Britannia' as they passed other British ships en route to or from Australia, they appear to have been a fairly patriotic lot. They appear to have preferred the longer, and hence potentially more dangerous, voyage to Australasia, even though their contribution (or deposit) towards the assisted passage and their mandatory outfit of clothing cost them as much as a fare to the United States or Canada. They were determined it seems, to make a new life in a far-off British colony to which they were attracted by its climate, its imperial connections and the prospect of full-time work. The promotional guidebooks, tracts, pamphlets and weekly newspapers dedicated to colonial emigration, appear to have been persuasive in this regard. Promoters of colonisation feared that emigrants bound for Britain's westerly colony, Canada, were likely to pursue life across the border in the United States, constituting a loss of valuable imperial manpower. Australia was the colonisationists' favoured destination, and their arguments appear to have been persuasive.

One of my objectives in this book is to explore how and why working-class assisted emigrants bound for Australia co-operated so fully with the emigration authorities that adult mortality rates were, by the 1850s, equal to, or even lower than, rates for the proletariat on land. This was a remarkable achievement, given the vicissitudes of a three- to four-month voyage over several oceans and climate zones, enduring horrendous seasickness in the notoriously rough English Channel and Bay of Biscay, enervating heat in the breathless, becalming tropics, and bitterly cold, stormy, conditions in the southern latitudes.

Simultaneously, the story of the successful containment of disease and death on government-assisted ships offers us clues about how and why the adult mortality revolution occurred in industrialising Britain, although lagging well behind the transition at sea. The question to propel us forward is this: How did maritime populations lead the way in demonstrating that public sanitation and private hygiene were the key elements to lowering mortality, long before medical science, with the exception of smallpox vaccination, could make very much difference to the comfort or longevity of crowded populations?

Before turning to contextual matters in the Introduction and first chapter, a few explanatory notes may benefit readers seeking aids to their own research. The convention followed from the third chapter is to avoid repetitive footnotes by citing the source of the diary, letter or journal the first time that it is mentioned as part of a sequence concerning only the diarist's experience. Whenever the diarist is mentioned out of sequence at a later point in the narrative, however, citation is again given. Hence, readers should be able to identify the source with ease. In some cases, emigrants offered very little information concerning their vessel. To complement their own testimony, I have filled in gaps by turning to tables published annually by the Colonial Land and Emigration Commission for each of the colonies, and appended to their annual reports. Information given for individual ships includes tonnage, dates of departure and arrival, number of days on the voyage, the name of the surgeon superintendent, the number of adult and child emigrants who boarded, by sex, and the deaths of adults and children, by sex, on board. From 1855, aggregate tables were also included of infants who were born and died on the voyage in each year. These reports and appendices can be found systematically produced in sequential volumes of the Irish University Press facsimile editions of *British Parliamentary Papers*, in the 'Emigration' series. Readers searching for particular ships or events should also consult the IUP 'Colonisation' series of *Parliamentary Papers*.

I have also turned to the Immigration Agents' Reports and tabular appendices published in each of the colonies' *Votes and Proceedings*. As well, *Government Gazettes* prove particularly useful. In South Australia, for example, the Immigration Agent's quarterly reports — often discussing individual ships, quarantine and so forth — were regularly published in the *SAGG*. For South Australia, too, the surgeons' summary reports from 1848 are housed in State Records (SA). Ronald Parsons' *Migrant Ships for South Australia 1836–1860* is a particularly useful source on the tonnage, dimension and dates of vessels, as is Ian Nicholson's *Log of Logs*, which covers all destinations. For the 19th century, essential emigrant shipping sources include Basil Lubbock, *The Best of Sail* and *The Colonial Clippers*. For the era of steam, indispensable reference works include TK Fitchett, *The Long Haul*, Stuart Bremer, *Home and Back* and Anthony Cooke, *Emigrant Ships*. I have sought to avoid tedious repetitive footnoting where one or more of these sources have added to the details concerning the specifications of a particular vessel, but full citations are included in the bibliography.

My purpose is to focus on the voyage; I have followed the emigrants' lives after arrival in cases where their narrative offers some insight into their state of health and well-being within weeks or months of disembarkation. Except where a précis was easily accessible, I have not made any attempt to trace their lives before embarkation, or to follow them after initial settlement. Such an attempt would have gone well beyond the brief for this book. The plethora of published family histories to be found in state libraries, however, will provide readers with a collective account of the joys and sorrows of many hundreds of 19th-century settlers.

In so far as the original letters and diaries are concerned, spellings given within quotation marks, or in indented quotations, are as transcribed from the original manuscripts or from archival typescripts. In an effort to communicate the richness of expression, I have deliberately avoided correcting spelling or punctuation. I have glossed only letters where the spelling or expression may be undecipherable to the unpractised eye, by placing the intended word or phrase in square brackets. I have also placed within square brackets connecting words that make better sense where, in the writer's haste, they have been omitted. On two occasions I have provided my transcriptions of letters where the original spelling is so idiosyncratic that the original may prove unfathomable. For such phonetically spelled correspondence, readers might find that reading the letter aloud with, if possible, as close to the regional accent as possible — using the ear as much as the eye — proves a satisfying way of deciphering it. Where emigrants crossed out words or phrases, I have followed the convention of striking through the word or phrase exactly as the writer has done. Asides in round brackets were transcribed exactly as expressed by the writer.

The third chapter begins with the 1820s, and each chapter proceeds, more or less, chronologically. Two chapters are devoted to the high volume decade of the 1850s, arising from both the breadth of experience in those years, and the richness of surviving correspondence. From the 1870s, new sailing ship design, the addition of auxiliary engines and the introduction of steamships travelling via the Suez Canal considerably shortened the time spent at sea, although, surprisingly, the canal route cut only 900 miles from the length of the passage. By then, the faster voyages were so successful that they received less attention from both imperial and colonial authorities. Nor did the experience differ substantially from the 1870s. Hence, I have brought together the observations of emigrants over the remainder of the 19th century into one chapter. During these decades, when steamships sailed through the Suez Canal, they stopped en route to refuel, creating new hazards for emigrants likely to pick up pathogens at several ports. Diaries from a few passages in the 1910s, 1920s and 1940s, conclude the book.

The chronologically structured narrative may help readers to draw conclusions about improvements to the comfort of the voyage within

Routes taken by emigrant ships
from before 1840 to c1960

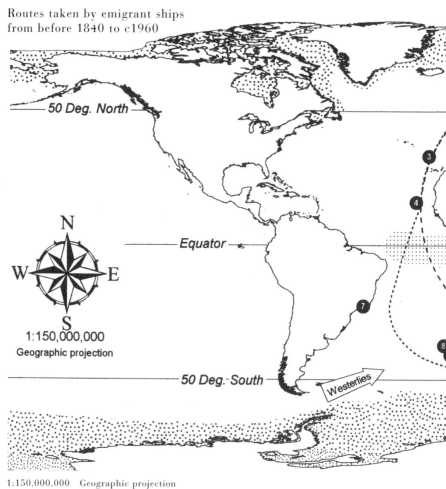

1:150,000,000   Geographic projection

VOYAGES	LOCATIONS		
- - - - Before 1840	1 UK	10 Crozet Is.	20 Townsville
······· c1840-c1900	2 Bay of Biscay	11 Kerguelen Is.	21 Rockhampton
— ·— c1880-c1960	3 Madeira	12 Gibraltar	22 Brisbane
	4 Cape Verde Islands	13 Malta	23 Sydney
	5 St Helena	14 Port Said	24 Melbourne
AREAS	6 Cape Town	15 Aden	25 Adelaide
⠿ The Doldrums	7 Rio de Janerio	16 Colombo	26 Perth
⠿ Pack Ice	8 Tristan da Cunha	17 Batavia (Jakarta)	
⠿ Shelf Ice	9 Gough Is.	18 Thursday Is.	
		19 Cooktown	

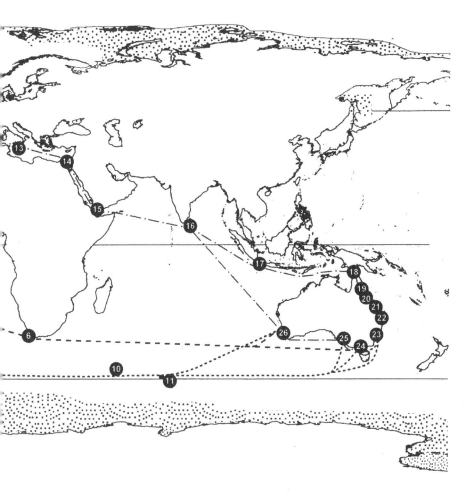

and between each decade. Where voyage letters and diaries describe the first few weeks of settlement, I have included their observations of diet, health and illness on shore as the writers settled into their new routines. This is important if we are to gain any insight into just how far the voyage — and the new, equally harsh environment for people fresh from a European climate — affected the health of settlers as they strove to establish themselves in a colony a world away from home.

Introduction

his book builds upon my earlier work on the mobilisation and voyage experience of Australia's government-assisted immigrants from the United Kingdom.[1] It also extends the work of two pioneering historians of the passage to Australia in the age of sail. Don Charlwood and Helen Woolcock, authors of, respectively, *The Long Farewell* and *Rights of Passage*, have each written about the voyage from the United Kingdom to Australia.[2] Charlwood, in his richly illustrated volume, threw his net wider than Woolcock, whose groundbreaking quantitative analysis focused on government-sponsored voyages to Queensland between 1860 and 1900. Along with an impressive array of sources — most especially the vast statistical resource analysed by Woolcock — they each dipped into the diaries of assisted emigrants and the medical logs of surgeon superintendents, to convey a picture of life at sea.[3]

A number of editors with an interest in genealogy or family history, often descendants of emigrant diarists, have published illustrated transcripts of a particular voyage diary. By no means all, but many, of these enormously interesting editions and scholarly analyses listed in the bibliography are the diaries or letters of the emigrating gentry or middle classes: those able to purchase a fare travelling in the expensive first, second or intermediate cabin accommodation, ministered to on the voyage by servants, and sharing the captain's table.

These editions, of both steerage and cabin passengers, which have found their way on to the shelves in the collections of state libraries and specialist bookshops, have made the experience more accessible for those unable to read this unique manuscript testimony in situ. Other writers have employed Australia-bound voyage diaries as a means of exploring cultural and literary perspectives to theorise about the ways in which diarists made sense of the challenging situation in which they found themselves at sea as they sailed towards an unknown future.

In this book, my focus is on the practical initiatives and outcomes in terms of health and mortality, of government-assisted emigrants travelling in steerage as revealed by both official documentation and the testimony of these shrewd eyewitness recorders of the process. But how representative of their fellow travellers was the evidence of these highly subsidised, yet eager observers of the passage? Did their voices typify those of the nearly 1.5 million immigrants from the United Kingdom who disembarked on an Australian shore in the 19th century? We can partially answer these questions by considering the representation of government-assisted immigrants among the numbers who arrived.

From 1831, under the auspices of various Colonial Office agencies including, most importantly, the Colonial Land and Emigration Commission between 1840 and 1878 — which acted in association with the individual colonies' Agents General from the 1860s — Australia's government-sponsored immigrants travelled on vessels chartered and financed by each of the colonial legislatures from funds collected from the sale of land. As a result of social engineering on a grand scale, about 740 000 immigrants, around half of all free arrivals from the United Kingdom, were assisted by colonial governments, and many more were privately subsidised by family and friends, and by philanthropic organisations.

During most decades of the 19th century, the legislatures of the major colonies, excepting Victoria, assisted well over half of their total arrivals from the United Kingdom. However, Victoria, which attracted a disproportionate number of gold-seeking private fare-paying travellers from the early 1850s — nearly triple the number of fare-payers arriving in any other colony — distorts the overall picture. Although, numerically speaking, Victoria received the third highest number of assisted emigrants from the United Kingdom following Queensland and New South Wales, these subsidised arrivals represented only 23 per cent of all British and Irish immigrants landing in Melbourne. About 88 per cent of all passengers disembarking after 1860 in the new colony of Queensland were funded by its legislature until 1900.[4] The vast majority of those who arrived at Australian ports bearing tickets paid for privately, on private ships, also travelled in steerage or its later equivalent, third-class accommodation.

We can see then, that although government-assisted immigrants represented, nationally, about one half of all arrivals from the United Kingdom, they represented a vastly higher proportion in all colonies but Victoria. They can be said therefore, to be representative of Australia's working-class settlers. The extent to which they spoke for their fellow passengers is unknowable, given the serendipitous nature of the survival of personal testimony. Still, as will become evident, their letters and diaries, which are a casual sample of many hundred that survive in archives in Australia and the United Kingdom — and we have no idea how many remain in private hands — are infused with common themes, suggesting that cautious generalisations are possible.

From the mid-19th century, unassisted emigrants travelling in steerage on private ships were governed by similar regulations to those enforced on government-chartered vessels since the 1830s. Owners of British vessels were required by the Passenger Acts to hire the services of a surgeon superintendent to oversee these regulations, an aspect of the voyage to which I have turned my attention in a companion volume soon to be published. It offers a view of the voyage from the surgeons' perspective, placing their role into its official and regulatory context, while examining what went wrong on the few high-mortality voyages of mid-century.[5] Private shippers voluntarily adopted the successful management routines conducted, since 1831, by various Colonial Office agencies charged with the mobilisation of government-assisted emigrants from the first year of subsidised passages. Emigration authorities, in turn, had adopted the successful regimes introduced on convict ships by the Admiralty in 1815, which had been further refined by the 1830s. The first official account to bring attention to the significance of ventilation, fumigation, sanitation, personal cleanliness, hygiene and the dietary on board Australia-bound convict ships was Assistant Colonial Surgeon William Redfern's report to Governor Macquarie on 30 September 1814, in response to the calamitous mortality on three ships recently arrived. His recommendations on the provision of adequately trained, competent surgeons with authority and power to challenge brutal, incompetent or drunken captains, and his suggestions for the immediate implementation of his draft reforms, precipitated the transformation on convict ships that saw the significant downturn in convict mortality from 1815, after which the average monthly death rate on ships carrying mainly adults rapidly declined from 11.3 to 2.4 per thousand, reducing even further to around 1.0 per thousand after the mid-1850s on convict voyages to Western Australia.[6] Similarly, the monthly death rate of adult assisted emigrants bound for Australia declined from an average of 2.4 per thousand between 1838 and 1853, to an average of 1.0 per thousand between 1854 and 1892, matching adult death rates in England.[7]

Owing to the adoption by private shipping companies of the regulatory principles introduced on government-chartered vessels, the on-board routines for fare-paying steerage passengers were similar to those followed by emigrants on government sponsored ships. However, not all private vessels followed the strict rules regarding set meal times, the timing of cleaning routines, and behavioural standards policed by the Emigration Commission. As one fare-paying emigrant travelling in steerage on a private vessel, the *General Hewitt*, remarked in 1852 of his 139-day, 16 000-mile passage to New South Wales,

> … the strict regulations and discipline on board the government emigration vessels is not observed in private passenger ships, and we were free to do just as we liked, so long as general good order was kept.[8]

The major difference between private vessels and those chartered by the Commission was that the reputation of government-operated ships was higher, and regulations governing hygiene and sanitation on board were strictly enforceable. Indeed, owing to the reputation for healthy voyages, and the safety record of ships chartered by the Emigration Commissioners, some private families possessed of abundant capital, including the well-off Clark family sailing on the *Fatima* in 1850, chose to fit out, at their own expense, special cabin accommodation on the upper deck of a government ship for their family's accommodation rather than travel on a private vessel.[9] This well-connected family, related to the promoter of the penny post, Rowland Hill, whose members were acquainted with Dickens and Thackeray, sailed in the company of 223 government-assisted emigrants. Among these steerage emigrants, three children died, while four infants born on board reached Australia with their parents.

It is worth mentioning at the outset that the terms 'emigrant' and 'immigrant' — about which there seems to be some confusion in the historical literature — are used here quite specifically. The first refers to the departure of people from their home shore. The second refers to people arriving at their destination. Hence, in this context, a person departing from the United Kingdom is an emigrant, and the same person arriving in Australia is an immigrant. At all stages of the process they are, of course, migrants. I have also followed the 19th-century convention of referring to steerage passengers as emigrants, whether assisted or not, and of referring to the better off, who occupied cabins in first, second or intermediate class, as passengers. These labels served then, as now, to delineate class differentials, although lower-middle-class emigrants occasionally chose to travel in steerage, rather than spend money on expensive cabin accommodation, thereby reserving enough capital to set themselves up in a style of modest affluence on arrival.

Those readers who wish to know more about the methods used on behalf of Australia's colonial legislatures by British government agencies, and later by colonial Agents General, to promote the colonies and recruit emigrants, may find that my earlier book *Emigration and the Labouring Poor* will provide much of the background material they seek. There they will find discussions of the means used to attract immigrants, including the involvement of various philanthropic bodies as well as the local parish poor law authorities. Also covered are the various bureaucratic pathways and turnstiles negotiated by potential government-assisted emigrants during the first 30 years of systematic emigration. Included are surveys of the extraordinary amount of published material (the equivalent of the modern guide book) designed to assist with decision-making about destination, colonial jobs and prices, and available to even the poorest potential emigrants. Not all of it was extravagant or misleading, as is often thought, confirming that emigrants were often able to make an informed assessment based on the availability of information produced especially for them.

Elsewhere, I have published analyses of the agencies that controlled the system, and systematic listings of the various schemes and regulations governing recruitment for the whole century. Criteria governing the selection of agricultural labourers, country tradesmen and their families, and young single female domestic servants — those eligible to apply for a government-assisted passage — are also covered there. Appendices and tables also provide the numbers arriving each year in each colony, both government-assisted and total immigrants arriving from the United Kingdom for the entire century. Readers who wish to know more about the origins, occupations, literacy, religious persuasion, age and family structure of emigrants arriving before 1861, can consult my *Emigration and the Labouring Poor* and the bibliography. FK Crowley explored similar themes and sources for the period 1860–1900 in a pioneering unpublished thesis written in 1951, and a seminal article published soon after.[10]

I have deliberately limited the use of scholarly apparatus in this book. I have chosen, instead, to direct readers interested in the more analytical complexities of counting deaths, unravelling causes of death, and the comparative analysis of voyage- and land-based mortality, to papers and articles where my methodology and results are described. Here, apart from providing a few illustrative tables, my aim is to distil the major elements useful for understanding the experiences of the emigrants whose voices bring to us the immediacy of their encounter with the system and with life at sea.

This book surveys the ways in which emigrant letters and diaries enhance our understanding of the official management of the voyage. My focus is on the processes and administrative instruments employed by

British and Australian authorities, from 1831, to promote a life-saving and health-enhancing routine on board the long voyage. It builds upon my recent analyses of mortality on slave, convict and emigrant voyages over the 18th and 19th centuries with my co-author, Ralph Shlomowitz. We have explained why a decline in mortality occurred in those spheres and examined the connections between the official methods employed to reduce deaths on those routes. This work, itself, was built upon earlier aggregate analyses by Shlomowitz and McDonald of voyage deaths between 1831 and 1900, which demonstrated that the Australia-bound emigrants — adults, children and infants — suffered far lower mortality rates than their peers travelling the much shorter route across the Atlantic to North America. Full citation can be found in the bibliography.

Analyses of Australia-bound voyages, at the individual level, have been possible only because of the survival of the mandatory reports of the surgeon superintendents who supervised each vessel bound for South Australia between 1848 and 1885. These reports, preserved in State Records (SA), represent an exceptionally rich and unique resource for studying mortality and institutional procedure, and they underpin the commentary below.[11] Surgeons were required to submit official logs of their voyage to colonial authorities on arrival. After scrutiny by emigration officials and the Colonial Secretary's office, logs were forwarded to London for auditing by the Emigration Commission. Surgeons were also required to submit a summary report of their voyage. These were retained in the colony and, in the case of South Australia's reports, were kept together. Each report records details of the vessel, the personnel on board, the name, age, sex and cause of death of each person who died on the voyage, a short commentary on the health and sanitation procedures enforced on board, and any other comments or advice recommended for adoption to preserve the health and comfort of emigrants.

Apart from scrutinising death rates in various age groups, either for particular years or over a period of time, we were able to link a great deal of information about the ships, the surgeons and the emigrants. This linkage also enabled an evaluation of the pattern of deaths over the voyage. Meanwhile, I sought explanations for why many voyages suffered no deaths at all. The majority of ships bound for Australia suffered fewer than six deaths over a three- to four-month period, while high death rates on a few horror voyages plagued by epidemics have skewed the overall picture.

Unfortunately, the surgeons' reports have not survived for ships arriving in Victoria, nor have the reports on vessels arriving in New South Wales been systematically preserved and catalogued. However, once the logs — from which the summary reports were drawn — were processed in the colonies, they were forwarded to London, where Colonial Office clerks compiled registers as they were received at the Commission's office for auditing. Using these Colonial Land and Emigration Commission manuscript registers housed at the Public Record Office, Kew, I have been able to evaluate the individual cause of death linked by name to each ship arriving in Victoria and New South Wales between 1848 and 1869, a period when the data were of high enough quality to enable analysis.[12] As well, the 33 general reports

Table 1

Proportion of emigrants who embarked in the United Kingdom
who died (loss rate) on voyages to New South Wales,
Victoria, South Australia and Queensland,
1848–60 and 1861–69, in percentages

	NSW			VIC			SA			QLD		
	Adults	Children	All	Adults	Children	All	Adults	Children	All	Adults	Children	All
1848–60	0.6	5.2	1.7	0.7	6.2	2.1	0.5	5.5	1.9			
1861–69	0.4	2.0	0.6	0.2	2.7	0.5	0.2	4.3	1.0	0.6	5.4	1.4

NOTES Children include ages 0–13 before 1856, 0–11 thereafter. Higher child mortality on South Australian ships (1861–69) may be related to the higher proportion of children (20 per cent), than New South Wales (15 per cent) and Victoria (13 per cent), leading to a greater number of susceptibles for the transmission of infection. No tables were included for South Australia in CLEC appendices for 1848, therefore South Australian data are inclusive of 1849–60 and 1862–67. No ships were despatched to South Australia by the CLEC in 1861, 1868 or 1869, hence gains made in New South Wales and Victoria in 1868–69 are not reflected in South Australian figures. Queensland-bound ships were included in New South Wales data before 1861, and only 27 ships were despatched to Moreton Bay by the CLEC between 1861 and 1867. Thereafter Queensland's Agent General was responsible for mobilisation and record-keeping. For a complete analysis of his data, 1860–1900, see Woolcock, *Rights of Passage*. So few ships were despatched to Tasmania and Western Australia that they have not been included here. New South Wales data are inclusive of 1861–68; no ships were despatched in 1869.
SOURCE Appendices to annual reports of the Colonial Land and Emigration Commission [CLEC].

of the Colonial Land and Emigration Commission, published annually in *British Parliamentary Papers*, allow an aggregate picture of mortality, although not of cause of death, allowing comparisons to be drawn between all major colonies.

Although figures given in this book rely largely on South Australian data, owing both to the wealth of resources and the systematic publication of the Immigration Agent's reportage of ships arriving, Tables 1 and 2 indicate that there is no reason to assume that the experience of the surgeons, or of the emigrants, was any different on ships bound for Port

Table 2

Emigrants who embarked in the United Kingdom who died on voyages to New South Wales, Victoria and South Australia, 1855–69, and to Queensland, 1860–66, by age

	Number embarked	Total deaths	Ages: Under 1	1-3	4-6	7-9	10-19	20-29	30-39	40-60
NSW	60 239	643	177	222	32	11	42	94	30	35
VIC	51 264	373	94	128	12	13	27	66	15	18
SA	37 056	421	149	154	14	8	20	45	14	17
QLD*	9 112	124	21	48	4	4	7	27	5	8
Total	**157 671**	**1561**	**441**	**552**	**62**	**36**	**96**	**232**	**64**	**78**

	Voyage loss rate %	% of all deaths: Under 1	1–3	4–6	7–9	10–19	20–29	30–39	40–60	Total
NSW	1.1	25	34	3	3	7	18	4	5	100
VIC	0.7	28	35	5	2	7	15	5	5	100
SA	1.1	35	37	3	2	5	11	3	4	100
QLD	1.4	17	39	3	3	6	22	4	6	100
All	**1.0**	**28**	**35**	**4**	**2**	**6**	**15**	**4**	**5**	**100%**

NOTES Victoria's lower percentage loss rate is probably related to the composition of ages on board: fewer children and higher proportions of adolescent and adult women.
*Queensland includes 1860–66, only. (27 vessels despatched by the CLEC)
SOURCE Appendices to Annual Reports of the CLEC.

Adelaide than on vessels bound for the other colonies. All vessels and their personnel bound for South Australia operated under the same system, departed from the same British ports under similar conditions, carrying people from similar regions and occupational groups, and often manned by the same personnel as ships bound for Sydney, Melbourne or the smaller colonies. Furthermore, the proportion of emigrants who died on ships bound for each colony (the loss rate) is broadly similar. Numerous surgeons superintended emigrants bound for a number of different colonies and undertook 20 or more journeys during their career with the service. Hence, voyages to South Australia, and their records, can be considered to be representative of all colonies. As well, the long career of the colony's zealous Health Officer and Immigration Agent, Dr Handasyde Duncan — a medical practitioner based at Port Adelaide between 1849 and 1878 — ensured continuity in reportage and policy implementation.

Ships and personnel bound for Moreton Bay in Queensland after 1860 operated under the control of the newly appointed London-based Queensland Agent General who, alarmed by high mortality on the first few ships he mobilised, successfully adopted the principles and practices that had proven so successful for the Emigration Commissioners and their predecessors since 1831.[13] Later, upon their appointment to London as Agents General from the 1860s, as each colony was granted responsible government, his inter-colonial colleagues also continued under the guidance of the Emigration Commission. From 1872, the Commission was gradually absorbed by the Board of Trade, whose officials were responsible for colonial emigration thereafter. With the demise of the Emigration Commission in 1878, emigrants of the late 19th century were never again to travel under the same scrutiny as that insisted upon by that body of enthusiastic civil servants since the 1830s. By the 1870s, the imperial and colonial governments were satisfied that, on the whole, the mobilisation and transit of emigrants to colonial destinations was working well; that the routines in place were saving lives, and that shipping companies were adhering to the Passenger Acts governing life at sea.

It is not my intention to rehearse my quantitative analysis here, other than in general terms in order to enhance our understanding of the trends in mortality and well-being, and to provide context. My aim is to revive the voices of working-class people travelling to Australia and to place their maritime and settlement experience into epidemiological and administrative context. The emigrants' letters, although often dismissed as illiterate, represent, collectively, a rare testament to working-class literacy. They confirm the statistical picture, which shows that Australia's 19th-century immigrants were extraordinarily literate. We know this because emigrants were required to state on their application forms whether they could 'read', 'read and write', or 'neither'. Although the application forms were disposed of long ago, this and other information, including their origins, religious persuasion, age and occupation, was transferred to passenger lists that were sent to the colony with each government-chartered ship, providing details on every emigrant. The Immigration Agents, who also interviewed immigrants upon arrival, then compiled tables appended to their quarterly and annual reports published in the *Government Gazette* and *Parliamentary Papers*. These reports have lent themselves, like some of the passenger lists, to quantitative analysis, allowing us a snapshot that can only be coloured by the testimony of the emigrants themselves. The more mobile the emigrants were, the more literate they tended to be. Their correspondence, and the evidence supplied by the Immigration Agents who interviewed them on arrival and compiled their profiles, show that they stand well apart from the image projected in many earlier histories of Australia as the ne'er-do-well sweepings of the alleys and workhouses of British and Irish towns. Many were autodidacts, self-taught readers and writers who, if Protestant, and especially if non-conformist, attended the enormously important Sunday Schools of Victorian England, where many an emigrant supplemented his or her primary education.

Many letter writers wrote fluent and stylish English. For others, spelling, punctuation and grammar were not their strong points. Some wrote phonetically, their syntactic constructions acutely attuned to the accent and idiom of their home county. Though sometimes barely comprehensible on first perusal to uninitiated modern readers, these letters, like those of their more literate fellow travellers, convey complex ideas and offer astute commentary. Surviving letters leave the impression of people alert to the sights and sounds surrounding them. They were eager to share every detail of the journey to smooth the way for prospective emigrants among their family and friends. Some, naturally enough, wanted to share their grief following the death of a child, and to confirm for anxious parents that in spite of their loss, their Christian faith remained undiminished. Others were eager to take advantage of home-bound ships, which picked up the emigrants' mail mid-ocean, to inform parents that their expected infant had been delivered successfully and was thriving.

Their observations of life on board ship were a tangible confirmation that their momentous decision to travel 15 000 miles had been validated by their experience, even when they had been shattered by the death of a child or spouse. They felt deeply the knowledge that unless their parents or siblings followed them they were unlikely to see or embrace them ever again. Yet, almost without exception, their strong religious convictions carried them through the vicissitudes of the voyage and settlement. Their faith was made manifest in their repeated declarations to their correspondents of certainty that reunion in a higher sphere was not only an inevitable but a joyous prospect. They were, however, determined to bind their earthly ties closer in the present by committing to paper a long conversation bringing immediate comfort to themselves and their families. A number carried on this conversation for many years after settlement. During the passage and after arrival, they remained ever mindful of their tenuous grasp on life, and looked to Providence for divine succour.

Numerous other voyage diaries, especially those written by young men, are often so formulaic as to concern themselves mainly with daily weather observations, sardonic character portraits of their messmates, descriptions of birds and fish studied or caught by passengers and crew, and their other amusements on board. These diaries tend not to yield the kinds of observations useful for understanding relations between the emigrants and their supervisor, the surgeon superintendent, whose word was law on the voyage. We learn little, if anything, about the environment in which emigrants negotiated their domestic lives during the three- to four-month passage. These revelations are made, on the whole, by married emigrants, those with responsibility for children, particularly women, although many fathers wrote evocatively about life between decks on behalf of their wives and children.

Many of the self-educated, religiously inclined emigrants organised lectures, sermons and lessons for their fellow travellers. Hence, those barely literate at the beginning of the voyage had a fair chance of functional literacy before its end, especially as the departments responsible for emigration placed books on board for the edification of the emigrants, in the expectation that they would attend classes run by schoolmasters on board. Philanthropists and religious organisations also provided, in bulk, biblical tracts, inspirational emigrant tales, and practical pamphlets with instructions and hints on employing their time on the voyage, in the hope of infusing and inculcating a Christian sensibility among the emigrants.

Surviving diaries suggest that this donated material was well used. Especially useful, it seems, were the hints and templates on how to write an emigrant letter. And the numerous editions of letters from the colonies published as promotional literature by empire-minded benefactors appear also to have been used as exemplars of style and content. It is probable that both the tracts, which were distributed on embarkation to emigrants, and the small volumes of published letters, designed to fit a pocket and widely circulated at low cost by the clergy, were read, and their format emulated, by many of the letter writers and diarists examined here. Education was the key to the future, according to these tracts, and emigrants appear to have been grateful for the opportunities offered on board.[14]

My analyses of literacy show that most emigrants were more than functionally literate. This is a term used to describe the ability to read at a fundamental level and to commit their own Christian and surnames and a few other words to paper. Many had received enough schooling, even if only for a few years at Sunday School, to continue their education using, mainly, the best primer available to them, the King James Bible, from which many could quote from memory, word perfect. And numerous correspondents — perhaps even most — were women determined to keep in touch with relatives, especially mothers and sisters, and to provide folk at home with practical information for their own impending journey.

Women, especially young, single Irish women, were often pioneers for their families, to whom they sent contributions towards the passage, saved judiciously from their wages as domestic servants. Both single and married women saw it as their duty to provide as much information about what to bring in terms of additional food comforts and recipes for making best use of the generous rations on board. High on their list were baking powder and bicarbonate of soda for indigestion, yeast for bread-making, jams and pickles to enliven the dietary tedium, and hints on how to pack jars and bottles to avoid breakages. Referring to their own experience, they also offered templates for the application process, helping those who followed to cut corners and to negotiate the official red tape.

My pursuit of emigrant letters has been propelled by an enduring interest in the health and mortality outcomes of voyages to Australia. Many were written by women, some of whom had heart-breaking stories to tell. I did not choose a formal method of selection, but simply transcribed letters and diaries held in various archives in Australia (and the very few I found in Britain) that described the health, dietary and sanitary routines on board. I have been left with the impression that the better off the traveller, the more likely he or she was to complain about the food and fellow passengers. Steerage emigrants were kept busy preparing food, attending to their rostered cleaning or mess duties, or caring for young families. Cabin passengers were, however, attended by their own servants and the ships' stewards.

Paradoxically, the comfort of their situation left well-off travellers the freedom to reflect at leisure on the adversities of life at sea, unaccustomed as they were, however spacious their cabins, to living at close quarters with strangers. Letters written in the cramped steerage deck tend to be livelier. For many labouring families, life at sea was, perhaps, not so different from the domestic situations that they had left behind. Many were determined to escape the spectre of destitution that haunted daily waged seasonal labour and to exchange their cramped dwellings for an independent livelihood funded by full-time work in the Antipodes, where their labour was in demand. They accepted any privation suffered on the voyage — even the loss of infants and children, whose grip on life at home was also tenuous — as the inescapable cost of relocation to a new and potentially prosperous life.

A number of writers remained optimistic and cheerful in spite of oppressive conditions. Their correspondence vibrates with the fortitude of people accustomed to hardship, used to making do under difficult and trying circumstances. Fearful they sometimes were. They were homesick, ill and dispirited. And they frequently described their idle, dirty, greedy or belligerent compatriots — the scourge of confined spaces en route still. Yet the letters show that the journey was also a welcome rest from ill-paid toil. In spite of the monotony of the diet by modern standards, many emigrants had never eaten better in their lives. They frequently paid tribute to the dietary comforts (provided under the strictly enforced government contract), which were prepared and consumed in a confined space whose amenities to a 21st-century sensibility, represent sheer purgatory.

Although we may generalise from them, these surviving letters do not speak for all emigrants. There must have been many who did not put pen to paper; who failed to keep in touch with family and friends; who did not prosper and whose memoirs, had they been written, would have dripped with misery. The more uplifting narratives of the passage and settlement that survive for public scrutiny today have, perhaps, submerged the stories of the less fortunate, those who remain silent, their letters, long discarded or slowly disintegrating in attics. The very survival of the testimonies explored in this book may have been determined by their writers' success as settlers. Original letters written home from the voyage, or following settlement in one or other of the colonies, but now housed in Australian archives, must have been brought back to Australia in the baggage of a successive migratory family member who had kept them as an affectionate symbol of kinship and as a repository of crucial information for their own journey. Perhaps descendants only kept the letters of forebears whose lives flourished, eventually donating them with pride to local collections. Maybe the recipients of letters from less fortunate emigrants, or their descendants, disposed of their dispiriting correspondence. Perhaps only the friends and relatives of successful emigrants followed, in an era when kith and kinship networks were all-important in determining who went where, and when. While we may never know what proportion of Australia's colonial immigrants viewed their own movement from one hemisphere to another as successful, the sheer volume of surviving letters and diaries suggest that the themes shared by so many of them are as close to representative as is possible. And even if we fail to meet the measure of typicality, each letter is historical evidence in its own right and worthy of its place in the annals of migration and settlement.

Few letters sent or received by working-class people — the static compeers of the more adventurous emigrants — survive in Britain or Ireland today. Nor is North America as well served as Australia with surviving epistolary evidence of its immigrant poor.[15] But the numerous letters, diaries and journals held in private and public archives in Australia allow us insights into the hearts and minds of people whose voices in history have tended to remain subdued.[16] The accents of the labouring poor are now enjoying a renaissance. Most recently, David Fitzpatrick's masterly exploration of a number of letter series has made audible again the voices of several of Australia's 19th-century Irish immigrants and those of their correspondents in Ireland.[17] Vibrant with nuance, their very survival invites us into their world. There, if we restrain that scourge of historical understanding — our modern preconceptions of the past — we can learn much. Emigrant letters are, in short, an extraordinary resource. They speak to us across the centuries, animating the experience of their writers as no other evidence can.

Besides viewing the voyage from the point of view of the emigrants, the other major aim of this book is to see how the regimes used to improve the comfort and reduce the risk of death on board government-chartered ships can illuminate the simple, yet effective means by which mortality was constrained in the age of sail. This was an era before medical science, with the key exception of smallpox vaccination, had made very much difference to the lives of the poor. Setting out deliberately to emulate the successful reduction of mortality on convict ships that carried adults with very few infants or children — the most vulnerable sectors of every population — the agencies responsible for emigration from the 1830s experimented with ways to reduce deaths and improve well-being.

The most effective life-saving measures on land before 1900 were preventative, in an age when prevention, not cure, was the catchword. These strategies, particularly in the last four decades of the 19th century, were mainly of an engineering or socio-environmental nature: commitment to improving sanitation, housing, clean drinking water, personal hygiene, and diet. The major medically related preventative strategies adopted from the early 19th century were the crucial provision of smallpox vaccination and the isolation of infectious disease, followed by the introduction of antisepsis in the last few decades of the Victorian era. Equally important for the health of infants, was an increasing emphasis on the health and well-being of their mothers, a strategy that may have contributed more, even than improving environmental conditions, to a revolution in infant survival in the United Kingdom in the late 19th century. At sea, this was a strategy that had engaged emigration and immigration officials since the 1850s.

These cornerstones of preventative, environmental and medical science were the tenets adopted by the convict and emigration services. Their tactics led to a substantial fall in the death rate of adults and children at sea on ships en route to Australasia, although the Grim Reaper continued to hover near very many infants at sea, as on land. The sanitary routines implemented by emigration officials are still the cost-effective procedures — with the addition of rehydrating saline drips for infants and children, and more sophisticated immunisation regimes — advocated for less developed countries today where the disease environment and life expectancy is comparable to those of industrialising Britain 150 years ago. Lives can be saved for extraordinarily small sums.

In the modern science-fixated world, high-tech invasive medical solutions absorb exorbitant funding, yet a glance at the triumph of engineering, social and environmental strategies of a less sophisticated era can still provide some lessons for the present.

That the fall in deaths on sailing vessels on the Australian route led the mortality transition in Britain, the first industrial nation, by about a quarter of a century, is perhaps surprising to readers whose genealogical research revealed that their ancestors travelled on one of the ships that suffered a horrible fate. On these atypical voyages, ravaged by an epidemic infection that crept silently and undetectably on board in its incubating phase with one or more of the emigrants, usually a child, the mortality was truly appalling. The major killer pathogens — diarrhoea, measles, whooping cough and scarlatina — were as ferocious at sea as on land.

Other readers may have taken as typical the more sensationalist literature of the recent past, and assumed that their forebears, or all emigrants, also suffered perilous voyages. Undoubtedly, it took time for the administrative machinery to mature to the point when the lives of adults on government emigrant ships bound for Australia by around 1850 were at no more risk of death at sea than on land. Loss of life by shipwreck, however, was rare. Although a number of ships carrying assisted emigrants ran aground at landfall with no loss of life, before 1872 only two ships were wrecked. These were the *Cataraqui* (privately chartered by the New South Wales government), while approaching Port Phillip Bay in 1845, with all 369 passengers lost, and the *Guiding Star*, which was lost without trace on the voyage and assumed to have struck an iceberg, in 1855. This ship, which went down with 543 emigrants on board, was the only one chartered by the Emigration Commissioners with loss of life by shipwreck among 853 vessels carrying 281 378 government-assisted emigrants to Australasia and South Africa before 1872, representing 0.2 per cent of emigrants on those vessels.[18]

Between 1873 and 1914, five government-chartered ships were wrecked, two with no loss of life in 1871 and 1890. The *British Admiral* lost 79 of 88 emigrants in 1874; the *Kapunda* lost 219 emigrants, 33 passengers and 33 crew in 1887; the *Northfleet* lost 293 of 379 emigrants in

1893. Hence, 591 emigrants from a total of 258 541 sailing under the auspices of the State, or 0.2 per cent — the same proportion as for the earlier period — were the victims of shipwreck between 1873 and the First World War. Among private passenger ships between 1863 and 1895, six were wrecked with only one, the *Wanata* in 1866, recording no loss of life.[19] It is conventional in analyses of death and disease in the maritime sphere to include only ships that arrived at their destination. Hence, figures given in this book, or the tables to which readers are referred, do not include deaths from shipwreck.

From 1831, many government-chartered ships suffered no loss of life to disease or ill health, even of children and infants. Rather than the 'coffin ships' of the popular literature and sensational journalism, this

Table 3

Ships classified by number of deaths per voyage to New South Wales, Victoria and South Australia, 1848–60

| | Deaths | | | | | | | Total ships | Voyages | | Average no.of emigrants per ship |
	Zero	1–5	6–10	11–15	16–20	21–30	31+		< 6 deaths (%)	< 11 deaths (%)	
NSW	41	149	57	17	9	3	5	281	68	88	317
VIC	43	159	57	18	7	15	12	311	66	84	328
SA	19	108	38	14	7	4	1	191	66	86	293
Total 1848–60	103	416	152	49	23	22	18	783	66	86	316

| | Deaths (%) | | | | | | | Total ships (%) |
	Zero	1–5	6–10	11–15	16–20	21–30	31+	
NSW	15	53	20	6	3	1	2	100
VIC	14	51	18	6	2	5	4	100
SA	10	57	20	7	4	2	0.5	100
1848–60	13	53	19	6	3	3	2	100
1861–69	28	57	11	4	1	1	0	100

NOTES For 1861–69 breakdown, see Table 4. Data for 1848 are not included for South Australia, but see Haines, '"Little Anne is very low"', Table 9, for 1848–85, based on manuscript records.
SOURCE Appendices to the General Reports of the CLEC.

outcome was a triumph by any standards in the 19th century, given that the voyage averaged over 100 days, traversing many different climatic zones and enduring extreme weather conditions, from suffocating heat to biting cold. The vast majority of voyages, as we can see from Tables 3 and 4, buried less than six emigrants at sea. Alas, mourners at these maritime funerals mainly grieved for children under the age of six, and particularly under three years of age, who had succumbed to one or more of those fatal childhood infections that remain the scourge of children in some regions of the world.

Hence, systematically operated voyages to Australia show, in a world dominated by the notion that medical science is responsible for the extraordinary decline in deaths in the modern era, that simplicity and

Table 4

Ships classified by number of deaths per voyage to
New South Wales, Victoria, South Australia and Queensland, 1861–69

	Deaths							Total ships	Voyages		Average no.of emigrants per ship
	Zero	1–5	6–10	11–15	16–20	21–30	31+		< 6 deaths (%)	< 11 deaths (%)	
NSW	10	31	5					46	89	100	366
VIC	26	27	1	1				55	96	98	278
SA	4	24	8	2		1		39	72	92	350
QLD	6	13	5	3	1			27	67	85	315
Total 1861–69	46	95	19	6	1	1		167	84	95	325

	Deaths (%)							Total ships (%)
	Zero	1–5	6–10	11–15	16–20	21–30	31+	
NSW	22	67	11	47	49	2	2	100
VIC	47	49	2	2				100
SA	10	62	21	5		3		100
QLD	21	46	18	11	4			100
1861–69	27.5	56.9	11.3	3.6	0.6	0.6	0.0	100
1848–60	13.1	53.1	19.4	6.3	2.9	2.8	2.3	100

NOTES   For 1848–60 breakdown, see Table 3. General notes as for Tables, 1, 2 and 3.
SOURCE   Appendices to General Reports of the CLEC.

dedication to the 'sanitary idea' were, and remain, the keystones to reducing adult and child mortality in an industrialising society. Most important, perhaps, is the experience of infants in the maritime environment. Children under the age of one year, like their cousins on land, failed spectacularly to share the life-saving benefits of their parents and older siblings. An exploration of the reasons for this, as we shall see, answers some questions and raises more, about why the lives of infants at sea and on land before the First World War, remained so horrendously at risk in spite of advances that had contributed so successfully to those who survived the first 12 months of life.

Before we turn to the testimony of the emigrants, the next chapter places the voyages into their 19th-century environmental and epidemiological context. It canvasses the state of our understanding of health and disease during a century when the corollaries of population growth, rapid industrialisation and urbanisation — the booms and busts of unfettered economic growth — brought havoc in their wake as well as great benefits. As the gap between rich and poor widened, sharply delineating for the first time the 'Two Nations', the four Ds — disruption (or dislocation), deprivation, disease and death — underscored the atrocious living standards suffered by the poorer classes in the burgeoning cities and towns as well as the rural hinterlands that serviced the developing manufacturing and commercial centres.[20]

It was from among these workers, subsisting at the lower end of the socio-economic spectrum (although by no means the lowest), that Australia's government-assisted immigrants were largely drawn. This survey of the environment they left behind may help to illuminate the interaction on government-sponsored voyages, between health, disease, official policy and the policeman of those procedures (the surgeon superintendent), with the adults and children under his control. The chapters that follow are devoted to the testimony of the emigrants on a journey that carried them, anxious and sea-weary as they neared their destination, to a landfall where many saw themselves as 'strangers in a strange land'.

'I never look at the sea without lamenting our dear children'

Sickness, health and the voyage in context

The immigrants

The 15 000-mile passage to Australia was expensive. From 1831, as we have seen, about 740 000 immigrants were assisted to reach Australian shores by funds allocated by the labour-hungry colonial legislatures. Before about 1860, the Colonial Land and Emigration Commission, a branch of the Colonial Office, selected people on behalf of individual colonies according to strictly regulated criteria. Married male agricultural labourers, rural tradesmen, miners and female domestic servants were most in demand. Respectability was also a high priority: testimonials were required from a clergyman or magistrate. Except under very rare circumstances, inmates of workhouses or recipients of outdoor relief were precluded.[1]

People who responded to recruiting drives were, essentially, self-selecting workers who put themselves forward for selection by applying through official channels for an assisted passage. We have no overall statistics on how many were rejected, but surviving evidence suggests that the rejection rate was quite high. Age was an important criterion for selection. Colonial authorities preferred married couples in the prime of life with older children poised to take up the slack in the job market. As for state of health, a medical practitioner was required to sign the application form, and the successful applicant was further examined by the ship's surgeon before departure for any sign of visible infection. Families with members considered to be too sickly to endure the voyage, or with a child showing signs of infection, were sent home at this stage. The emigrant had also to show proof of smallpox vaccination, or smallpox scars, before being allowed to embark. Until about 1860, recruitment was directed mainly at rural regions and small towns; manufacturing and industrial regions were not seen as appropriate recruiting grounds for Australia's developing agricultural economy.

From about 1860, the majority of assisted emigrants travelled under nomination or remittance schemes whereby friends and relatives in the colonies could, on payment of a substantial deposit, nominate individuals or families.[2] Under these schemes, it was more difficult for the Emigration Commissioners and the London-based colonial Agents General to control the age and sex of the immigrants. Before 1848, about half of the government-assisted arrivals to the two major colonies, New South Wales and Victoria, were Irish, about one-third were English and about one-sixth were Scots. (Welsh immigrants, never numerous, were counted as English.) Following the revival of government assistance in 1848, after a lull of about five years during an economic downturn, English arrivals predominated. From that time, about half of Australia's arrivals were English, around one-third were Irish and roughly one-fifth were Scots.

Although Australia-bound non-assisted voyages were far more highly regulated than vessels sailing to North America, little is yet known about the unassisted travellers, those who could afford as much as £30 for a one-way adult fare in steerage in some years, a sum higher than the annual wage of an agricultural labourer in southern England in mid-century.[3] Little notice was taken of the fare-payers (whether they were berthed in a cabin or steerage) by imperial or colonial legislatures, beyond reporting annual aggregate numbers departing and arriving. However, Australia's assisted immigrants, like its convicts, are among the most scrutinised of all 19th-century populations.

Travelling under the protection of the State, they were counted, examined and reported upon, both on departure and arrival. And their health and living conditions on board represented a crucial component of this scrutiny. Consequently, candidates for government-assisted passages voluntarily assented to a diminution of their domestic liberty that could only have been envied by a Medical Officer of Health on land, where resentment against domestic intrusion by public officials or philanthropic sanitarians prevailed.[4]

Regulations, superintended by the surgeon, enforced hours of rising, dining and retiring. Days were set aside for compulsory bathing, washing clothes and changing linen under-clothing. Bedding was required to be aired daily in fine weather. A matron, initially chosen from among the married women and who was paid a gratuity on arrival, assisted inspections by the surgeon superintendent and acted as the moral guardian of the single women. Later in the century, professional matrons were employed. Volunteer constables, chosen from among the emigrants, were also paid a gratuity on landing. They supervised the fumigation and drying of the steerage decks with swinging stoves burning a range of disinfecting and deodorising substances, and co-ordinated meals, organised the daily cleaning, scrubbing and disinfecting of the mess tables, the berths, the floors and the water closets in steerage. They co-ordinated the collection of boiling water for tea and the retrieval of cooked meals from the galley, for both the married and single quarters. And the extent to which many emigrants entered into the routine with enthusiasm is recorded in their diaries and letters, as we shall see.

Many emigrants resented the lazier of their compeers and showed initiative in keeping their sleeping and eating spaces clean and well aired, and in caring for their children. They attempted to coerce others to do the same, or complained to the surgeon superintendent when co-operation failed. The poor were seldom passive ciphers.[5]

Emigrants are invariably a biased sample of the land-based population: far fewer left the United Kingdom's shores than stayed. They may have been healthier than those they left behind; they received the imprimatur of a local medical practitioner on their application form, and before departure there was the official medical examination to pass, however cursory by modern standards. It was at this point that those with observable deformities, or who presented as weak or ill, were refused passage, strengthening a bias towards the embarkation of the healthiest of the applicants. On the voyage, however, they were exposed to new health risks, owing to the crowded nature of the steerage accommodation. Seasickness during the first few weeks compromised their well-being for the duration of the long voyage. And they endured extreme climatic conditions on board. Moreover, at the port of embarkation and in the emigrant depots, many people, especially children from isolated regions, were exposed to childhood diseases never before encountered, against which they had little, or no, resistance. Hence, the bias towards health brought about by the official selection of self-selecting candidates was probably countered by the vicissitudes of the voyage.

Death rates on Australia-bound vessels chartered by the Home Office from 1815 for convict voyages, and Colonial Office agencies for government-sponsored ships from 1831, were extremely low in comparison with other transoceanic voyages on British ships. These included the transatlantic slave trade and other non-slave voyages, such as indentured labourers voyaging from India to Fiji, Mauritius, Natal and to the West Indies, and voyages crossing the far shorter transatlantic route to North America. This successful containment of disease and death on Australia-bound vessels was brought about by stringent sanitary measures, with an emphasis on cleanliness, supervised on board by the officially appointed surgeon superintendents, who were paid a substantial gratuity for each emigrant landed alive. Their generous ascending pay scale, rising incrementally with each voyage from ten shillings to a maximum of one pound per emigrant landed, acted as a strong incentive to perform well.

Empirically gained knowledge, first gathered and disseminated by experimenting surgeons on naval, merchant and slave ships in the second half of the 18th century, and monitored by the Admiralty and the Home Office, was transferred to ships carrying naval surgeons in charge of convicts to Australia under the auspices of these departments. In turn, the Emigration Commissioners adopted their strategies. Like the Admiralty and Home Office, they kept strict surveillance over the outcome of each ship, instituting inquiries following high-mortality voyages. The implementation of regulations governing sanitation and hygiene were monitored at both ends of the voyage, as was the surgeon's conduct. The colonial Agents General, who gradually assumed responsibility for recruitment from the 1860s, adopted the Emigration Commission's policies, assuring continuity of procedures that had proven so successful. To broaden our understanding of the novelty of health management in the maritime sphere, a glimpse of the epidemiological situation on land will provide some context.

Epidemiology and the mortality transition on land and at sea

The connections between a high death toll and the disamenities of an increasingly urban, industrialising society include inadequate housing and sanitation, environmental hazards, such as contaminated water, industrial waste and smoke, poor wages and undernourishment. There are manifold difficulties associated with analysing causes of illness and death in the past but, despite the problems associated with shifting disease aetiology (the assignment of causes and names to specific diseases), and the development of new nosological taxonomies (the systematic classification of diseases), historians and historical demographers have assessed reasons for the mortality decline of the last few decades of the 19th century. This transformation in the industrialising world heralded an era when both children and the survivors of childhood could look forward to far greater longevity.

There are also sundry problems related to the collection, compilation, editing and manipulation of published data, especially that of Britain's General Register Office and its subsidiaries. What did the diagnoses, names and perceived causes of diseases mean in the past? How have these meanings changed? To what extent can modern demographic analyses of the distribution of morbidity (the rate of illness in a society) and mortality throw light on past experience? How far can we recognise in disease symptoms today the diagnoses of the past?

Just as importantly, we might ask why state authorities, sometimes even without the co-operation of physicians, assumed the mantle of public health to the point of developing nosological classifications and sophisticated statistical systems in an attempt to understand and ameliorate the consequences of disease. From the 1840s in England and Wales, about one half of all recorded deaths were children under five years of age and about half of those were of infants under one year (and since these deaths were significantly under-recorded, this figure is an underestimation). It is evident that if we are to further our understanding of disease both on land and at sea, our focus must be directed at the health and mortality of young children. Embodying the experience of thousands of parents travelling to the other side of the world in the 19th century, Sarah Brunskill's cry of grief three weeks into her three-month voyage to South Australia, ten days after the burial at sea of both of her children, echoes throughout this book:

> I never look at the sea without thinking of and lamenting our dear children. I was in hopes I would feel their loss less as time wore away, but I feel their loss more every day.[6]

Recent studies have examined the social, economic and regional environments within which infants and young children were nurtured, revealing widely differing experiences across time, class and location. They have pointed to the significance of the development of the infant welfare movement around the turn of the 20th century as a major contributor to saving infant and early childhood life. And recently there has been an emphasis on the significance of the mother's health and nutritional status during pregnancy, and in the immediate aftermath of delivery, for the health of her infant. There have also been calls to avoid looking at the past through 21st-century spectacles, imposing modern preconceptions upon it. We must not overlook the genesis and influence of the privately promoted shift towards cleanliness and domestic hygiene in the private sphere in the mid-19th century.

The last two decades of the 19th century saw a specific emphasis on the importance of personal cleanliness, maternal health and infant feeding in improving infant and child welfare in the urban regions and large towns of the industrialised world, including North America, the United Kingdom and Australasia. As in the United Kingdom and Australia, infant mortality rates in the United States failed to decline substantially before the first decade of the 20th century. Putting into practice the recommendations of the public-health-minded sanitarian reformers for saving infant and child life was easier said than done in the tenements and slum pockets of New York, Philadelphia, London, Birmingham, Liverpool, Sydney, Melbourne, Adelaide and similarly sized towns and cities of the industrialising world, in spite of the 'culture of cleanliness' that had been advancing among the health-manual-reading middle and upper classes since the last decades of the 18th century.

Oppressed by crowding, lack of running water and adequate drainage, insufficient and appallingly inadequate lavatory facilities and sewerage, and lack of funds to purchase soap, heating and fuel, the poor could not emulate their better off neighbours during the period of rapid urbanisation. In London, for example, high-mortality working-class districts failed to enjoy improvements in the provision of water until the 1890s. Despite exhortations by working-class magazines to preach cleanliness to the poor, slum dwellers in cities, towns and villages had no choice but to queue at the local pump for water of dubious quality and haul it over long distances, and frequently up several flights of stairs, rendering its fetching a major problem. Queues were also inevitable at the abysmally few ash or earth closets shared, in urban areas, by dozens of families whose jerry-built dwellings were damp and disease-ridden slums.

Nonetheless, the gospel of cleanliness was making its mark, even if infants and younger children were not to share in its benefits, for reasons that are still not entirely clear. However, it would seem, both from the evidence of Australia-bound ships and land-based data, that until the health and maternal education of mothers improved substantially, cleaning up the environment made little impact on infants, whose lives were so crucially mediated by their mothers. Yet, ought we not expect the youngest to enjoy at least some of the life-saving benefits gained by their older siblings and parents? In the healthier locations, they appear to have done so. But, nationally, improvements to infant health were dependent on a number of related factors besides maternal education, including, most importantly, legislation governing the systematic purification of the milk supply and the provision of milk depots for working-class mothers.[7] Even then, the inefficacy of regulations governing milk purification in the United Kingdom and the adulteration of liquid, powdered and condensed milk, meant that 'white poison' dominated available supplies until after the turn of the 20th century.[8] The role of flies in spreading diarrhoeal infection while exacerbating the epidemic cycle is also an important consideration. Their attraction to sweetened condensed milk, a cheap alternative infant food favoured in many working-class districts, was particularly harmful to weanlings.[9]

Hence, whereas sanitary improvements from mid-century brought benefits for older children and adults, these reforms, and the increasing focus on the health of mothers, were not enough to enhance the life chances of infants, the most vulnerable members of London's population, before the 20th century.[10] Summer diarrhoea, and its consequent weakening of infants' defences against other opportunistic infections, continued to prevail, although the risks were variable, depending on class and location. No infant diseases showed such a marked seasonality as diarrhoea, with its pronounced summer peak, reflected, most of all, in the deaths of the offspring of unskilled workers.[11]

Conquering rickets, which lowers the resistance of weanlings under the age of one to diarrhoeal and respiratory infections, was one significant step towards saving the lives of infants and toddlers. This bone-deforming deficiency disease was involved in the symbiosis between whooping cough and measles. Broadly speaking, although changing attitudes to child care may have stimulated a fall in child mortality in Britain during the 1860s, this seems not to have extended to infants and toddlers under the age of three, whose survival appears to have depended on less identifiable environmental dynamics, including a deficiency in vitamin D.[12]

Although there may have been a higher consumption of fish oils and animal and dairy fats among the artisan and middle classes, the nutritional quality of the diets of poorer working-class mothers, children and infants was unlikely to have improved before about 1914.[13] Little is known about the quality of human breast milk in the 19th century, but given the prevalence of rickets among children, it is likely that women (and thus their breast milk) suffered, like their children, from vitamin D deficiency. Hence, in urban regions, overcrowding, lack of sunshine, environmental pollution, cultural practices that kept children and toddlers indoors, and lack of adequate knowledge about infant foods, formed a tragic combination. Although there is little evidence to suggest a change in the dietary practices of the poor before the First World War, it seems that, in the last decades of the 19th century, health visitors may have had some impact in promoting both breastfeeding and the efficacy of outdoor play, leading to a decline in both rickets and whooping cough. On land, as at sea, we need to acknowledge the complexities of the epidemic cycle, the symbiosis between childhood infections, particularly whooping cough and measles, and the underlying conditions that profoundly affected both.

There are also strong arguments for considering the question of fertility as germane to the question of infant mortality.[14] Fewer children meant fewer people per dwelling, and this reduction in domestic congestion can only have ameliorated the rate of disease transmission within the household, let alone the health of mothers.[15] While the principal diseases of childhood were fatal in all age groups under five years, there were distinct differences between the major causes of death for infants and children in Britain. As late as 1891–1900, wasting diseases carried off infants under three months old, while diarrhoeal disease, convulsions (which may have been a symptom of the latter) and respiratory disease were largely responsible for the deaths of infants over three months old. Children from one to five years of age were fatally vulnerable to the four major infectious diseases of childhood: measles, scarlet fever (often referred to as scarlatina), diphtheria/croup and whooping cough.[16]

Given that childhood epidemic disease was rife among crowded families, with attacks from one infection leading to vulnerability to another, the survival of infants depended not only upon a reduction in the number of children per family, but upon cultural and social shifts which, in essence, predetermined the fate of the infant. On land it was not *just* fewer children per family that increased an infant's chances, but the modernising currents that brought about fertility control, and new perspectives on maternal health and infant upbringing. These conditions, and the new directions taken by health authorities towards the health of mothers and babies in the last years of the 19th century, reflect procedures introduced at sea on the route to Australia several decades earlier. We ought not underestimate the role of the State in bringing about reforms in areas over which it had jurisdiction, even in an age of laissez-faire.[17]

Disease causation and the environment

In recent years, we have learnt much about the epidemiological transition. This is a term used to describe the transition from a high to a low mortality regime among human populations owing to the decline of infectious disease. New quantitative methods in urban, social and medical history have demonstrated that only cause- and age-specific data can fill in the gaps in our knowledge of the patterns of infection among human populations. Most studies of age- and cause-specific death rates, however, focus on the period following 1870 and are hampered by failure to discriminate by sex in the official published data sources.

An analysis of the medical daybooks of an Ontario doctor between 1851 and 1881, demonstrated that the highest risk of dying was among his child patients. Parents appear to have waited until the situation was desperate before calling the doctor, thus his 'child patients may have been sicker than his adult patients' by the time the doctor visited.[18] The health of infants and young children remained at its riskiest prior to cultural, social and economic shifts that placed a higher value upon their lives. Moreover, the gap between the life chances of the poorest and other classes had widened markedly during the later 19th century, so we need to look backwards for the initiatives that ushered in the gains that only gradually accrued for the youngest in the population.

The public health movement of the United Kingdom in the late 19th century can be better understood if we seek its genesis not in the 1870s, but a century earlier. The focus on the late industrial era tends to overlook the efficacy of Georgian campaigns to clean up British cities, in both the public and private spheres. The pioneering health historian, MC Buer, implored readers to judge each century from the perspective of the one before rather than its successor. She observed a reduction in infant mortality from the mid-18th century 'which has only been equalled in the [first two decades of the] 20th century'. This observation places into perspective the fall in infant deaths around 1900, reminding us that infant mortality, horrendously high before 1800, fell in stages, separated by a century of industrialisation. Although industrialisation brought higher living standards for the better off, stagnating, even declining, conditions were endured by those living in the shadow of the 'dark Satanic mills'.[19]

The Victorian era of rapid urbanisation, internal migration, rural dislocation, de-skilling and transition to new industrial occupations created a plateau in disease ecology between about 1840 and 1870, during which average heights, previously rising, were held in check and mortality rates failed to improve. This stark reality emphasises the point that rising wages concomitant with industrialisation, 'although a conventional proxy for improved standards of living — [do] not always or necessarily translate directly into a greater availability of food or an improved diet'.[20] Regional variations also distort the picture. Agricultural workers — the lowest paid in the economy — suffered stagnating wages, often living under appalling conditions in hamlets and villages, failing to share the economic gains of their town and city compeers. Hence, differential mortality between age groups and sexes in and between rural and urban areas suggests that many rural dwellers were as unhealthy as their city cousins.

Numerous advances were made in the 18th century, brought about by the reformation in public manners and the revival of classic civic virtue in the late Georgian age. This was an era that ushered in an advocacy of domestic and public hygiene, focusing primarily on cleaning up London's metropolis in an effort to reverse the highly visible human wastage. Gains in health and mortality appear to have been achieved via the building of stone, rather than fire-prone wooden, buildings, stone or brick flooring, wider paved streets, street drainage and cleaning, and an increased use of water, soap, disinfectants and ventilation. Changing views on infant nurture and isolation of the sick, the enthusiastic advancement of disease management via preventive practices, and the dissemination of educational tracts and guides on household management also appear to have contributed. And we ought not underestimate the impact of newly available, mass-produced washable cotton underclothing.[21]

In rural regions, a thorough understanding of the efficacy of swamp drainage to reduce malaria (the ague), and an intuitive understanding of the dangers of cesspits, piled garbage and dung heaps, may have contributed to better health and a reduction in mortality. Miasma theory (simply put: if it smelled bad, it was bad), although intuitive and lacking the bacteriological science of the post-1870s, led the way to the benefits of cleanliness long before germ theory was substantiated by Koch and his colleagues in the 1880s. Furthermore, if we investigate the impressive peacetime life-saving gains won in the mid-19th century by the military at home and abroad, and on convict and emigrant ships bound for Australia — all spheres operating under the jurisdiction of the State, where sanitary discipline and hygiene were authorised and regulated — we can observe a sophisticated understanding of disease transmission and developments in preventative strategies, including infant nurture, long before the germ theory of disease had been accepted.

Campaigns for cleanliness, both personal and public, emanated from miasmatist ideology practised by sanitarians in Britain in the 1840s. Their zealous campaigns for improved engineering and a cleaner environment gathered pace from mid-century. An analysis of capital expenditure on sanitation in 36 British towns, using Local Taxation Returns, suggested that a surge in spending from the mid-1890s on sewers, drains and water supplies coincided with the fall in infant mortality and may largely have contributed to it. It is no accident that these reforms occurred after the introduction of the franchise for most male workers in 1867, in an era sometimes referred to as 'gas and water socialism', when working-class males were given a voice in the management of their public affairs, contributing to local regulation of sanitary infrastructure.

In the late 19th century, high levels of investment in sanitary infrastructure contributed both to the effectiveness of regulatory environmental reforms and the life chances of infants.[22] Hence, the earlier mortality decline in other age groups, it has been argued, 'must have been a consequence of less directly interventionist factors than sanitary reform.'[23] Yet local public health initiatives covered more than just advances in sanitation and piped water. It would be a pity to direct attention away from earlier efforts including housing, water, road work and paving, food and drug adulteration, and regulation of environmental hazards, before the era of 'gas and water socialism'.

The difficulties of identifying the precise causes of the fall in infant deaths have not been resolved. Contributing factors include the consolidation of mother and child welfare movements, the domestic education of mothers and a focus on their health, improving standards of living, purification of dairy milk supplies, improvements in artificial feeding and so forth. Care still needs to be taken in attributing the enhanced life chances of infants at the turn of the 20th century to novel regulatory initiatives implemented by state or local government agencies.

However efficacious, these public reforms for older children and adults may simply have coincided with life-saving initiatives aimed at domestic hygiene and maternal welfare by sanitary reformers for the best part of a century. Infant mortality had been declining in some rural areas during the 1870s, but in the absence of public investment in sanitary infrastructure in the overcrowded urban environment, a parallel decline in large towns and cities had been inhibited. The well-being of infants born in these areas awaited a substantial commitment of resources. Only analyses of specific cause of death will clarify the extent and timing of the influence of sanitary reform on declining infant deaths in various town and city environments. Yet, given the decline in infrastructure-poor, less urbanised areas, it will remain difficult to determine whether a decline in deaths from infantile diarrhoea at the turn of the 20th century, for example, can be attributed to numerous reforms focusing directly on mothers and babies. A better understanding of health, disease and death on voyages to Australia may contribute to a further understanding of these interactions.

Death causation

One problem related to relations between doctors and their patients concerns the broader social context in which causes of disease and death were recorded in the past.[24] This problem inevitably leads us to question the motives of the recorder — the medical practitioner — in an era when changing nosological fashion (the naming of diseases) meant that causes of death could be variously described, depending on the predilection of the recorder, as profound changes in medical thinking occurred during the 19th century. Moreover, there were subtle and not so subtle shifts in interpretation of the symptoms associated with various diseases, possibly linked (as we can see with the benefit of hindsight) to changes in the virulence of specific infections, creating a puzzle for the observers in an age before the maturation of bacteriological science. We must consider the purposes to which death statistics were put, a problem seen as 'the shifting use of death records and statistics'.[25]

Although physicians agreed over the diagnosis of well-defined diseases such as cholera, plague, yellow fever or smallpox, there was little accord when it came to various other conditions with symptoms that were apt to cause confusion, including a range of fevers, cancers and wasting diseases. However, by the mid-19th century, doctors were familiar with Registrar-General William Farr's nosologies and his regular updates, and most diseases were readily identifiable. Whereas the symptoms of phthisis (tuberculosis, sometimes referred to as consumption) could mimic several different diseases, there were many conditions with such widely different characteristics that they gained general recognition and were seldom confused. This widespread knowledge and consensus about causation meant that diseases were probably diagnosed more, rather than less, accurately.[26]

By 1853, the Registrar-General of Victoria, WH Archer, had produced his own nosological index based on William Farr's. His intention was to promote 'as far as possible, scientific accuracy in the returns of "Cause of Death", and secondarily to secure uniformity of statistical practice both here and in England'.[27] Over the next decade, Archer adopted Farr's modifications to disease and death tables in the search for accuracy in tabulating mortality in the colony. By 1863, he thought it proper to produce a new index 'in accordance with the latest statistical improvements', designed for the use of his own officers, although he hoped that medical practitioners in Victoria would also find it serviceable. Archer's adoption of Farr's nosologies, immediately upon his appointment to establish the Registrar-General's Office of Victoria in 1853, gives some insight into the uniformity of nomenclature disseminated to the Australian colonies at an early stage. That Farr's nosology was used widely is evident in the causes of death recorded by surgeon superintendents on ships sailing to Australia.[28] Nevertheless, we must remain aware of the vagueness of diagnoses, the difficulties of interpretation and the competence of the recorders.

On Australian voyages surgeon superintendents observed their patients daily for three to four months. By the time of cure or death, they probably believed their diagnoses to be unambiguous, even when they reported two or three interacting causes. While disease labels have changed markedly in the last 150 years or so, we ought not underestimate the certainty of experienced observers in daily contact with their patients. Moreover, accuracy was enhanced because, unlike doctors on land, surgeon superintendents were constrained by official procedures including the auditing of their logs, journals and reports on arrival, and by the opportunity given to the emigrants to complain about personnel and conditions on board. This minimised any prospect of hiding maternal deaths, or failure to record premature births and perinatal deaths (occurring within one month of birth), as happened so often on land.

Nevertheless, the low number of recorded stillbirths on Australian ships is puzzling, though given the virtual impossibility of estimating stillborn rates in England, it is difficult to know just how far they were under-recorded at sea. In England, a considerable number of infants who drew breath but soon died were buried uncertified, with the connivance of midwives, doctors and cemetery officials, suggesting that the number of neonatal deaths may also be considerably under-reported in England. In the West End of London, for example, one large private practice recorded one in 30 births as 'stillborn', many of which were probably premature live births.[29] Given that research for 1946 showed a higher rate of premature babies born to agricultural workers, we would expect a high rate to have prevailed in the 19th century, and this is borne out on voyages to South Australia.[30] Curiously, however, a higher rate of stillbirths among the voyaging population was recorded after 1873, compared with the earlier years.

Five of the eight recorded stillbirths after 1873 were reported in 1876. The high number in that year may suggest either that pregnant women were less healthy (following a period of agricultural depression and lock-outs in the southern English counties), or that the weather was particularly boisterous, causing severe seasickness among the most vulnerable women, compromising the life-chances of their unborn infants. The higher rate, however, may simply reflect an era of more accurate reportage of stillbirths. There is reason to doubt, though, that surgeon superintendents consistently reported stillbirths. Emigrants were interviewed on arrival, at which point parents could complain if a proper burial service was not performed (thus alerting the Immigration Agent to inadequate reportage by the surgeons), restraining the likelihood that

Table 5

Stillbirths on voyages to South Australia, 1848–85

Year	Number of voyages	Number of births	Number of stillbirths	Stillbirths as % of births	Average births per vessel
1848–54	138	726	3	0.41	5.3
1855–67	115	444	3	0.68	3.9
1873–85	70	266	8	3.01	3.8
1848–85	323	1436	14	0.97	4.7

SOURCE Haines, "'Little Anne is very low'", Table 17.

stillbirths consistently remained hidden. Yet, given that no stillbirths were reported in several years when many births occurred, it may have been the case that — just as on land — parents, like surgeons, did not expect the stillbirth to be officially reported, or that a formal burial would be held. Furthermore, it seems likely that surgeons simply assumed that there was no point in recording a full-term stillbirth in their statistical death summaries unless they also recorded a birth. A cause of death such as 'marasmus' or 'inanition' (failure to thrive) may thus have been attributed to an infant who had not in fact drawn breath, to simplify and balance their figures.

It is therefore likely that, rather than overlooking stillbirths altogether in their reports, surgeons included them among the neonatal deaths, so inflating their figures on death in comparison with reportage on land, where stillbirths were not included in mortality statistics. It is also possible that surgeons had no option but to record a stillbirth when the mother also died during delivery or shortly afterwards, in order to record a cause for her death. On the *Nepaul* bound for Victoria in 1852, one emigrant diarist described the burial of a stillborn child, whom he included in his own tally of deaths, and in doing so he was probably following the surgeon's example.[31] In the next section, we turn to the experience of infants and young children who were most likely to suffer the consequences of the voyage.

The voyage and its consequences: mothers, babies and children at risk

At sea, as on land, infants and young children accounted for most deaths in the age of sail, as we saw in Tables 1 and 2 on pages 29–30. On government-chartered voyages to South Australia, procedures directed at saving life — including the prevention of families with an excess of young children from boarding — failed to reduce infant losses. Yet it is worth stressing that, had families with numerous children under the age of seven been permitted to embark, infant losses would have been far higher, as is made manifest by several disastrous passages in 1852–53 when regulations covering age and size of family were temporarily relaxed. The Emigration Commissioners emphasised, time and again, that their calculations showed that it was not the number of children on board that influenced mortality on the voyage, but the number of children under the age of seven *per family* on board. And the children who gained from policies to limit the size of families on board were the infants' siblings, particularly those over the age of six.

Emigrant ships carried a large complement of infants and children whose health was in far more danger than those of adolescents or adults. And the childhood diseases brought on board by children occasionally affected the health of parents and older siblings. This risk was far lower on convict ships, which carried very few children. Yet, in spite of the risk of cross-infection, by 1854 adult death rates on convict and emigrant voyages had been reduced to equal the death rate for similar classes on land. Supervised sanitary and hygiene measures, which were continuously refined on government-assisted vessels following suggestions from surgeons and colonial immigration agents, continued this trend. By 1876, Queensland's immigration authorities were moved to publicly extol the benefits of public health reform. As one official put it, 'in contrast to the powerlessness of curative medicine, the power of preventing disease is about the happiest possession of science'.[32]

On all voyages bound for the Antipodes, however, the death toll of infants and young children remained higher than on land and declined much less markedly than the adult death rate. The steeper decline from about 1880 for infants and young children may have been associated with a marked reduction of births on board. Hence, with far fewer babies born at sea, the average age of infants (in total) was increased, contributing to a slight decrease in their vulnerability. Also important was the introduction of steamships, which considerably shortened the time spent at sea, thus reducing the time that infants were at risk.

Following high child mortality in 1852 and 1853, the Emigration Commissioners sought advice from medical specialists on child nutrition and, for the first time, introduced a special diet for infants and toddlers over the age of four months, as can be seen in Table 8 on page 203. Before then, infant rations had not been specified, the assumption being that women breastfed their infants or made do with available rations. However, the ration of powdered milk and powdered eggs and special farinaceous foods to compensate for loss of breast milk was insufficient to save infant life. These innovations appear, though, to have contributed to the slight improvement in the life chances of babies and young children over the age of one.

A slight rise in the average percentage mortality in the 1870s across all ages on South Australian voyages may be due to chance, given the small size of the sample, but it may also suggest that when the colonial government took over the organisation of vessels and personnel, they lacked the experience gained by the Emigration Commissioners over four decades of mobilising emigrants bound for the colonies; they soon turned to the Commission's personnel for assistance. As well, the 1870s were troubled years in the southern regions of rural England. A depression in the agricultural regions, coupled with the refusal by farmers to employ labourers involved with rural agricultural unions, meant that times were as hard as they had been in the 'hungry forties'. These regions had always been highly represented on ships bound for South Australia. Hence, the slight rise in mortality on these voyages may have been related to hardships encountered, in terms of health and well-being, in the regions where the most desired occupational groups resided. This was also a period when there was less control over the selection of candidates according to the usual health and occupational criteria, as colonial residents took advantage of remittance regulations to sponsor family and friends by paying a substantial proportion of their fare in advance. Under these conditions, it was possible that less robust people were boarding ships bound for Australia in the 1870s.

The health of children and adults on land, and their responses to life-threatening disease, appears to have been profoundly influenced by domestic and public hygiene and sanitation. Infant survival had to wait for a confluence of cultural shifts accelerated by fears of national degeneration in the wake of health surveys conducted during the Boer War, which produced a stark picture of the poor health of Britons and their children. On government emigrant ships to Australia, these cultural shifts that benefited mothers, babies and toddlers, seem to have occurred far earlier in a milieu in which state authorities on both sides of the world were monitoring each other's activities.

At sea, the percentage of births compared with the number of adult females embarked fell over time. It is probable that a contributing factor to the lower birth rate after the 1860s was that single female domestic servants were highly represented among female emigrants during the 1870s, reducing the number of pregnant women on board. The declining birth rate from the 1860s was also linked to the self-imposed decision by prospective married seekers of a government-assisted passage to delay departure until after the birth of a child. Parents-to-be may well have been persuaded by authorities of the wisdom to defer their passage even though there were no rules to prevent the embarkation of pregnant women. However, notices distributed by shipping companies in the 1830s and 1840s that, among other things, cautioned women to delay departure if they were advanced in pregnancy, appear not to have made a great deal of impact given the numerous births recorded. Hence, it is curious that an official Colonial Office minute, in 1877, argued (in response to a private letter that drew attention to the importance of preventing the embarkation of pregnant women), that

> although we have never before heard of any complaints on this subject, there can be no doubt that it would be a prudent thing if pregnant women near their confinement could be induced to defer for a time their emigration …When we conducted all the assisted emigration to the Australian and South African Colonies, we had it in our power to attach such conditions to the grant of free and assisted passages as we thought conducive to the interests of the emigrants and of the public. It was our practice, accordingly, to decline to accept as emigrants women who were likely to be confined during the voyage, and we took measures to ascertain that fact at the time the application for a passage was preferred, and before preparations for departure were made by the applicants.[33]

The number of births at sea did decline over time but, given the numerous births throughout the period, some of them within days of boarding, this argument seems somewhat disingenuous. The completed application forms have not survived, nor have the letters of acceptance to candidates advising them of their departure date. It is possible that these letters of embarkation suggested that women advanced in pregnancy delay departure, but I have not found evidence for this, nor does a caveat appear on the list of regulations for eligibility for an assisted passage, nor on the application forms. On board one high mortality voyage (the *Sultana*), to Queensland in 1866, were 40 expectant mothers among 112 married women.[34] Yet women travelling on ships chartered by the Queensland Agent General were, 'strongly advised not to travel until after confinement'. Some may have taken this advice from the 1880s, when the more regular schedules and faster voyages of steamships rendered delay more acceptable to emigrants.[35] However, as the Colonial Office 1877 minute went on to argue, there was little power under the Passenger Act to prevent pregnant women from embarking:

> The Passengers Act, it is true sanctions the rejection of persons who by reason of any bodily or mental disease is unfit to proceed or is likely to endanger the health or safety of the other passengers — but this provision of the Act has never been applied, or held to apply, to the case of pregnant women as pregnancy is not a disease, nor a cause likely to endanger the health or safety of the other passengers.[36]

Moreover, over one-quarter of all infants born on Queensland-bound vessels were primigravidae — that is, they were first-born children of mothers who were prepared to face their first confinement at sea.[37] Although colonial Agents General from the 1860s were at liberty to attempt to persuade pregnant women to delay departure, the Minute went on

> It is however to be borne in mind that the Passenger Acts require that Immigrant ships should be properly fitted with hospitals, both male & female, and should carry duly qualified medical practitioners, so that in fact poor

women have really a better provision at hand in their
confinements on board, than they can always command
on shore.

Many emigrant women who gave birth at sea and who kept diaries
or sent letters home certainly agreed. They appreciated the treatment
they received in the ship's hospital. Surprisingly, as we shall see from
their own evidence, many women believed that their confinement and
recovery was far easier at sea than previous births at home had been. It
seems, nevertheless, that during the last three or four decades of the century, some women were voluntarily delaying departure until after their
confinement. As a result, the number of embarked infants rose relative
to voyage births.[38] This delay may have contributed to the declining
number of infant deaths on board, because babies born at sea were at the
greatest risk of death. Between 1847 and 1872, on government-assisted
ships to all Australian colonies, 'the death rate of infants born on the
voyage was 66 per cent higher than that of infants embarked': fewer
births meant fewer deaths.[39]

In spite of the horrendous loss of life of infants at sea, we might bear
in mind that, according to the published figures, during 15 years in mid-
century, 90 per cent of babies born at sea survived their days, weeks or
months on board, as we can see from Table 6 on page 66. From 1860,
too, 88 per cent of male babies and 89.5 per cent of female infants born
on Queensland-bound ships were landed safely. Faster steamship voyages
in the 1880s halved the rate of infant deaths and reduced adult deaths
three-fold.[40]

In South Australia, where manuscript figures are available between
1848 and 1885, we know the date of birth of 787 of the 1436 infants
born on board and that the average duration of the passage in that period
was 95 days. About 60 per cent were born in the second half of the
voyage, among whom 15 per cent were born in the last two or three
weeks. Among the 151 infants born on board who died, 76 per cent
were buried during the second half of the voyage, among whom 28 per
cent died in the last two or three weeks of the voyage.[41] It is note-

worthy, though, that of those 787 babies born on board for whom we have the date of birth, 48 were delivered within the first nine days, and another 101 within the first month at sea. Women whose confinement was looming were not afraid to set foot upon an ocean-going vessel although, sadly, on Queensland ships between 1860 and 1900, 32 women who gave birth died, representing 1.95 per cent of live births on board.[42] On South Australian vessels, 20 maternal deaths were recorded and another seven women died within two months of giving birth, for whom the cause of death was reported as either diarrhoea, dysentery, general debility or enteritis. Of those seven deaths, four occurred well over a month after confinement. If, however, we include the three deaths of mothers who died within a month of delivery, we can stretch maternal deaths on SA voyages between 1848 and 1885 to 23 deaths. Hence, the maternal percentage loss rate relating to the 1436 live births on South Australian ships, is 1.6 per cent, marginally less than that on Queensland-bound vessels. It is also noteworthy that, among those seven women who died within two months of delivery on South Australia-bound ships, all of their infants also followed them to a watery grave. Likewise, of the 20 women for whom surgeons assigned 'childbirth' as their cause of death, 12 of their infants were also buried at sea.[43] The remaining eight infants appear to have been hand-reared by friends or relatives on board, perhaps wet-nursed by another nursing mother. Their fate in the colony is, as yet, unknown.

While maternal mortality averaged 1.6 per cent on South Australia-bound vessels, in England the percentage loss rate in the mid-19th century was 0.5 per cent, three times lower. There are, however, manifold reasons, apart from problems relating to the calculation itself, for remaining cautious about the quality of the data on land, owing to the attribution of maternal deaths to other causes, and to hidden deaths. Nor is it possible to know how many pregnant women remained uncounted in the calculations; hence the land-based rate may have been drastically underestimated.[44] On voyages, maternal deaths could not be hidden. The maritime death rate approximates that of lying-in hospitals in England (2 per cent) where transmission of puerperal fever, related to the organism responsible for scarlet fever, was prevalent. Doctors probably contributed to maternal infection in a pre-antisepsis era when home delivery by a midwife was the safest option. The prevalence of scarlet fever on emigrant ships may also have had some bearing on maternal deaths. The women were, of course, unaware that hospital deliveries were dangerous, and looked forward to medical attention in the ship's hospital.

Although it is fair to raise questions about why women put themselves and their infants at such risk, we ought not imply that 19th-century travellers applied the same risk-assessment to their own international movement as we might today. Life at home for many was grim, and infant life was tenuous at the best of times. The presence of a qualified medical practitioner on board was a comfort for many women who believed themselves to be better placed than their friends who remained behind. They did not, however, anticipate the scale of the seasickness they were about to face, which could prove so disastrous both for themselves and their infants.

Table 6

Infants born on voyages to New South Wales, Victoria, South Australia and Queensland who died at sea, 1855–1860 and 1861–69

	1855-60			1861-69		
	Born	Died	% loss rate	Born	Died	% loss rate
NSW	515	43	8.3	116	8	6.9
VIC	377	39	10.3	110	9	8.2
SA	297	37	12.5	144	17	11.8
QLD	-	-	-	97	10	10.3
All	1189	119	10.0	467	44	9.4

NOTES   The deaths of infants born on board were only reported between 1855 and 1869.
Until 1861, Queensland data were included in New South Wales tables: Data for Queensland is for 1861–67 (27 ships mobilised by the CLEC); no data were collected for Queensland by the CLEC thereafter, but see Woolcock, *Rights of Passage*, for a complete analysis of the Queensland Agent General's Data, 1861–1900.
No separate table was included for South Australia for 1848, and no CLEC ships were despatched to South Australia between 1868 and 1869, therefore South Australian figures are inclusive of 1849–67.
South Australian ships included a higher proportion of children, 1862–67 (20 per cent, compared with 15 per cent for New South Wales; 13 per cent for Victoria; 16 per cent for Queensland), suggesting a higher transmission rate for infection among susceptibles and a subsequent impact on their infant siblings.
SOURCE   Appendices to the General Reports of the CLEC.

Although tragic, maternal mortality — the death of a mother in childbirth or from a childbirth-related cause in the days following parturition — was not one of the most significant causes of death at sea. Of 195 females aged over 11 years who died on ships travelling to South Australia between 1848 and 1885, 20 deaths were recorded as childbirth-related. Among women under the age of 20, the four maternal deaths followed, in order of importance, deaths from fever, tuberculosis and brain effusions.

Whereas in England and Wales childbirth-related deaths among adult women followed in importance only tuberculosis and typhus, among the 16 women aged 20 or over who died during childbirth at sea, maternal deaths were lower in importance than causes related to fever, tuberculosis, diarrhoea and conditions related to kidneys and liver. The care given to women, including rest in hospital, a surgeon and matron's attendance and superior food, seems to have helped, as their diaries suggest.

Deaths in childbirth, however, like the deaths of newborn infants, may be related to the climatic conditions endured by women on board. They suffered seasickness far more acutely, and for longer periods, than men. This is a theme played over and again in letters and diaries written by both sexes for the entire century. The surgeons also referred to the dreadful seasickness suffered in the first fortnight of the voyage as the vessel wallowed in the English Channel and traversed the notorious Bay of Biscay, and at other stages during heavy weather. Many emigrants, but especially women, also succumbed to exhaustion during the debilitating weeks in the tropics. This had not changed in the post-war period in the 1950s, when women still suffered far more than men from seasickness. Modern medical opinion also confirms that not only do women and girls suffer more acutely, but pregnant women are particularly susceptible to motion sickness.[45] Hence, severe seasickness in the early stages of the voyage and thereafter, or collisions with furniture during rough seas, may have contributed to premature labour, increasing the chances of death of both mother and baby.

Expectant mothers whose delivery followed a long spell of seasickness or exhaustion were undoubtedly much weakened, and some, like

Bridget Coghlan on board the *Edward Parry* bound for Adelaide in 1854, were unable to withstand the rigours of labour. Dr Cornelius, the surgeon superintendent, reported that she died of 'premature labour & exhaustion from sea sickness'.[46] The deaths of two more of the 20 women who died in, or following, childbirth during the passage to South Australia between 1848 and 1885, were specifically attributed to seasickness, which may well have been involved in the deaths of a number of others.[47] Those women who had faced debilitating seasickness but who were strong enough to withstand labour undoubtedly produced weaker babies, and were possibly unable to suckle them. The cumulative effects of an excruciating bout of sickness early in the voyage on the health of expectant mothers and babies ought not be underestimated. Few diaries fail to describe, in vivid detail, the horror of those early days.

In summary, assaults on the health of both mothers and babies can be explained. Acute infectious diseases could sweep through the narrow confines of the vessel; weaning was more difficult at sea, owing to the lack of adequate substitute baby foods; diarrhoeal diseases were prevalent in the tropics, leading to the dehydration of babies; poorly ventilated steerage quarters exacerbated the vulnerability of babies who were already in danger of suffocation and overlay while sleeping in their parents' berth in a rolling vessel. The serious seasickness and stress of expectant mothers during heavy weather, and the oppressive heat of the tropics, probably induced premature, low weight, weak babies. Severe motion sickness may have caused mothers to cease breastfeeding, or to be too ill to care for them, placing their babies at greater risk, especially as other lactating mothers who might otherwise have nursed the infant of a sick mother were, probably, themselves, prostrate.

Accidents to expectant mothers, or to mothers dressed in cumbersome Victorian costume, carrying infants while attempting to climb ladders to the upper deck on a heavily rolling ship, also placed mothers, mothers-to-be and infants at greater risk. Lastly, the effects of cross-infection induced by soiled and infrequently washed nappies within the close confines of the family berth, were also significant. It was the infants, however, rather than their mothers, whose tiny bodies slipped over the side of the ship in alarming numbers. Parental neglect may have played its part.

We need a closer understanding of the extent to which the value of infant life had to be officially acknowledged before advances in life-saving regimes could be formally instituted on land. For example, as late as the 1890s, parents or carers who neglected, harmed or killed infants were often dealt with far more leniently in the courts than poachers and petty thieves. It was not until the turn of the 20th century, following exposés of the appalling health of infants in the United Kingdom, that medical students received training in infant care, including diet. Until then, their dogmatic advice on artificial feeding may have proven more harmful than helpful. Apart from a developing (and systematic) interest in improving the health of mothers, two important contributions to the fall in infant deaths around 1900 may have been a diminution during the 1890s of both the widespread dosing of infants with adulterated opiates and the common practice of bleeding and lancing gums during dentition, with its attendant risks of introduced infection.

Increasing female education and the gradual rise of the mothercraft movement from the 1860s — particularly from the 1890s — may have educated doctors as much as mothers, contributing to the (variable) impact of home visiting.[48] This may have been the most progressive improvement in human health in modern British history, during a period when eugenicist thought led to a clearer understanding of the impact of poverty on maternal and infant health. In the United Kingdom and Australia, the years between 1901 and 1911 saw an unprecedented surge in infant survival. Besides environmental improvements and emphasis on mothercare, an infant's life chances were probably also associated with a decline in female deaths from tuberculosis, associated with rising living standards and higher nutritional levels among women of childbearing age. Not only were women healthier, but the fate of their newborn infants was largely dependent on the mother's fitness: 'the environment may well exert its most powerful influence through the history of the mother before her pregnancy and what she passes on to the child'.[49]

In the case of assisted-emigrant ships, the official agents of the State initiated the increased value placed on the life of infants and young children as early as the 1830s, placing particular emphasis on infant nurture from the early 1850s. By imposing regulations on crowding and family size on board, and refusing, after 1852, to bow to colonial demands to charter double-decked ships, which carried too many vulnerable children, and by placing particular emphasis on the diet and the health of mothers, the Commissioners undoubtedly helped bring about the lower mortality regime of children at sea thereafter. It must be borne in mind, that however efficiently the surgeons managed the sanitary routines on board, airborne infections, including measles and whooping cough, could sweep through ships, carrying off numerous infants and young children.

Families at risk

The Emigration Commission was always mindful of the risks attached to embarking families with more than two children under seven, or three under ten years of age per family. Following the arrival in Port Adelaide of the *Morning Star* in 1862 with 26 deaths, among whom 25 were children from 16 families, including 22 under the age of seven, who succumbed mainly to measles, scarlatina and marasmus, the Emigration Commission's secretary reminded the South Australian authorities, whose Agent General had approved the nominated emigrants, that 'We find that the number of young children in each family has more to do with the mortality than the relative proportions of the whole number of children and adults in the ship'.[50]

The 1860s were a transitional period for the Emigration Commission; the Australian colonies had each begun appointing Agents General to take responsibility for the recruitment and selection of emigrants. The Commission's Secretary, Stephen Walcott, who had gained a wealth of experience over many years, was worried, as mortality began creeping up, that the South Australian authorities were becoming lax. A number of enquiries over the past decade or more had given him ample reason to reject families with an excessive number of young children. Reprimanding South Australia's Agent General in 1863 for allowing families with numerous young children to board a ship that had suffered high mortality, he explained that

> From a large experience we find that families containing more than two children under seven, or than three children under ten years of age, embarking on so long a voyage as that to South Australia, greatly increase the risk of sickness and mortality on board; we unhesitatingly, therefore, reject all families of that description when applying to us for passages. The value of this rule was unmistakeably shown when on one occasion, and upon the pressure of numerous Colonists, we consented so far to modify as to admit families with four children under twelve years of age, the average rate of mortality on our ships immediately jumped up from about one and a-half per cent, at which it stood before the change, to about five per cent; we then reverted to our old rule, when the mortality again dropped to the previous rate.[51]

Eight years earlier, in 1855, the worried Commissioners had warned the colonial authorities, who had declared their intention to relax the rule about family limitation in the case of nominated emigrants, that they were heading for disaster. Fresh in their mind was the bitter experience of 1852 when, under pressure from the London-based Australian Agricultural Company, they relaxed the rules. Three-quarters of the mortality on ships despatched in 1852 prevailed among children of four years and under, most of whom succumbed to scarlatina, measles and whooping cough, which, in turn, produced 'a good deal of low fever among the adult emigrants'.[52] However, sighed the Commissioners in 1855

> As this request is made by the [Australian] authorities with a full knowledge of the circumstances, we shall comply with their wishes, although we have thought it right to record our apprehension that some increase of sickness and mortality must be looked for in consequence. ... In carrying out the system, we shall endeavour so to distribute large families as not to have many of them in the same ship.[53]

In 1866, South Australia's Immigration Agent again made the point, following the arrival of a few ships with a surfeit of children per family, that when the Commissioners had been solely in charge of selecting emigrants: 'there was a limit put to the numbers of children in each family principally on account of the very great mortality amongst children of tender age; this most salutary rule has been lately ignored.'[54]

Before departure, emigrants who already had certification from a local physician or surgeon that they were fit, were superficially examined by the ship's surgeon upon their arrival at the emigrant depot at Plymouth, Southampton, Deptford or Liverpool. He looked for symptoms of disease or visible weakness, and vaccinated those with no signs of previous vaccination or smallpox scars (those who survived an attack were immune for life), or who were unable to produce a certificate of vaccination. Candidates who showed symptoms of infection of any kind, or who were considered too weak to endure the passage, were sent home. Nevertheless, incipient (and thus undetectable) infection, including measles, scarlet fever, whooping cough — all airborne pathogens — and cholera (carried in the water barrels in epidemic years) frequently accompanied passengers up the gangway to irrupt days or weeks from shore. Families who were sent home to await the recovery (or death) of an infected family member, almost certainly left infection in their wake, having mixed with the other emigrants before expulsion. Despite inspection of inoculation points or scars, smallpox also occasionally travelled on emigrant ships, brought on board before its symptoms were visible — perhaps even spread by the vaccinating process itself.

The colonial Immigration Agents interviewed the immigrants and the ships' officers and inspected the ships. They produced regular reports on the condition of the ships, on the performance of the surgeon superintendent, master and crew, on the emigrants' fitness as settlers and their state of health on arrival. These reports, which were processed by the Colonial Secretary, were forwarded in the Governor's regular despatches to the Colonial Office to be processed again by the Emigration Commission. Correspondence and reports between the various colonial governments and the Colonial Office were then included annually in the *British Parliamentary Papers* (reproduced and distributed to a wide readership as Blue Books) as were the Colonial Land and Emigration Commission's 33 annual reports with their comprehensive statistical appendices, beginning in 1840. Locally, the colonial Immigration Agents' reports were published in each colony's *Government Gazette* and *Parliamentary Papers*. Owing to extraordinary press scrutiny, emigration and the plight of emigrants were kept constantly before the public.

Voyage mortality to all destinations was always a focus of attention in the Emigration Commission's annual reports. As assisted emigration to Australia was reviving in the late 1840s, after a lull of several years, the Commissioners, in 1847, were keen to demonstrate the success of measures implemented to protect the welfare of the 'humbler classes':

> In order to show how far the attention bestowed on Australian emigration led to improvements in the art of conveying people successfully, we may be permitted so far to enter into detail as to mention, that in the Government emigration which falls within our own knowledge, there has been a progressive and unceasing diminution in the rate of mortality; and that this rate which, in 1838, was so high as 4.84 per cent, was in 1839 reduced to 2.71 per cent; and in a small emigration last year to South Australia, was no more than 0.62 per cent. In 641 souls, the only deaths were of three children and one infant. We believe that the passage to Australia may now be made by large bodies of the labouring classes, with less risk of death by disease than amongst the same number of persons living on shore in England.[55]

In the following year, 1848, the volume of assisted emigration had picked up following economic revival in the Australian colonies whose legislatures were footing the bill for introducing labour. In that year, 3073 men, women and children — mostly agricultural labourers — arrived in South Australia, and the Commissioners were

> happy to perceive that the voyages have been effected rap-
> idly and in safety, and that the health of the passengers has
> been as good as in former years. The rate of mortality was
> about 0.3 per cent. amongst the adults, and 3.31 per cent.
> amongst the children embarked.[56]

This was, indeed, a superlative achievement, given the vicissitudes of
weather, climate and environmental conditions in steerage during the
three- to four-month passage across several climate zones.

On only 17 of the 323 voyages to South Australia between 1848 and
1885 were more than 16 emigrants buried at sea. Eight per cent of ships
suffered no deaths; 54 per cent recorded five or fewer deaths; 25 per cent
recorded six to ten deaths; 8 per cent recorded 11 to 15 deaths; 3 per
cent recorded 16 to 20 deaths, and 2 per cent buried between 21 and
65 emigrants at sea.[57] The mortality profile for South Australia, as for all
colonies, is skewed by epidemics of childhood diseases on a minority of
ships between 1849 and 1854, and one or two thereafter. On the positive side — with 1829 deaths among a population of 104 368 immigrants between 1848 and 1885 — we can see that over 98 per cent of
assisted emigrants bound for South Australia were delivered safely to the
colony. Ninety-eight per cent of emigrants bound for New South Wales
and Victoria between 1848 and 1860 disembarked alive. The proportion
for Queensland was similar. The proportions landed alive for all colonies
increased to over 99 per cent from the 1860s, a superlative achievement
in the age of sail.

'The mother will be very unpleasantly situated'

Life at sea and at home

t sea the emigrants' senses were assaulted on every front. Leaving aside the odours seeping from the cooking pots in the galley, one needs little imagination to conjure up the smells in the married quarters in steerage, where often one-third of the emigrants were children, many of them untrained babies and toddlers travelling in a regime where supervised clothes washing was allowed on deck only twice weekly, and where diarrhoea prevailed. And we might consider that diarrhoea needed no pre-existing condition on board to be fatal. Emigrant medical manuals advised mothers to make up many dozens of nappies from old linen donated by friends and relatives. These were to be thrown overboard directly after use to join the detritus surging in the wake of passenger ships, which included the bedding and clothing of infected patients, as well as kitchen slops, garbage and sewage. Disposable nappies, foreshadowing the 20th century, represented one more environmental hazard in the maritime sphere. Dumping infective material in the ocean, however deleterious for the marine environment and its inhabitants, undoubtedly saved lives on board.

If one computes just one nappy change a day for a voyage of 110 days, or nine dozen nappies, their bulk would have absorbed much of the space available for the clothing of an infant's parents, leaving aside the clothing requirements of siblings.[1] If there was another untrained toddler in the family, the problem was magnified. Thus it is unlikely that more than a dozen or so nappies were brought on board for each infant. This is what one emigrant medical manual advised:

> The mother who has to take an infant on board, or she who expects to be confined on the voyage, should, for some time before her embarkation, obtain from her friends all the old cotton or linen she can procure, and manufacture them into napkins, of which she must have very many dozens; for, *as these cannot be used again* on board ship, and must, the moment they are removed, *go through the port-hole*, unless she be *well* supplied, the mother will be very unpleasantly situated.[2]

The manual also advised families to bring some quires of common brown paper to be made ready for use and kept handy, but did not mention what 'this most requisite article' was to be used for. Undoubtedly, its readers understood. The manual's insistence that soiled nappies (and menstrual napkins) go through the port-hole suggests that cabin passengers, rather than emigrants for whom there was no accessible porthole in steerage, were expected to harken to this advice. It was only the well-off who had space for many dozens of nappies. Even three changes a day for one infant on a 100-day voyage amounted to 25 dozen nappies to be disposed through the port-hole.

Curiously, no mention was made of nappy supplies either in the regulations or in the ship's stores. Thus a small supply of nappies was brought on board, or they were supplied from the limited calico yardage in the surgeon's stores. They were changed infrequently and either thrown overboard or stored beside the family berths for the twice weekly washing days. In either case, the stench below decks, where families were separated only by curtains or partitions, must have been dire, given the number of infants and toddlers on board; the potential for discomfort and cross-infection was acute. Although childbed linen was supplied with the surgeons' stores, no official mention was made in the mandatory clothing kit for emigrants of the provision of menstrual napkins for women. These were probably supplied in the form of used linen sheets, and dealt with in the same way as babies' nappies, by the women themselves.

The water closets, sometimes malfunctioning or overflowing, added another stench barely comprehensible to the modern sensibility. Take into consideration, too, the severe seasickness at the beginning of the voyage and on entry to the Southern Ocean after the calm of the tropics, and a modern reader's stomach may begin heaving in sympathy. Permeating the fetid air produced by numerous adults and children living in close proximity were the daily fumigants smoking away in charcoal and tar-burning swinging stoves. Other malodorous disinfectants, sprinkled liberally on the decks and bottom boards of the berths, including chloride of lime or zinc mixed with vinegar and other solutions, would be familiar to anyone who has ever smelled creosote.

Yet a curious omission from the commentary of emigrants and surgeons — especially on stormy voyages — is the extent to which seasickness early in the voyage and on entry into the Southern Ocean, as well as the presence of so many babies on board, created what we might think of today as a vile and stinking purgatory below decks. Rarely do emigrants or surgeons mention (except on the few ghastly fever ships of the early 1850s) the horrendous smells created by a combination of vomit, faulty water closets and diarrhoea below decks. Nor do even the most intimate diaries focus on lack of privacy for married couples — nor the reactions of neighbours to ardent coupling by those accustomed to crowded conditions at home. Undoubtedly, many did not abstain from copulation during the three months at sea in spite of the narrow, three-foot-wide bunks shared by couples; single women occasionally entertained lovers chosen from the crew.

It is important to recall that, even though Australia-bound emigrants were self-selecting individuals who were screened for their health and respectability, life at home was generally crowded, and domestic arrangements uncomfortable, even wretched, for the classes from whom many emigrants were drawn, especially before the 1870s. They were accustomed to living in close quarters with large families; their incomes were low and they had little to spare for even the humblest luxury. Their

lives could be hell on earth, as Anthony Wohl demonstrates so evocatively. Quoting Sir John Simon, one of the most eminent medical officers of the Victorian age and an enthusiastic promoter of preventative
public health, Wohl offers some insights into the state of the urban environment in Britain. This description, written by John Simon in 1849,
was true of many towns, too, and some rural villages provided their own
environmental horrors:

> It requires little medical knowledge to understand that
> animals will scarcely thrive in an atmosphere of their own
> decomposing excrements, yet such ... is the air which a
> very large proportion of the inhabitants of the City are
> condemned to breathe ... in a very large number of cases
> [the cesspool] ... lies actually within the four walls of the
> inhabited house; the latter ... receiving and sucking up
> incessantly the unspeakable abomination of its volatile
> contents ... where the basement ... is tenanted, the
> cesspool lies — perhaps merely boarded over — close
> beneath the feet of a family ..., whom it surrounds unin-
> terruptedly, whether they wake or sleep, with its fetid pol-
> lution and poison.[3]

These conditions, John Simon observed, were 'a removable cause of
death', and he might well have been echoing the sentiments of the
various government departments who had successfully ameliorated conditions on convict and emigrant ships since 1815. In market towns,
cesspools and drains were awash with foul-smelling effluent from pig
and cattle slaughter houses and dairies, and as late as 1900, ten million
tons of horse manure were deposited annually on the streets of English
towns.

Street cleaning alone was an almost insoluble problem, as a reading
of Dickens' *Bleak House* will confirm. 'Jo the crossing sweeper' represented a legion of boys operating in the alleys and streets of Britain's
commercial and industrial towns in the 19th century: 'Tom All Alone's'
was recognisable to most lower-class Victorians. On market days in
country towns, and even in large cities including London, dairy and beef

cattle, sheep and pigs were herded through the streets. In 1873, 1500 slaughter houses were daily despatching beasts in London alone. Annually, nearly 350 000 cattle, over 1.5 million sheep and nearly 15 000 pigs were brought to the central London market for domestic consumption and to Deptford for foreign trade. The excrement they left in their wake, augmenting the vast drifts of horse manure, was prodigious, creating enormous problems for disposal even though much of it was sold as fertiliser to farmers. Respectable Victorian householders — who walked the same streets and breathed the same air as their servants, shopkeepers and tradesmen — kept their windows closed in summer.[4]

Rail transport had promoted, rather than limited, horse-drawn transport as ever-increasing networks of railway lines increased the rate at which produce and people were ferried around the country to be picked up and delivered by carts, drays and cabs. Thirteen thousand cattle and sheep were slaughtered weekly in London's abattoirs in 1892; blood and waste products had long flowed along the drains, augmenting 'the filth and stench of the city'. In the 1870s, when a Southampton doctor

> visited a patient who lived within 7 feet of an open cesspool into which flowed all the wash and blood of a local pig-killing establishment, he reported that the 'smell was so pestiferous that he (not being stink-seasoned) could not remain five minutes without fainting'.[5]

We may infer from conditions on shore that life below decks — except on ships encountering the stormiest weather — when hatches were battened for days on end during an excessively unfavourable season at sea — was tolerable for most 'stink-seasoned' emigrants and their surgeon superintendents. Many even enjoyed the voyage, which suggests that the cleanliness and hygiene routines worked well. Otherwise, over a three-month voyage, mortality would surely have been far higher, and complaints vociferous. The swinging stoves and their sulphurous fumigants, the daily scrubbing, and the buckets of disinfectant sloshed about, together with vigilant supervision by the sanitary constables, must have worked to the satisfaction of most diarists, whose complaints about the noise and pollution below decks are rare. With the daily scrubbing and fumigating routines, and adequate ventilation, numerous emigrants found that the fumigants and disinfectants sweetened the air considerably. Many well-disciplined ships appear to have avoided the noisome stenches reported on those pestilent vessels that seriously tested the patience and temper of their human cargo (and of the authorities who examined the ships on arrival).

Noise, too, was fearful at times: the creaking timbers, the cracking masts, the thundering sea boiling over the decks as giant waves crashed over the superstructure and poured down every crevice. This, together with the sinister sound of tearing canvas in heavy weather, was terrifying. Many emigrants enjoyed a relatively uneventful, fair-weather passage. But the pitching of the vessel and its groaning frame, the flapping and banging of the sails, and constant shouting of the crew, let alone the squabbles of children and adults, combined to create a racket from which many emigrants sought retreat by finding relatively quiet corners under the lifeboats or behind coils of rope.

The ship, in reality, constituted a tenement block of two to five hundred people or more, with a similar mix of ages, the main difference being that the seafarers were under the strict supervision of an authority to whom submission was mandatory. And there was no escape. For four decades and more from the early 1840s, except under special circumstances, ships sailed directly to the Australian colonies, calling at no ports en route. Hence, for around 100 days, the incessant din, uproar, movement and vile odours, which would defeat a modern passenger, accompanied the emigrants as they rolled, lurched or sped their way to their new lives in Australia.

'Poor Little Alfred
was the first that died'

The 1820s and 1830s

From Leith to Hobart, 1820

By 1820, fares to Australia were exorbitantly high. Terms demanded for a voyage to New South Wales or Van Diemen's Land (Tasmania) on the *Skelton* in that year were 70 guineas for a cabin and 40 guineas for a steerage passage (one-third less to the Cape of Good Hope). By comparison, a steerage fare in the high volume 1850s varied between £15 and £20. Even with ship owners finding provisions and livestock for consumption on the voyage, the fare remained beyond the means of a British or Irish worker.

On the *Skelton*, just four weeks after departure on the 22-week voyage, a passenger was 'delivered of a fine boy'. James Dixon, a diarist on board, wrote 'Her recovery was speedy and complete; so much so, that she said, jocularly, a ship was as good for ladies in that way, as the shore, where there was so much attention paid to them'.[1] This is a refrain that, in spite of the tragic loss of infant life in the maritime sphere, echoes throughout the following chapters.

Although measles, typically, broke out among the children on this vessel, with a number of adults also attacked, 'the distemper proved of a very mild kind'. Thirty-six children and five adults were sick, 'yet no death occurred'. James Dixon believed that the medical officer was responsible for their recovery:

> Here it may be observed, that in this malady, attention
> to air, diet, and medical experience, is of utmost

consequence to children; and in this instance, considerable advantage was derived from the skill of a Medical Gentleman of experience, who was on board as a passenger. The disease began in the family of Mr Headlam, and had been communicated to that family by travelling in the same coach from London, with a child who had just recovered.

This is the earliest example I have found of an emigrant testifying to the importance of a good medical officer on board. James Dixon understood, as did his peers, the dangers of infection met on the way to the port of embarkation or during the days prior to boarding. The communication of infection was well understood, in spite of theoretical debates during the 19th century between contagionists and anti-contagionists. The latter followed the miasmatic theory that germs spontaneously erupted in filthy, damp, musty or marshy areas and argued against the communicability of disease from person to person, with the exception of specific diseases such as smallpox and measles. This was not as obtuse as it might look today, given that their catchcry was a sensible one: if it smells bad, it is bad. Many medical men planted a foot firmly in both camps, and numerous miasmatists, or anti-contagionists, led the sanitarian charge against dirt and disease in the early to mid-19th century; as we have seen, mortality — especially infant mortality — remained appalling in the United Kingdom's cities and industrial towns until after the turn of the 20th century.

Published accounts of experiments and experiences at sea on slave, merchant and convict ships in tropical and temperate zones from the late 18th century were crucial in disseminating knowledge about the communication and containment of disease. Public health reformers of the mid-19th century looked to these and to successful methods long used by the British army during peacetime to promote health among its troops. They were also influenced by the zeal of reformers in prisons and other public institutions, in their attempts to clean up slums and push forward the 'sanitary ideal', including the introduction of clean, piped water and sewerage systems.

The medical officer on the *Skelton* was a beneficiary of this maritime expertise. The routines on board this pioneering emigrant ship on the Australian route had been recommended for convict ships by the Redfern report of 1814. Dancing to music played by emigrants — there were always musical instruments on board — was recommended as an excellent exercise for alleviating ennui, reviving the spirits and promoting appetite and good health. Water, typically, was a problem. Casks taken on at Leith at the beginning of the voyage had tasted bad, although 'not injurious to health'. Better water had been taken on at Portsmouth, which improved in flavour once the ship reached colder climates.

On reaching Table Bay, at the Cape of Good Hope, 14 weeks into the passage, the ship was forced to hoist its quarantine flag, having admitted to the presence of measles, although the last case had recovered three weeks earlier. The families on board were bitterly disappointed; they had looked forward to taking the children ashore for a romp, washing their linen and taking on refreshments 'as would be conducive to health for the further prosecution of the voyage'. Only the captain, the doctor and a few cabin passengers were permitted to go ashore to organise fresh stores, and a few young men left the ship to take up employment at lucrative rates of pay. No children or 'foul linen' were allowed off the boat and all washing had to be done on the upper deck. Although the port's Health Officer and the Colonial Secretary were polite to the passengers and emigrants, the officials refused to release the ship from quarantine because the Dutch at the Cape

> having a number of slaves, on which, perhaps, no inconsiderable part of their incomes depended, were dreadfully alarmed at the idea of a ship where the measles had prevailed coming near them.

Slavery was declared illegal in the United Kingdom in 1772 and, after decades of agitation, an Act of Parliament abolished the British slave trade in 1807. In 1795, the British conquered the Cape from the Dutch East India Company, and later returned it to the Dutch — the Batavian

Republic — before repossessing it permanently in 1806 until Union in 1910. In 1833, slavery was abolished throughout the British Empire. British naval vessels patrolled the oceans for ships carrying slaves travelling under other national flags, liberating them in Liberia or Sierra Leone. Emigrants in mid-century occasionally saw slave ships, noting that the vessels were designed to lie low in the water to avoid detection. British authorities at the Cape Colony were unwilling to upset Dutch slave-owning inhabitants at the time that the *Skelton* visited in 1820. A few years earlier, introduced measles had 'carried a great many of their slaves off, as well as a number of free inhabitants and children'.

The 260-ton *Skelton* sailed from Leith in Scotland on 19 June with 57 passengers and a crew of 17, taking on another 21 passengers at Portsmouth. They arrived in Hobart on 26 November 1820, with no mishap after leaving the Cape, apart from the death of an elderly man a day before reaching port — his health had been declining since sailing from Table Bay. Naval officers inspected the ship: 'the arrival of a vessel with so many settlers was an object of some importance in the colony', Dixon wrote. The *Caroline*, carrying around 40 passengers, arrived on the same day, intensifying the excitement. Bowing to etiquette, all settlers immediately called upon Governor Sorrell, who determined the extent of land grants to each arrival. Although he was fascinated with everything he found in Hobart, James Dixon's snobbery got the better of him once he was among polite society again. He found Hobart's 'small society' stifling and lacking in good will. Tasmanian Aborigines, he wrote in a tone typical of his era, 'are distinct from New Hollanders [he was probably referring to mainland Aborigines] both races are in the lowest scale of human beings'. He was, however, impressed with convict children, whom he saw as far healthier than their counterparts in England, being 'tall and well made'. Moreover, they

> speak a better language, purer, more harmonious, than is generally the case in most parts of England. The amalgamation of such various dialects assembled together, seems to improve the mode of articulating the words.

The Australian accent, it seems, was already audible.

'*A most beautiful voyage*' *to South Australia, 1838*

Eighteen years later, another reasonably well-off family travelled to South Australia as intermediate cabin passengers (roughly equivalent to a second-class passage) along with a few other cabin passengers in both intermediate and first class and a number of steerage emigrants on a ship chartered by the South Australian Colonisation Commissioners. All of the emigrants and passengers were subsidised by the South Australian Company. Although it was soon to become bankrupt, and would have to be bailed out by the Colonial Office, which took over its administration, in 1836 the Company had set up the new non-convict settlement of South Australia on Wakefieldian lines, whereby the sale of land and the introduction of labour and capital were to be kept in balance. This meant, according to the principles of the system's architect, Edward Gibbon Wakefield, that capitalists with ample means should be introduced under favourable terms to purchase land and to employ the agricultural labourers, domestic servants and rural tradesmen who were to be conveyed on free passages to work on the farms, service the colonial households both indoors and out, and erect the buildings necessary for the social and economic development of a new colony.

Sarah and George Brunskill, aged 26 and 40, and their two young children sailed for the two-year-old colony on a subsidised passage from Plymouth on the 355-ton *Thomas Harrison* in November 1838, with over 100 other emigrants on a passage superintended by Dr BH Yate. They arrived in February 1839, after a voyage of 15 weeks, having buried both of their children at sea, as we have seen. Yet, despite their distress and grief, and in spite of the deaths of many more children at sea — 30 in all — Sarah Brunskill, like many emigrants who endured similarly heartbreaking experiences, maintained a sense of optimism about her future in the colony. Her keen observations, rural middle-class in tone, expectation and sense of dutiful largesse, reflect the experiences of the better off subsidised travellers on emigrant vessels. Her descriptions, like those of her fellow diarists, again remind us that conditions that 21st-century observers would find intolerable were not exceptional to people of her class and time. Writing home to her parents in Ely, Cambridgeshire, Sarah described their voyage.

Having sailed from Plymouth with a fair wind, she suffered a sore throat, which, she believed, was cured by the application of leeches. Her children too, had sickened with sore throats. Sarah thought their health was improving, but within eight days of sailing her infant son died. Less than 24 hours later, her two-year-old daughter, too, was buried at sea; her anguished response is recorded in the Preface. Her servant, possibly employed as a housekeeper, who was travelling in steerage with her own family, was a tower of strength:

> without her we must have laid out our darlings: without her we should have wept alone. She did all in her power to soothe and comfort. She has 5 children of her own but has never known the pang of losing one. Is this the lesson given to wean our hearts from this world? May it work in us the means of salvation![2]

The Brunskills' infant son died following a night of 'strong convulsions'; he had suffered an acute attack of diarrhoea. Thirsting for water during that last night,

> the last spoonful I gave him appeared to choke him. For two days he grated his teeth dreadfully — he had 4, poor dear. Three or four hours before he died his tongue looked all over white scales and it appeared to rattle against his teeth. He was nothing but bones, not a shadow of himself.

Their daughter succumbed to measles

> from which we thought she was recovering nicely, but inflammation seized her throat, and the agony she suffered you can never fancy. We applied a linseed poultice mustard plaster to her chest, and a blister — but all to no avail; her heavenly spirit was in haste to join her brother and

meet her God. The heat she was in before she died was great, it was painful to touch her, her arms were covered with blisters about the size of a pea or a cowpock and she had a few on her forehead. They were quite white. I should not have known her, had I not been always with her. When dead she looked like Ann: two little angels they looked, so beautiful in death. She, like her brother, was thrown into the deep about the same time on the Thursday. The Union Jack was thrown over them, and the burial service performed.

Many emigrants used the term 'thrown into the deep' to describe a burial at sea, although for the most part both children and adults were buried with sincere respect in the presence of the captain, crew, passengers and officials on board. Many diarists describe the weeping of the captain and crew during the burial of children. Captains, who were usually responsible for reading the burial service, frequently broke down, unable to continue, handing the prayer book to another officer to officiate. Bodies were encased in a shroud made by the sailmaker, weighted and slipped over the side in the most decorous way possible, dependent on the state of the weather and the ocean. Most surgeons assembled the emigrants for the burial service as a mark of respect to parents; music and dancing were suspended for the day. Sarah told her parents, 'The night our Missy died it blew a very strong gale, the most stormy night but once since we have been on board'. Under those conditions, and given the urgency with which — for the sake of the passengers' health — bodies had to be interred at sea, it is little wonder that the disposal of the dead often looked perfunctory, especially in heavy seas where it was dangerous to assemble the ship's company and passengers on deck. During storms, which sometimes raged for days, bodies were committed to the ocean through the surgeon superintendent's porthole after he had read the burial service.

Fourteen days into the voyage, Sarah recorded the death of 'poor Mrs Richman's third child'. At least, she sighed, they had three left. Eight children had died within the first fortnight of the passage, either from diarrhoea or sore throats, possibly scarlatina. Sarah believed that she, too, would have died had it not been for the application of leeches: 'My tongue began to swell, and I could scarcely speak or breathe, but now both George and myself are well, with the exception of weakness'.

The weather began to get warmer after the first fortnight. 'But', she wrote, barely able to articulate their suffering, 'we have no children to enjoy the change. Everything reminds us of them and reminds us we are alone'. Ten days later, however, Sarah's natural stoicism had returned. In spite of her sorrow, she was alive to the confined world that she temporarily inhabited. Having finished her previous journal entry by referring to their bitter loneliness, she told her parents that nothing particularly worth mentioning had happened during the past ten days, although the weather was too warm even for summer clothing. She was determined, however, to give them 'a slight sketch of how we spend our time'. After describing her fellow intermediate passengers, among whom there were petty jealousies and class differences that she found odious, Sarah outlined their daily routine, in which the preparation and cooking of meals was shared by the families in the intermediate section:

> We have to prepare our own meals, fetch our water, and
> in fact do everything we require except sweep our cabin,
> and that one of the boys does every morning. We have
> agreed to take a day to ourselves to do everything, so
> every third day comes my turn.

The fine, warm weather and fair winds brought with them a sighting of the Canary Islands. The spectacle of the phosphorescent sea that so delighted countless emigrants, including Sarah, inevitably reminded her of her children ('around the vessel it looked like liquid silver and every little billow appeared tinged with the same'). Her vivid descriptions and growing optimism were interwoven with her lamentations for her son and daughter:

> every box I open contains some kind gift or something
> belonging to our darlings. Little do you (now that I am

writing) know what we are suffering. My days appear so long and heavy. My patchwork will get finished now.

Rallying her spirits again, she told her parents that 'This is a life that would do William [possibly her brother] a world of good'. She continued,

it would teach him a lesson he could never forget. He would be able to drink after his <u>mother</u> at his journey's end, and eat with a steel fork which only gets cleansed by washing in dirty, greasy, salt water. We cannot get fresh water to wash up in, as we often fall short without. It is very bad now — all live, and stinks worse than our Ely soft water ever did. This voyage would be quite the making of him, as it would teach him to work in every way and put up with inconveniences he now never thinks of.

But in saying all this, do not think I mean to say we are badly provided for — we are not. Our provisions are of the best kind and more than we ever can consume. Twice a week we have 3 lb $^1/2$ of preserved meat to which we put a quart of water and it makes a most excellent soup. Our North-Country woman [their servant who was such a source of strength during the illness and deaths of the children] makes yeast, so we bake fresh bread every day, a great luxury I can assure you. Twice a week we have salt beef which is not good — the other days pork and as fine meat as I ever wish to eat; potatoes one day, and rice the next; a plentiful supply of raisins, so we often have good puddings. The flour and suet are as good as I ever had at home. In short our provisions are of the best kind, but we have as great a thief for a steward as ever was born. On Sunday the sailors struck, swearing unless they had their full allowance they would not stir a hand, and the Captain was obliged to accede to every thing. George had a great quarrel with him the Friday before; the steward gave our servants a pound and $^1/2$ short, which was carrying the joke too far, so George took it up and told the

Captain the steward was a d— rascal. The Captain said he would make him remember saying such a thing, but he repeated it, and told the Captain he was not afraid of anything he could do when he held with such a thief. The provisions are weighed out in our cabin, and we often see the steerage passengers cheated of a pound and a $^1/_2$ of sugar and different quantities of other things.

Ten days further into the passage, a ship was sighted in the distance, but did not come close enough to exchange letters. They had now been at sea for six weeks,

and ten children have died, and before many weeks are past there will be many more, all from the same complaint. George has been suffering the last three days, but I hope he will now lose it, or I shall be afraid it is something of the same kind as what they call the dysentery which disease carries off whole armies. The heat is now great, but nothing to what we are to expect. ... I have made George a straw hat, and a very good one it is, so if we cannot succeed well in farming we shall turn straw-bonnet makers. George has learnt to plait the straw from one of the sailors, so fancy us employ'd. The warm weather here brings out swarms of flies, cockroaches and bugs, the last mentioned in comparison are trifling inconveniences.

A month later, Sarah was tiring of the voyage and had endured a serious falling out with another family, but was comforted by the 'magnificent beauty of our sunsets — they are most glorious'.

The captain, in Sarah's eyes a rogue, had quarrelled with her husband and taken to letting the family's fowls loose on deck in the hope that they would fly away. But the steerage emigrants to whom the Brunskills had been solicitous looked after the fowls, fed them and prevented their loss: 'the sailors all mean to leave him at Australia on account of his shabby treatment, so I think our fowls are safe.' Moving straight on to tragic matters, she recorded the death of another child, making 17 so far, 'and I believe all could have been saved with care and proper medical attention. Ours I am sure would have been alive had we been on shore'. Sarah did not mention the medical officer, so it is difficult to know what kind of attention the children received; had he been at all comforting, she surely would have recorded it.

On the eve of arriving in South Australia, while the ship tacked up and down the coast waiting for a favourable wind to enter harbour, Sarah's spirits sank as she anxiously contemplated the next phase of settlement. Nevertheless, she reassured her parents, 'altogether we have had a most beautiful voyage since we left the Channel, even you would have enjoyed it. No one has been ill from sickness since we left the Channel'. Able to separate her private grief from the experience of the voyage as a whole, she was determined to make the best of the opportunities offered them. Reminding her parents that she and her husband remembered all of the birthdays that had occurred at home since their departure, Sarah did not doubt that the family at home, assuming the best, had also drunk the health of

> our dear children, alas they were not with us. The day our dear girl was thrown over George was standing hearing the service performed, and during the time he pulled out his handkerchief and with it his silver snuff-box, which went into the sea, so he has quite left off snuff — has not had any for months now and never intends to take it again. It appeared like a warning for him to leave it off, his losing his box at that time, did it not?

The first mate's death from consumption (tuberculosis) had brought the toll to 20, 'and almost all from want of attention'. Sarah had tried to comfort him with lozenges, and she cooked him arrowroot pudding, gruel, sago and other treats such as rusks and soda water, all without the captain's knowledge, and all to no avail. Three children had been born on board, one stillborn, but the other two infants and their mothers were doing well by the end of the voyage. 'The ship is like a little town, as much scandal and ill-nature prying into each other's affairs, you would hardly believe'. Had she the spirits, Sarah 'might have written quite a history of our voyage, as we are looked up to as the chief persons on board, although there are cabin passengers'. She recommended the efficacy of fresh barm (a yeast made from 'porter bottoms', the dregs from barrels of beer or stout), and offered to send the recipe for this excellent rising agent for cakes and bread. But

> we have found the preserved meat the last 11 weeks so bad that we cannot eat it, and that is served to us three times a week. What a treat will a little fresh meat be to us, but this voyage will reconcile us to many things on shore we should have thought very hardly of had we gone from England to Australia without it.

Sarah, though, was fortunate in her servant, who not only helped her with preparing yeast and meals for the intermediate passengers when it was the Brunskills' turn, but cared for her own family of five children in steerage.

Having arrived at Holdfast Bay on 24 February 1839, Sarah wrote on 12 March, 'Glad enough I am to address you from this place', which they had glimpsed as their first landfall since sighting the Canaries during the first fortnight of the voyage:

> we landed on one of the most sandy plains you can imagine, swarming with fleas. The sand is alive with them [perhaps she encountered the ubiquitous, viciously biting sandfly]. The bedroom that was shown to us was perfectly clean to all outward appearance, but before we went to bed we thought we would look — like fleas . . well, we turned the counterpane down and if you will believe me we killed until we were tired, so we resolved not to undress, but lay on the outside of the bed with our clothes on and tucked the counterpane in all round to keep the fleas to themselves, but that was impossible — they found us out, and by daybreak we had the appearance of small-

pox. I need not tell you we left the den as soon as we could, and walked after parts of our luggage they had landed, saw it packed on a bullock-cart of which there are not a few, five and six bullocks to a cart. They charge 25/- a load 7 miles, and only one load a day [to the township of Adelaide].

Having secured their section of land from the South Australian Company (as a quid pro quo for paying part of their passage), they found lodgings at a hotel while they waited for their temporary house to be built. Although the hotel building was not much to look at

they feed us uncommonly well — hot meat for breakfast and fish and meat for dinner, for which, with tea, bedroom and glass of porter at dinner, they charge £2 each a week. It is a great price, but what could we do? We could not get lodgings under £12 for three months, and when we find everything — meat 1/- a lb [one shilling per pound weight], fresh butter 3/6, salt 2/6, eggs 6d [sixpence] each, wine 6/- a bottle, brandy [blank] a gallon, no rum or gin, beer 3/6 a bottle. ... You cannot get a carpenter under 12/- to 20/- a day, and then they only work eight hours at that. We have engaged a young man who came out with us for £1 a week and find him everything for six months, so we think ourselves fortunate. Our house is not yet laid out. I shall not be able to tell you anything about it this time, as I wish to forward this by the first opportunity.

Despite swarms of flies, Sarah found the countryside in mid-summer 'more beautiful than I ever formed any idea, more like a gentleman's park than anything'. With her new farmhouse in mind, she anticipated lawns and a very good garden even though 'the weather in the middle of the day is suffocating, but the mornings and evenings are delightful' and were her family there, she would 'not wish to return'. Within weeks of landing, the Brunskills' workmen had sunk a well and begun digging the gardens. Although still in mourning, their pioneering spirit overcame the shock of a new climate and the hot, dry, environment:

> George has killed only one snake, I have not seen one, so I hope we shall not be troubled. Parrots, cockatoos, lauries [lorikeets, small brightly coloured birds] and magpies abound, kangaroo is very scarce. I have not seen any, but those who have tasted it pronounce it delicious. Parrot pie is very good, very like pigeon. Fish 3/- a pound. No fish in appearance like the English, but in flavor like turbot — it is called snapper, in shape like tench, and weighs from 8 lbs to 24 lbs. Smaller fish in abundance, like mackerel to look at but in taste like trout. Very few oysters. Hens 10/- each, geese 13/-.

Within weeks the Brunskills were settled on a property close to Adelaide, which they named *Sandford* after George's birthplace. Their dwelling, which they shared with their servants, was a temporary modular structure brought from England on the ship. This may have been a Manning house, one of various designs carried in kit form by better off settlers, in which they lived until a permanent, grander structure could be built.

The sun dried Sarah's washing faster than she could hang it out, 'and it whitens more than a week's frost would in England. There is no end of washing here, as clothes are dirty with dust as soon as on'. Although 'the heat is great and I get so tired that I hardly have strength … we never were so well in our lives'. Settlers often endured poor health during the acclimatising or 'seasoning' phase, as the early settlement period is sometimes called, as they adapted to their new environment, but the Brunskills fared well in this initial phase. Yet the summer brought eye infections or ophthalmia, the curse of settlers in dry, dusty regions of Australia, which Sarah blamed on wood smoke and the consumption of too much salt meat. In spite of the disadvantages, she wrote, 'anyone with care and industry may get on well here'.

Sarah, with grapevines in mind for her garden, reminded her parents to 'let me have the recipe for champagne, and whatever you send us, let it be packed in small barrels, as they travel best. ... I shall like some acid and soda when you send, as it is more refreshing than anything'. Women frequently asked for stocks of tartaric and citric acid and baking soda. These were used on the voyage and in the colony for medicinal purposes — as a refreshing effervescent drink to combat dyspepsia and constipation — as well as for baking. With an assurance that they maintained their Christian faith, that they and their servants took it in turn to attend church on alternate Sundays, she saluted her parents on behalf of her husband with 'God bless and keep you all alive until we return'. With a postscript ending 'Again God bless you and preserve you', Sarah's journal came to a close.

Like numerous settlers, the Brunskills' intention was to make their fortune and return home with it. But, typically, they stayed on. George was buried in the West Terrace Cemetery, aged 67, having described himself in official records as a farmer and merchant, and having lived at various residences. Sarah lived another 34 years; she died in 1900, aged 87, having outlived three of the eight children born to her in the colony, only one of whom, her last born daughter, did not survive childhood. Three of her daughters died before the age of 50, the others at 68, 84 and 96. Her only son lived for 73 years.[3] For a couple who arrived bereft of their two first-born, and who faced the unforgiving climate in a harsh environment devoid of even the basic necessities of life in the new settlement, their migration had proven extraordinarily successful in terms of fecundity and longevity.

The surgeons' strategies

The emigrants' moral and spiritual health was seen as an integral component of their physical and mental well-being. In 1834, Surgeon Superintendent Charles D Logan had sailed with female emigrants bound for Hobart on the *Sarah*. Owing to the success of this voyage in terms of health, his statement of the system he adopted was copied and circulated for the use of other surgeon superintendents, and most followed his routines. This zealous surgeon conducted religious worship every day and twice on Sundays. He read to the emigrants from 'Burders

Village Sermons' and organised hymn singing, scripture and tract read-ings.[4] Women among the cabin passengers on board conducted the Sunday School. Services were tailored to the rhythms of shipboard life and held on the poop deck, weather permitting. Classes were formed for schoolchildren and adults, many of whom 'were unacquainted with the alphabet at the beginning of the voyage, [but] were enabled to read the scriptures at its termination'. Dr Logan distributed Bibles and testaments to each mess, where literate emigrants took it in turns to read a chapter to the others daily. He believed that the efficacy of daily worship should not be underestimated: it 'arrested the attention of the most volatile, and influenced the conduct of all during the remainder of the day'. Most of all, he emphasised, if the surgeon superintendent was to gain the respect of the emigrants, his own conduct ought to be a model for others to fol-low. As one of many amusements, he encouraged emigrants to write short essays on particular texts, 'offering a trifling premium for the best exposition next morning'. In this way, he found, bad habits were curbed by diversions of a higher moral tone.

Mrs Logan, the surgeon's wife, superintended the single women, who were employed making up clothing provided by the ship owner (who was paid a bounty for the delivery of the single women and families to Hobart). Dr Logan's object was to use the voyage for improving the edu-cation, skills and morals of all on board, but health was his main concern:

> The hour of rising varied from 5 to 6 o'clock. Before breakfast all Beds and Blankets neatly folded up, the Deck swept, and personal cleanliness attended to, after Breakfast all order'd on Deck but the appointed cleaners, who uni-formly washed and scrubbed the lower Deck, bottoms of berths etc. — ventilation and occational fumigation also rigidly attended to.[5]

The women's virtue was always a principal concern of the surgeons, the colonial authorities and the women themselves, who demanded the protection they had been promised from the unwanted attention of sailors and male emigrants:

> An order being issued on the Voyage prohibiting females from going near the forecastle, none were allowed access to the Cook's coppers without a Pass Ticket on the special leave of the Superintendent when Tea or Cocoa were served out a married passenger was station at the Coopers 'foreward' and another at the Main hatchway, beyond which the female was allowed to pass till the number of her Mess was called. When, on receiving her allowance, she was obliged at once to retire. At Dinner the Meat was always brought from the Coppers in a Tub and served out near the Capstan ... All females were ordered off Deck immediately at Night fall, and in warm latitudes when obliged to relax this rule, a watch was placed at either side of the Deck to patrol from the Main Hatch to the Forecastle and thus impede all intercourse thither but generally speaking when evening came the Single Females were ordered on the Poop further aloof from the Seamen.

Dr Logan always mustered the male emigrants after the women were sent below, and later patrolled with a female attendant, to ascertain 'that each berth only contained its proper occupants'. He was unhappy with railings placed over the hatchway to deter the ingress of sailors by order of the London Emigration Committee, the body responsible for chartering the ship and selecting the single women. The railings interfered with the circulation of air below decks, where it was crucial for health. Once the railings were removed, Dr Logan induced the married men to act as guards at the hatchways on a rota system every night, which he believed to be invaluable in protecting the women. Any single woman found conversing with a sailor was confined 'two or three days to her berth and her Wine stopped'. A repeat offender was confined under the same conditions for a week on a bread and water diet. In exchange for a free passage to a new life of full employment abroad, women were expected to toe the line.

Surgeons frequently — for the next half-century or more — deprived emigrants of food treats, or confined them to a strict diet, as a

Quarter deck of an emigrant ship: The roll call
(*Illustrated London News*, 6 July 1850)

form of punishment for insubordination: draconian by modern standards, but order on board ship was crucial. Petty jealousies could lead to serious disruption of the routines and to the collapse of discipline altogether, leading to a seriously unhealthy voyage. Dr Logan even suspended the distribution of medicinal wine to emigrants — male and female — who failed to appear at Divine Service, or for late rising. Daily rations were issued at 5 am or 6 am to encourage early rising, so that emigrants got on with their chores before spending most of the day in the fresh air on deck. Married men were rostered on cleaning duty, water delivery to the messes, preparing potatoes and meat for the cook, and so forth.

Following naval procedure, separate messes were formed for families and single women, six to a mess, a routine that was followed for many decades. On embarkation, each mess was issued with a card of the names of its members. This ticket was produced when rations were issued by the surgeon superintendent with the assistance of selected married men, who were chosen at random every day to prevent jealousy among them and to promote confidence 'as to the justice of the distribution' of supplies. Dr Logan's object, he wrote, was to watch over 'the employment, conduct and conversation of all on board'. It was a surgeon's duty, he believed, to superintend 'without cruelty' and to be kind to the deserving. A demonstration of

> true solicitude, for the temporal, and eternal welfare of the entire, will on all occasions procure for the Superintendent, the respect, and esteem, of those placed under his supervision and produce at the end of a long Voyage, the delightful attestation that all have been comfortable and happy.

Dr Logan's statement of his system was copied and handed to a surgeon who followed him the year after on a voyage to Launceston also chartered under the auspices of the London Emigration Committee. Dr William Ronald, on board the *Amelia Thompson*, also carried a copy of the Committee's instructions. Many surgeons worked on both convict and emigrant vessels from 1831, and the Committee was anxious to stress the differences between the two human cargoes. Dr Ronald was charged with responsibility for promoting the 'domestic happiness' of all on board. He was to treat the Commander of the vessel 'with deference and respect', to co-operate with him and to seek his advice and consent over rearranging ventilation and fittings on board. The Committee cautioned Dr Ronald against treating the emigrants as convicts: no use of force 'as expedient for convicts' was to be employed. Although 'under pecuniary obligation', having been given free passages, emigrants were entirely free and independent, and the surgeon's 'means of compelling obedience on their parts proportionably limited'. More respectable than convicts, 'their moral sense of propriety will, it is hoped, in most cases obviate the necessity of coercion — conciliation consequently will supply your most effective engine of operation'. His duty was to show by example that submission to the disciplinary routines on board was the route to a healthy voyage. Nevertheless, numerous surgeons on larger vessels found mildly coercive tactics not only necessary but crucial to the success of the voyage.

Dr Ronald was instructed to avoid favouritism, promote harmony, be accessible, make allowance for error while checking insubordination, to conciliate all and to be harsh to none: 'Such a demeanour will hardly fail to gain the esteem of the great majority of the young persons in question'.[6] Most of all, he was enjoined to cultivate good feeling; to make good use of the matrons chosen by the Committee to guide the women, and to be mindful that many single young women were, for the first time, free from the constraints of 'relatives, friends, or superiors'. While he might follow the example of convict ships by choosing one woman as a sub-matron of her mess, to be responsible for ensuring that berths were kept clean, utensils cleansed, and general sense of order and punctuality kept,

> Great attention must be paid to cleansing and ventilating the Decks occupied by the Females, and to airing the beds, etc.; if possible facilities should be afforded to the females of bathing, and occasionally washing their clothes [dependent on weather ...] — cleanliness, however, should be inculcated and enforced on every practicable occasion.[7]

Dr Ronald was, in essence, to follow exactly the principles laid down by Dr Logan on the *Sarah*. Male relatives were allowed to consort with single women during the day and to visit them in the hospital in the presence of the doctor or matron. He was also reminded to keep a diary of the voyage, sending interim reports to the Committee via any ship they crossed on the way. On arrival in Launceston, he was to send his diary and further reports to the Committee by the first available ship. He was, they emphasised, under close scrutiny. He was not to allow curious onlookers to board the ship on arrival and was to mediate all on-shore communications. Primarily, he was to guard against 'improvident connections', which an inexperienced young woman might find 'too readily acceptable and which she might subsequently have reason to deplore'. It was the surgeon's duty to oversee the employment of the women and to ensure that none were taken advantage of by Launceston's reprobates — hotel keepers looking for barmaids or prostitutes, or settlers with less than honourable intentions.

Finally, the Committee appealed to Dr Logan's 'honour, rectitude, and humanity', reminding him to be ever mindful of his 'solemn responsibility' and to strenuously endeavour 'to promote the happiness of the numerous friendless beings under your protection, and to guard against the hazard of [moral] contamination'. These rules were essentially those demanded of surgeon superintendents for the remainder of the century.

'Four months to a day on the great deep', 1839

Three years later, on 10 December 1839, another emigrating family arrived in the company of 318 others on the 821-ton *Moffatt* at Holdfast Bay, seven miles from Adelaide; they too had travelled under the auspices of the South Australian Colonisation Commissioners. Ellen Moger and her husband Edward and their daughter Emily disembarked, 'having been just four months to a day on the Great Deep' on a passage superintended by Dr E Wren. Ellen addressed her parents in words throbbing with grief:

We had a safe, and many would say, a delightful voyage; but as regards myself, for the first five weeks I was scarcely able to move my head from my pillow with sea-sickness, which brought me so low that I could render but very little assistance to the dear children, as I was obliged to be helped on deck by two persons, from sickness. Edward and another Edward and the children suffered but little from sickness. But as we entered on a warmer climate, the dear children became relaxed (with the exception of Emily) gradually getting weaker and, for want of proper nourishment, became at last sorrowful spectacles to behold. They could eat none of the ship's provisions and our vessel was not like many that are sent out, provided with one or more cows for the accommodation of the sick; and had I the voyage to take again, I would make that a first consideration as I firmly believe that the dear children would have lived, and much sickness been spared, had we experienced proper attention from our Doctor and been provided with a little natural nourishment.

Poor little Alfred was the first that died on the 30th of Oct., and on the 8th of Nov., dear Fanny went and three days after, on the 11th, the dear babe was taken from me. I scarcely know how I sustained the shock, though I was certain they could not recover, yet when poor Fanny went it over-powered me and from the weakness of my frame, reduced me to such a low nervous state that, for many weeks, I was not expected to survive …

Our Captain took great notice of our children, when he saw them gradually wasting away and would send for them into his Cabin and give them port-wine, almost daily. In fact, wine and water was the only nourishment they took for weeks and that was given them too late. I would advise everyone who came out for Australia to bring nourishing things with them and take in turn with what is allowed on board, for the change is so great and so sudden to what we have been accustomed that the constitution, unless very strong, sicks under it.[8]

Table 7

Scale of victualling of ships carrying government-assisted
emigrants leaving England and Ireland, 1839

MALE EMIGRANTS

Days.	Biscuit.	Beef.	Pork.	Flour.	Suet.	Raisins.	Split Peas.	Tea.	Sugar.	Water.	Oat-meal.	Vinegar.	Soap.
	lb.	lb.	lb.	lb.	oz.	oz.	pint.	oz.	oz.	qts.			
Sunday	3/4	2/3	–	1/4	1	2	–	1/4	1 1/2	3			
Monday	3/4	–	2/3	1/4	–	–	1/3	1/4	1 1/2	3	1 pint weekly.	1/3 pint weekly.	1 lb. per lunar month.
Tuesday	3/4	2/3	–	1/4	1	2	–	1/4	1 1/2	3			
Wednesday	3/4	–	2/3	1/4	–	–	1/3	1/4	1 1/2	3			
Thursday	3/4	2/3	–	1/4	1	2	–	1/4	1 1/2	3			
Friday	3/4	–	2/3	1/4	–	–	1/3	1/4	1 1/2	3			
Saturday	3/4	2/3	–	1/4	1	2	–	1/4	1 1/2	3			

FEMALE EMIGRANTS

Days.	Biscuit.	Beef.	Pork.	Flour.	Suet.	Raisins.	Split Peas.	Tea.	Sugar.	Water.	Oat-meal.	Vinegar.	Soap.
Sunday	2/3	1/2	–	1/4	1	2	–	1/4	1 1/2	3			
Monday	2/3	–	1/2	1/4	–	–	1/3	1/4	1 1/2	3	1 pint weekly.	1/3 pint weekly.	1 lb. per lunar month.
Tuesday	2/3	1/2	–	1/4	1	2	–	1/4	1 1/2	3			
Wednesday	2/3	–	1/2	1/4	–	–	1/3	1/4	1 1/2	3			
Thursday	2/3	1/2	–	1/4	1	2	–	1/4	1 1/2	3			
Friday	2/3	–	1/2	1/4	–	–	1/3	1/4	1 1/2	3			
Saturday	2/3	1/2	–	1/4	1	2	–	1/4	1 1/2	3			

And so on in regular succession throughout the voyage, issuing beef and pork on alternate days.

Children of ten years of age and upwards are to be victualled as adults.

Children under ten years of age, whether male or female, are to have half of men's allowance, excepting in the article of water, of which they are to have full allowance.

There is also to be provided for each one of such children, fifteen pounds of rice, three pounds of sago, and four and a half pounds of sugar.

Table 7 continued

Scale of victualling of ships carrying government-assisted
emigrants leaving England and Ireland, 1839

The medical comforts are to be as follows:-

Preserved meats and soups	150 lbs.	
Lemon juice	648 "	
Sugar to mix with lemon juice	486 "	
Scotch barley	64 "	for every 100 persons.
Tea	8 "	
Sugar	48 "	
Vinegar	8 galls.	
Oatmeal	4 bush.	

To the above-mentioned medical comforts will be added the following, which in the case of ships fitted at Deptford will be supplied from the medical department, under the separate name of "Necessaries".

Arrow root	8 lbs.	
Sago	8 "	
Rice	32 "	for every 100 persons.
Pearl barley	16 "	
Whole ginger	4 oz.	

There is also to be on board each ship, five dozen of port wine, twelve dozen pint cases of preserved milk, twenty-four dozen of bottled porter, or a substitution of part of the supply in cask, if specially ordered, and a quantity of wine in cask, not less than two gallons for every person above ten years of age.

The only difference in the scale for Scotch ships is, that the allowance of oatmeal is half a pint daily to men and to women, and that molasses may, if convenient, be substituted for part of the allowance of sugar, by issuing one ounce of molasses and one ounce of sugar daily, in lieu of one and a half of sugar.

For the information of the passengers, a printed scale of victualling is hung up in every Government ship, which, after the weekly tables printed above, contains the following explanatory remarks:-

Table 7 continued

Scale of victualling of ships carrying government-assisted
emigrants leaving England and Ireland, 1839

Rice and Sago.
The surgeon superintendent may, at his discretion, substitute a quarter of a
pound of rice or sago, and one ounce of sugar, three times a week, for the salt
meat of each of the children under ten; and it shall be determined by him
whether to make this substitution for all the children under ten years of age, or
only for those under some earlier year, as, for example, seven.

Medical Comforts.
An ample supply of medical comforts is placed on board, none of which can
be claimed by any person as a right, but the whole is under the direction of the
surgeon superintendent, who will manage it in such way as he thinks best for the
passengers, and will account for the discretion he exercises in this respect on
his arrival in the colony.

Wine.
The wine is also under the entire control of the surgeon superintendent, by
whom its issue will be regulated according to the health and good order of the
passengers, and may be stopped from any individual or mess for misconduct. It
will generally not begin to be issued until after the first month or six weeks at
sea, and will then be served at the average rate of three or four times a week;
but probably seldomer in the hot latitudes, and oftener in the cold, according to
the discretion of the surgeon. The quantity used during the voyage is not to
exceed two gallons for every passenger above ten years of age; and no wine is
to be allowed to children under ten. The amount of each issue is not to exceed
a gill to each person.

Water.
The surgeon superintendent will, if circumstances admit, endeavour to
make some increase in the allowance of water while between the tropics.

Fresh Meat.
When fresh provisions can be issued, one pound of fresh meat to each
man, and two-thirds of a pound to each woman, with half a pound of vegetables,
is to be issued instead of the allowance of salt pork, flour and pease, or of salt
beef, flour, suet and raisins. Half the men's allowance to children under ten
years of age.

Table 7 continued

Scale of victualling of ships carrying government-assisted
emigrants leaving England and Ireland, 1839

Potatoes.
The surgeon superintendent is at liberty, if he think proper, to lay in a sufficient stock of potatoes for the first month of the voyage, to be issued, instead of
the flour, suet, and raisins, on the same day as the beef; but the providing of this
article must depend entirely on the markets and seasons. If it be used, the
allowance is to be two pounds to each man, and one pound and a half to each
woman.

Substitutions.
In case the surgeon superintendent should deem it expedient, or any other
circumstance should render it necessary, the following is the scale according to
which one article of diet may be substituted for another:-

1$^1/_4$ lb. of soft bread
1 " flour
1 " rice   } are equivalent to and
1 " sago   may be substituted
1 " scotch pot or pearl barley   for 1 lb. of biscuit.

1 " pease
$^1/_2$ " suet   } are equivalent to and
$^1/_2$ " currants   may be substituted
1 " raisins   for 1 lb. of flour.

1 " rice   } are equivalent to and
1 quart of oatmeal   may be substituted
                                      for 1 pint of pease.

$^1/_4$ lb. of onions or leeks equal to 1 lb. of any other kind of vegetable.

SOURCE Appendix to Annual Report of the Agent General for Emigration, *BPP*, 1839
(536.II), vol. XXXIX.

Working-class emigrants adapted to the food much more readily than the better off, whether they travelled in intermediate accommodation, like the Brunskills, or in steerage, like the Mogers, who probably chose the cheaper option in order to retain more capital for settlement. Both types of passage required a deposit, graduated according to the class of accommodation. Their middling-class gentility was manifest in their disgust at the provisions. For poorer emigrants, though, the food was richer and more abundant than most were accustomed to. But both Sarah and Ellen appear to have been very unlucky in the South Australian Colonisation Commission's choice of surgeon superintendent. The inefficacy of the medical officers on board their ships may, after all, have accounted for the high mortality of children on their passages, although Ellen Moger's own poor health may also have contributed to her children's death, since she was ill for the first five weeks and barely able to care for them. The doctor was, she wrote,

> a young and very austere man, and during the first half of the passage very careless and inattentive to the health of the passengers, till there were many alarming deaths, when he became more solicitous, respecting them.
>
> During my last illness he appeared quite an altered man towards me, allowing me more brandy, arrowroot or whatever I could take. In turn, and as a recompense on my part it seems, I invited him (whilst in a state of delerium) to my wedding dinner of roast pig and turkey.

After the deaths of her children, Ellen had taken 'strange fancies' into her head, fixating on her mother's easy chair, about which she talked for hours on end:

> I was bled and blistered, or rather, plastered and continued in that weak state until within a week of landing. I think I never should have recovered at Sea — you can have no idea of the effect the sea has upon some constitutions. Mine, for instance, it was a sort of sea consumption.

Surgeons — like doctors on shore — carried leeches and bleeding apparatus for the letting of blood, commonly thought to rid the body of bad humours. In their medical kit were various sized glass cups for blistering, a practice still used in some medical traditions. Plasters were bandages spread with adhesive curative substances (as in Sarah Brunskill's 'linseed poultice mustard plaster', which was used to alleviate inflammation and irritation), and were thought to have a therapeutic or healing effect on various ailments.

Undoubtedly, Ellen Moger's poor health on board, brought on by incessant seasickness, was exacerbated by her distress over the deaths of three of her four children, and anxiety about her surviving daughter, Emily. Having broken the terrible news to her parents, Ellen remembered that she had not described their routines on board. Again, like Sarah Brunskill, she overcame her own misery to offer a lively account of the daily routine, all the while placing herself above the general melee of the steerage deck:

> I have given you but a poor description of the voyage from the fact that little transpired worthy of comment, for it was, I assure you, one continued scene of confusion. I will, however, give you a faint description of one day and you will then be able to judge the rest.
>
> The bell calls 'the watch' off at six o'clock in the morning when down comes the Steward to give out the rations for the day, 'Ho Mess!' (six persons comprise a mess for rice, biscuits, flour, suet and raisons, or such as it may be reiterated through the ship), till one is stunned with the sound. Then comes such a rush of meagre looking visages till all are served. Then immediately follows the cry of 'boiling water'. Then there is a scamper, with piles of soap, biscuits, and slices of pork to roast at the Galley fire which, many having to wait full half an hour to accomplish, return metamorphosed into Blackamoors, with smut and smoke. When the great treat was over, those who were able to go, were ordered on deck to break-fast and there kept the

whole of the day. Great was the difficulty to keep the emigrants above, not withstanding there was an awning to shelter them from the scorching sun. ...

Ere the sumptuous repast of biscuits or port, or biscuits and butter is over, down comes our Commander, the Dr, ordering all beds on deck, after which the ordinary deck cleaners commence their operations by throwing chlorides of lime and scouring out, which you may suppose is quite necessary and with all they were in a sad state of filth, frequently finding vermin, but could not tell from whence they came. I spared no trouble to get fresh and clean changes of clothes for the dear children, whilst alive, but to no purpose.

The death toll on the voyage was 30, including a quiet and reserved young gentleman cabin passenger who threw himself from his cabin porthole. Nevertheless, Ellen found time to describe the magnificent weather on board, wishing that her parents were there to enjoy it with her,

to contemplate the beauty of the setting sun — its splendour was beyond description, and in a few moments you turn to behold the moon rising in silent majesty and shedding her glorious rays over the fast and mighty world of wonders. Whilst gazing on the beautiful scene you are, perhaps, interrupted by the sad tolling of a bell, informing you some poor victim to sickness and privation was about to be launched into a watery grave; such events are not uncommon, but the mind, I assure you, soon becomes hardened and callous on board a ship.

Ellen was not at all impressed with the new colony, believing that emigrants were deceived by 'the many flattering accounts respecting the beauty of the country and fine salubrious air of South Australia'. She would, undoubtedly, have thought the local tag 'Port Misery' an apt one for Port Adelaide. Though aware that arriving during the summer's extreme heat had influenced her assessment, Ellen understandably drew a picture of relentless wretchedness. However, she admitted to being treated very kindly by the Cornish family with whom they temporarily lodged while building on their half acre of land two miles from Adelaide, where her husband was employed at a phenomenal ten to 12 shillings daily as a sawyer. The hot winds and 'whirlpools of dust' were

> like clouds of smoke, extending as far as the eye can reach, it causes an over-powering lassitude which I am unable to describe. When the rain comes it decends in torrents, we have not had much. Winter here is considered the grow-ing season. At the present time everything is scorched up, or I should say bears the appearance of barreness for I have not yet seen anything to scorch.

Neither was Ellen impressed with the inflated price of provisions. Not only would expensively bought meat become fly-blown within hours, but

> Bugs and fleas we have by thousands everywhere. Some nights I can get no rest for them. When we came first I was in that horrid place, the Square [the immigrant depot], and caught from 100 to 200 of a night and still they were swarming. Ants and mosquitoes are also very tiresome, these are a few of the comforts of 'Australia'.

All the same, there were advantages. Wages were high. Within three years, many people who arrived on the first ships were rich, 'those with money now may do well here'. Builders were in great demand, and already mile-long streets were full of 'tidy brick and wood houses one storey high'. Ellen was disappointed to find no fruit grown. Apples were imported from Van Diemen's Land, selling from threepence to sixpence each.

Ellen Moger, too, continued her voyage journal for some weeks after arrival until the next ship departed carrying letters for England. She had brought letters for friends already in the colony, and was able to send news of them to her family. Her surviving daughter's health, which had declined on the voyage, remained poor:

> My dear Emily now seems more precious to us than ever, and I feel very thankful I did not leave her in England. Her health is not as good as formerly having something [like] Scurvy, the effects of Salt diet. She is also troubled with weak eyes, a complaint exceedingly common in this town, from the great degree of heat, light and dust …

Adaptation to the harsh summer environment was exacerbated by the scarcity and expense of fruit and vegetables, leading to undernourishment and scurvy-like symptoms. Ellen also asked for some comforts from home to assist with the family's adjustment to the unforgiving climate. She hoped they would send these items with another friend who was soon to embark for Australia:

> A few articles that with you cost but little, with us are very dear. A few dozen boxes of Lucifers matches would be very acceptable, and a few score yards of Dun's straw plait for hats and bonnets are very expensive here. Common gauze veils are almost indispensable to protect the eyes from the sun, dust and flies. I already regret leaving my parasole behind, they are most desirable and cost from one to two pounds apiece. I shall also be glad if you can send me a few drugs, many sorts not being able to be got for money. Carbonate of Soda is 6d. per oz, Tartaric Acid 1/6 oz. and in this warm climate they are very refreshing. Senna, salts, cream of tartar and Rhubarb are most useful in this inflammatory country. Our bodies are, at the present time, in a complete state of irritation — poor Emily is quite an object. I trust it will soon die away. My hair has fallen off my head and the little that is growing appears to be grey. You may fancy me a fine figure, people dress very gaily here, and at Church you would be surprised at the elegance that is displayed.

George Moger had not regained his vigour since disembarking, and took days off. Ellen supplemented their income by earning a handsome 16 shillings weekly at needlework and planned to open a school once she had regained her health. In spite of the stresses they faced, she recommended that her brother consider bringing his three sons to the colony once they were older: 'A son is a fortune to a father in this new colony', and she believed that other friends might do well. Having taken the momentous decision to emigrate, she was determined to make the best of it in spite of the tragedy and misfortunes that overshadowed their settlement. Nevertheless, she concluded, 'I shall cherish the hope of ending my days in England and seeing you all once more'. That Ellen Moger could even contemplate a return voyage so soon after landing confirms that, apart from the heartbreak of the children's deaths, the passage held few terrors for her.

Surgeons, parents and children

Notwithstanding the Moger and Brunskill families' experience, maritime surgeons in the 1830s often showed great sensitivity to parents. Dr Patchill, superintending the *Crescent* bound for Sydney from 3 October 1839 to 12 February 1840, discovered that a child on board had not been vaccinated against smallpox before departure. He vaccinated his patient (using an attenuated powder or serum manufactured from the scabs of cowpox pustules carried on board by all surgeons for vaccination during the voyage); subsequently, the child became unwell, and Dr Patchill took full responsibility for sponging him, and feeding him barley water and light gruel.[9] Stomach complaints and bowel disorders, mainly constipation and headaches, kept Dr Patchill busy. He found that the health of many women had become 'delicate' from suckling their infants. Most children suffered from diarrhoea, which he put down to the change in diet, and by the end of the voyage ophthalmia among them was severe. But, of the 235 emigrants who embarked, only two children 'sank low enough to die'.[10]

The emigrants lined up for treatment in such numbers that Dr Patchill was unable to take notes for his official report. For many working-class emigrants, the proximity of a doctor to whom they had free and unfettered access was a novelty, and they determined to take advantage of it. Never had they attracted so much medical attention in their lives and this, perhaps, gave the thousands of women who gave birth on board ships added confidence during their confinement. The surgeon on board the 478-ton *Warrior*, bound for South Australia in 1839–40 with 300 souls, distributed medicine to emigrants who lined up in great numbers for their dose, which was free of charge and freely given.[11] Surgeons were mostly concerned that their charges kept their bowels open to guard against constipation, hence 'opening medicine' and purgatives were distributed frequently.

Emigrants also eagerly consumed their daily lime or lemon juice, an integral component of their diet, known for centuries as a preventative against scurvy. To make the preserved citric concentrate palatable, surgeons often mixed it with a little rum. The *Warrior*'s surgeon also fostered dancing on the deck and oversaw the cooking of provisions. Supervising the bathing of children regularly, this anonymous surgeon also insisted that the adults take shower-baths whenever it rained. Rainwater was caught in canvas and a private space was made on the deck for emigrants to take it in turn to use buckets to shower themselves. As the voyage progressed, an ailing woman was dosed first with brandy and water, then with quinine, and the surgeon dressed her bedsores with poultices. The captain allowed a fowl to be killed to make broth for her and the other invalids. The surgeon and a travelling colleague visited her each day, administering a range of medicines, but, in spite of attendance by the doctors and two of her women friends, she died. As usual, her bedding was immediately thrown overboard, her berth disinfected with chloride of lime, and she was buried as soon as decently possible. The surgeon insisted that the women who attended her bathe immediately. Isolating and containing infection was his primary aim.

Worried about the dreadful condition of the water closet in the women's quarters, believed responsible for the dysentery, this vigilant surgeon removed it — probably to the upper deck — and was even more insistent than ever on scraping and cleaning. Many surgeons, and numerous diarists, described with disgust the problems caused by overflowing water closets, especially in heavy weather, and we ought, perhaps, to be surprised that diarrhoeal illness on ships was not far more severe. Although no deaths occurred in the first seven weeks of the voyage, thereafter three women, aged 17, 18 and 28, died — of bilious fever, typhus fever and consumption respectively — and two men, both aged 46, had died — one of consumption, the other of dysentery — before the *Warrior* arrived in South Australia almost five months to the day after departure. Although there were 37 children under the age of 15, including six infants, among the 102 souls on board, no children died, perhaps owing partly to the surgeon's solicitous and compassionate treatment. The absence of measles, scarlatina, whooping cough and other childhood infections at the beginning of the voyage must also have contributed to such a successful passage.

London to Holdfast Bay, 1839

In 1839, Hugh Watson, a Scot, sailed from Leith to London. There, he boarded the 1469-ton *Buckinghamshire* in the company of '700 souls in all', including his 28-year-old wife Mary and daughter Isabella, among the 512 emigrants.[12] Manned by a large crew, it was a huge ship for its time (about double the size of an average emigrant ship before mid-century), which also carried cabin passengers. In his first letter home, Hugh advised his friends 'to come by London, as you fare better in an English ship. I sold £1 worth of provisions when we came ashore that we could not use'. Rations on board had been so liberal that he had not needed to break open his own supply of comforts, netting him a small profit on arrival. 'There are no dangers at sea', he told his parents, 'I saw more tossing between Leath and London than all the rest of the way':

James Collinson, Answering the emigrant's letter,
1850 (Christopher Wood, *Paradise Lost:
Paintings of English Country Life and Landscape
1850–1914*, Grange Books, London, 1993,
p. 112, Courtesy of Christopher Wood Gallery).
The father holds both the letter and
a map of Australia.

> We were only 14 weeks on the sea in which we were all
> very healthy and happy. We had a minister aboard and had
> sermon each Sabbath day. We had 400 immigrants and a
> great many cabin passengers and the crew and the ship's
> company, 700 souls in all. … We had 6 births and 10
> deaths, all young children except one and he was far gone
> in consumption before he came away. … We were all very
> merry for every one of us got a little grog to mix with our
> water as it is allowed by the Commissioner when the
> water gets bad, and Mary had a pint of London porter
> each day all the voyage out.

Although Hugh does not say so, Mary was pregnant. Her condition accounted for her allowance of porter, even though she was not due to give birth on board. Hugh had spent his last shilling at Gravesend on two more Bibles to add to his 'little stock of books for the children, and very glad we were for books are scarce here'. Having described the sailors' celebration upon crossing the equator, and the arrival of Neptune, Hugh made it clear that the sailors 'were not allowed to meddle with the immigrants'. With fine weather, and pleasing gales, the voyage passed splendidly for Hugh and his family, who were excited by the sight of whales and dolphins.

Like most diarists, Hugh related his experience for the benefit of friends and relatives whom he expected to follow.

> I would advise any person coming to take a bottle of good
> Scots whisky with him and take a little now and then in
> the hot weather about the line; and for dress a pair of
> breeches made of packsheet [probably a type of light can-
> vas or duck] and a vest with sleeves the same.
>
> Have two suits and wash one in salt water when
> the other is on; and a pair of carpet shoes or none at all. I
> went most of the way barefoot for salt water spoils shoes,
> but they are very cheap here. Women's are from 3/- to 6/-
> per pair, and men's from 6/- to 12/-.

> If any acquaintance about Newbegging was asking
> for me, you can tell them I am well and invite them to
> come here whether it be tradesmen, farmer or laborer.

Hugh Watson's maritime experience was one of excitement and awe: 'It was truly grand to see the wonders of the Lord in the deep, and his works in mighty waters'. He was no less enthusiastic about his new country: 'This is a good place for a rich man as well as a poor one to build a house in the town of Adelaide'. Houses built for £50 returned £1 weekly in rent. Engaged by a gentleman farmer as a shepherd three miles from the township of Adelaide, at £1 weekly and rations, including 14 pounds of flour, 10 1/2 pounds of beef, two pounds of sugar, 1/2 pound of tea, with a free house and garden, Hugh could not believe his luck. Moreover, Mary Watson was taking in washing, which was sent weekly from the town to their cottage on the banks of the River Torrens, where water was plentiful: 'She is earning £1 per week which I am sure she would not do in Scotland in a month'. His young daughter Isabella was also keeping fowls, earning sixpence for each egg, and the family, within a few months of landing owned a cow, two swine, one with piglets, and twelve hens.

Hugh urged his parents to come out, assuring them that a number of people in their seventies had survived the voyage. Wages were high for dairymaids, and all of his family would quickly find work and prosperity:

> We would be glad to see you all here, every one; our
> brothers and sisters would do well. We want no idlers, no
> drunkards; but sober, industrious men and women, and
> they will be independent in a few years.

Independence, for working men like Hugh Watson and their wives, was a crucial motive for emigrating:

> Any person may begin work the next day he comes to
> land; there is plenty of work.
> If they do not get work at first people work for
> the Government at a reduced wage at 9/- per week and

their rations [higher than the average wage for a rural labourer in England]. Which I think no man can starve here as the poor immigrants at New York did when they arrived there in poverty. I am very glad I went not to America, but that was not the place where my grandfather's blessing lay, for he said: keep thou to the South and thou shalt prosper.

Hugh did not doubt that he would prosper: 'Town acres that were sold for £5 two years ago, this day is sold for £1,500, so I would advise anyone that intends to come, the sooner they come the better. I wish I had come sooner'.

Food was plentiful and for the taking. Like numerous emigrants, Hugh Watson felt liberated by the lack of constraint on hunting, shooting and fishing, all punishable offences in the United Kingdom:

> Every man here has freedom to shoot what he pleases. The kangaroo bounds with amazing swiftness over our plains, and the emu, little inferior to the ostrich, stalks along amongst the trees, and the cockatoo is flying like the crows in Scotland, and the parrots are noisesome above our heads. But as the wages are high, few men have time to shoot them unless it be shepherds, and as not every man brings a gun with him, one can buy one as cheap here as in Scotland.

Lacking a modern sensitivity towards the natural environment or understanding of their contribution towards the extinction of species, settlers bagged game at every opportunity, supplementing their diet and their income with feathers, pelts and skins: 'We have the Opossum here which is so valuable for its skin in Britain for ladies muffs and boas'. Hugh, though, was more interested in cultivation:

> The land is sold in this country at one pound per acre, and there are extensive plains that the plough may run

for miles without touching a tree, and so smooth that you can see from end to end. ... We have two crops in the year, and what has been done in our own little garden and then see it in its natural state would astonish you. I can compare it to nothing but the old Mansion seat of some gentleman on the River Clyde, that has been in cultivation for a thousand years and, used then as a pleasure ground for one hundred years.

These three pioneering emigrants to South Australia in the 1830s were linked by their Christian faith. But as working people, the Watsons found little to complain about the voyage or the privations of settlement. Not having buried a child at sea, the entire experience was one of adventure and a determination to succeed. Hugh assured his parents that although his family arrived penniless, they were not friendless, having found many Scots who were fond of talking 'of home and their father's house'. For the upwardly mobile Mogers and Brunskills, accustomed to the attention of servants, and burdened by expectations of — or aspirations for — a semi-genteel life, the adjustment to both the voyage and arrival was far more severe. In addition, they landed in a state of mourning, which overshadowed their new lives. Arriving in midsummer added to the horror of their situation, whereas the Watsons arrived in autumn, unbothered by whirlwinds and scorching sun. By spring, Hugh's admiration for the landscape and climate had not diminished. It was, he wrote,

the most beautiful country I ever saw; the trees are always green here and our winter is nearly over. It has never been colder than your May in Scotland. We have no pinching frost here and the heat does not go to an excess although it is hot yet the clearness of the atmosphere makes it that any man could work all the year round. I wish all my friends were here.

Hugh Watson was yet to experience an Adelaide plains summer, and was probably giving an opinion based either on hearsay or promotional pamphlets. Either way, his letter home, written six months after landing — perhaps designed to impress upon his family that he and his wife had made the right decision to place their faith in a colonial future — may have read quite differently had he disembarked in midsummer.

The risk of death to future infants born to Mary Watson, Ellen Moger and Sarah Brunskill in the young colony was as high as that of infants born to their kith and kin at home. Whereas in England, 50 per cent of all deaths were among the under-five-year-olds, in the 1840s in South Australia, 50 per cent of all deaths were those of infants. By the 1880s, 220 in every thousand infants born in the colony would not survive childhood. Adelaide's appalling infant mortality rate matched England's as sewerage and public health initiatives failed to keep up with the rising population and subsequent urban development.[13]

As it happens — although Hugh did not mention the sad news in his first letter home — within three months of arrival, Mary Watson had given birth to a daughter, who died almost immediately. Three years later, aged 31, Mary herself succumbed to consumption and was buried with her daughter in the West Terrace Cemetery. At the time of her death, Hugh described himself as a cowkeeper at Brownhill Creek, near Adelaide. Having faced the tragic loss of his wife and infant daughter so soon after arrival, Hugh Watson eventually remarried and produced at least one son. Like so many of his brethren, this optimistic Scot progressed from shepherding to cow-keeping, to ownership of his own farm at Delamere on the Fleurieu Peninsula, where, in 1871, he assisted with the building of St James Church of England. His life ended in 1882, 43 years after setting foot on South Australian soil.

'Both Doctor and Captain
was very kind to me'

The 1840s

Surgeons, fever and public opinion

n 14 February 1842, after a voyage of almost four months, the 673-ton *Manlius* sailed into Victoria's Port Phillip Bay, a province of New South Wales until 1851. On board were the survivors of the 245 souls who embarked at Greenock, Scotland, on 21 October 1841. Initially, the 245 emigrants were composed of 39 families (147 souls in all), 61 single men and 37 single women. They were superintended by Dr John Patterson and, during the 116 days that he cared for the emigrants, he delivered eight infants and buried 44 emigrants at sea, including 11 adult men, 15 adult women, two children under the age of 14, nine children aged between one and seven, and seven infants.

Upon arrival, the ship was quarantined at Gellibrand's Point, near Williamstown, when a further nine adult men, six adult women and two children aged between one and seven died, bringing the death toll among the 245 emigrants to 61. Owing to the severity of the illness on board, the government initially refused to reimburse the shipowner; however, following an enquiry, he was adequately compensated. Perhaps immigration officials recognised that he was not to blame for the outbreak of fever, and were anxious about the possibility that other shipowners might lose confidence in a system capable of leaving them out of pocket after an expensive undertaking.[1] Smaller, but significant, fines were far more efficacious in ensuring that charter parties were honoured and regulations observed. Alienating too many shipowners by depriving them of the total cost of the voyage would have proven disastrous for the importation of much-needed emigrant workers to the colony.

The fatal pathogen on board the *Manlius* was typhus, a highly infectious organism of the *rickettsiae* family, which is transmitted via the bite of the human body louse, *Pediculus humanus corporis*. Also known as spotted fever, jail fever, ship fever, putrid fever, colonial fever, camp fever and famine fever, typhus was the curse of jails, the military, and people gathered together in unsanitary, confined spaces where clothing was changed infrequently. It was particularly prevalent among travellers, and it was not until 1907 that medical scientists understood that the disease vector, or carrier, was a ubiquitous insect. Until then, the mode of transmission was not understood. Among the symptoms of typhus are high fever, prostration, aching body and head, and a reddish rash covering the trunk and limbs. Although it attacks people of all ages, typhus is generally mild in children under 15 years of age. Mortality increases with age. Until late in the 19th century, it was often confused with typhoid fever, another highly infectious disease caused by a bacterium, *salmonella typhi*, transmitted by water and sewerage, and sometimes transmitted by asymptomatic carriers.

Two sets of parents on the *Manlius* died, one couple leaving five orphaned children aged two to 12, and the other leaving five orphaned children aged seven to 13. The *Port Phillip Chronicle*, undoubtedly pointing a finger at the surgeon superintendent, raged that 'there is obviously somebody very grossly to blame in this matter'.[2] The Scottish contractor, Alex Laird, also expressed his deep sympathy, and made it his business to contact the next of kin of those who had died. He also added his weight to claims for the humanity of the captain and owners of the ship. Moreover, he pointed out, HM Emigration Agent at Greenock had examined the stores and could not fault them, and the ship sailed from the Clyde with far fewer numbers than her tonnage and the law permitted. He had paid an extra 2/6d per barrel of beef to ensure the best quality. The ship was, in all respects, a model one.

The captain, who faced an official enquiry and was tried and sentenced by the press, nevertheless received his full gratuity of three shillings each for 245 souls boarded. The surgeon also received a full gratuity of 10/6d per emigrant and was exonerated from any blame. Tight regulations, official enquiries and the passionate engagement of the press placed the onus of responsibility on shippers to care for the emigrants in their charge. Newspaper reporters trumpeted any transgressions, and their reports were carried back to London by the next ship leaving port, to be picked up by the British press, which called the Colonial Office to account for all misdemeanours. Thus voyages to Australia — the longest in terms of transoceanic passenger traffic — were kept in the public's view, inhibiting gross negligence by shipowners while keeping the regulators under close scrutiny.

The Colonial Office was well aware that the arrival of bad reports severely affected recruitment in the United Kingdom, especially in regions personally affected by a maritime tragedy. A few years later, for example, when the bounty ship *Cataraqui* impaled on rocks off King Island in Bass Strait when approaching Port Phillip Bay in 1845, with the loss of all emigrants on board, including 23 from one small Cambridgeshire village, Guilden Morden, the surrounding population was so shaken that the village did not produce another Australian emigrant until 1867.[3] There was wide local and national press coverage, and a fire-and-brimstone sermon preached by Guilden Morden's vicar, who saw the tragedy as God's judgment on the sins of pride and envy: his parishioners had attempted to break out of their station in life by seeking prospects abroad, attracting heavenly wrath. Even lesser tragedies drew ample newspaper reportage, ensuring that authorities in both hemispheres remained alert to their responsibilities.

In the case of the *Manlius*, the enquiry was conducted by a colonial surgeon, Dr Henry Morton, assisted by Dr Patterson, the ship's surgeon — a serious breach of impartiality: Dr Patterson was, after all, passing judgment on his own performance. After interviewing the survivors, the duo concluded that

Emigrant ship between decks
(*Illustrated London News*,
17 August 1850)

> The immigrants in question after their long ordeal are all
> restored to health and look very well. They represent the con-
> duct of the Surgeon Superintendent and the other officers of
> the ship as being kind and attentive during the voyage.
>
> Under these unhappy circumstances we must
> decline recommending the payment of Bounty and leave
> that question for the decision of superior authority.

As one might expect, the medicos were keen to draw attention to
the ship, rather than to the medical attention. They went on

> The first case of fever occurred on board whilst the Vessel
> lay at Greenock Bay on the point of sailing and that dur-
> ing the entire voyage it continued to spread. 27 deaths
> took place from fever during the voyage and 14 deaths
> after the ship's arrival at Port Phillip.

Other illnesses accounted for the remaining 20 deaths.

In March 1840, Richard Reid, from Cavan, was just five years old
when he embarked in Dublin on the 409-ton *William Nichol* with his
parents and nine siblings, including three brothers and six sisters, and
about 140 other souls. Given his age, his reminiscences in later years
must have been conflated with the memories of his older siblings and
parents. He vividly remembered, though,

> One of the characteristic points with regard to our
> Doctor was his great care about the sanitary condition of
> the ship, — the wholesome nature of the food, the per-
> sonal cleanliness of the people. But I took a strong per-
> sonal objection to one of his modes of giving a salt water
> bath to young boys. Two or three of us were stripped, and
> then placed in a large wooden tank or barrel. In a few
> minutes a couple of sailors brought sundry buckets of salt
> water which they dashed down upon us. We were rebel-
> lious and that may have had some influence in causing
> such a rough shower bath to be seldom employed.[4]

In spite of such protests, surgeons often took matters into their own hands if parents failed to bathe their own offspring. Lack of cleanliness was one of the transgressions most commonly punished by surgeons. People unused to bathing were by no means always persuaded of its benefits unless mild coercion was used.

Cleanliness, coercion and punishment

Another ship to sail into Holdfast Bay on 7 July 1840, the same day as the *William Nichol*, was the 570-ton barque *Fairlie*, carrying James Bowley, who was to make his name as a builder in the new colony. On this ship, within hours of weighing anchor in the Thames on 4 April, a rebellious group of single men had refused to clean the married quarters, creating a disturbance on board. James Bowley does not reveal the outcome, but three weeks later he recorded another commotion when Lavinia Sawyer was 'made fast to the main mast' by a group of emigrants after she had refused to clean the hospital when her turn came around. The emigrants often took matters into their own hands if their fellow travellers failed to pull their weight. This may, in some cases, have reinforced the surgeon's authority.

On that day of high drama, during which a male champion drew a knife in Lavinia Sawyer's defence and blows were exchanged, James Bowley went on to report two other events:

> in the evening about 9 o'clock a child died. Spoke the Barque 'Donpedro' from the East Indies a great number of emigrants wrote letters in expectation of sending them by her, she proved to be a French ship so was very much disappointed.[5]

For James Bowley, the events of Lavinia Sawyer's punishment bore equal weight in terms of recording events on board, with 'speaking' the French ship, and the death of a child. Again, about ten days later,

> Spoke the ship 'Arab' from Van Diemen's Land homeward bound out 92 days, lowered the boat and sent letters to

her, this was at 4 o'clock in the evening of Sunday.
Another child died, of the measles. Steady breeze during
the night, rather cold, Latitude 4.

As Ellen Moger observed, one could not help becoming 'hardened
and callous' on an emigrant ship.

Another diarist noted that, on the subject of child deaths, 'It is
astonishing how soon the occurrence is forgotten on board. Much more
stir is created by the discovery of some stolen flour on one of the
Emigrants, for which he is put in irons and confined'.[6]

On crossing the equator, the sailors on the *Fairlie* performed their
usual boisterous ceremonies, and the emigrants were permitted to throw
buckets of water at each other, a sure way of encouraging some contact
with water. To encourage exercise, rewards were given by the surgeon
superintendent for competitive racing around the deck.

More than anything else on board — even storms — the threat of
fire most unnerved emigrants. Two months into the *Fairlie's* voyage, on
a tempestuous evening, with the ship rolling violently,

> amidst the confusion the awful alarm of 'Fire' was given,
> which caused the greatest confusion, men women and
> children were seen running up and down the deck in
> most awful alarm, the cause of the alarm was upsetting the
> medicine chest when the aquafortis oil of vitriol and
> other drugs getting mixed together which caused a great
> smoke hence the alarm, at ¹/₂ past 11 order was restored
> and all confusion subsided.

Some women, as we shall see, never recovered from their fear of fire
after similar alarms on board.

After 90 days at sea ('the shortest passage ever known'), the *Fairlie*
anchored in South Australian waters, having buried 24 emigrants at sea,
mostly children. Days earlier, the doctor had stopped all rations of grog
after a malcontent had cut down the men's hammocks. With their nog-
gin cut short, the men themselves soon discovered the culprit, and the

surgeon settled the matter. Democratic punishment of this kind proved a boon to surgeons, whose discipline was easily threatened by the ganging up of bored and restless young men.

Within months of his disembarkation, James Bowley had married in Holy Trinity Church and entered into a business partnership with his new brother-in-law. He went on to build the first bridge over the River Torrens. He also built the Lunatic Asylum, which was later to become the Infectious Diseases Hospital, an institution made necessary by the diseases that disembarked with emigrants such as its builder.

Warwickshire to Melbourne, 1840

In 1840, Thomas and Maria Wade arrived in 'Melbourn, Port Philip, Australia Felix' after emigrating from Barford, in Warwickshire, after a comfortable voyage of nearly six months. Like many diarists, Thomas Wade enjoyed the voyage and, much to his satisfaction — like that of several of his fellow diarists — gained weight before its end. Writing to his brother from Melbourne, Thomas told him that

> We arrived at Port Philip on the 6th of May 1840 a voyage of nearly 6 months we had a very pleasant one tho' a long wone, our Doctor was a nice man on which the comfort of the emigrants entirely depended we staid at the Cape of Good Hope 11 days had nearly 300 on board, 2 deaths, & 6 births, on board I was very sick for the first month my wife was very ill part of the way, but now we are both in good health, I have got so fat you should hardly know me the end of the voyage, Port Philip, is the name of the harbour it is a beautiful Bay 50 miles long and 30 wide with an entrance half a mile wide, it is considered one of the best harbours in the world. Melbourne is the capital town of Port Philip 5 years ago it was on[ly] inhabited by the Natives now it is a large town beautifully situated on the banks of a fresh water River Yara yara [Yarra Yarra] is its name it has been traced 200 miles up

the country, the streets are much wider than at home. in the principle streets of Melbourne land has been sold at £19 a foot. Land in the town is very dear but 5 miles out reasonable so the villages round are forming, the newspapers are published twice a week.

It was, perhaps, a testament to the doctor's discipline on board that at least four, and perhaps all, of the infants born on board this unusually long voyage, perhaps even all of the children (Thomas gives no clue as to the ages of the dead), survived — a triumph by any standard. The Wades' enthusiasm and state of health had not been dented by the voyage.

Typically, Thomas — anxious to convey a picture of civilisation reminiscent of home — described in great detail the churches, chapels and shops. He gave the usual account of food and house prices, and wages earned by various types of tradesmen and labourers. Praising the fertility of the soil and the flourishing vegetation, Thomas, like his fellow correspondents, boasted about the size and weight of oxen and sheep:

> Sheep and beast are very cheap and those that keep them in the interieor make large fortunes in 2 yeaers know dear brother I have gave you an account of the colony you may please yourself about coming but if you do come bring as many tools as you can for sale as well as for use for you may make double price.

He had been taken on by a carpenter who agreed to 'learn me the trade'; his wages were excellent and Maria had apprenticed herself to a dressmaker, offering her employer three months' free labour in return for the apprenticeship. This robust couple, for whom the voyage seemed like a vacation — an unimaginable luxury at home — were determined to make good. Strongly urging his family and his wife's kin to follow them, he assured his relatives that well-paid work was plentiful for industrious people, moreover

During our voyage we had good food and every accommodation that could be expected on board a ship you
might bring some flour as perhaps you will not be able to
eat biscuit while you are sick and [bring] cheese or any
thing you like this is [illegible] much as you will eat but
you will not regret as you may sell them for twice as
much as you gave but put them in boxes and lock them
such things are so tempting tis just as well to go free as we
had just the same treatment, as those who paid their voyage and as for been in bondage [in the colony] it is … just
[the same] as when at home you pays the board which is
no inconvenience whatever for your house you want a tin
pint and plate spoon knife and fork and take care of the
rest an you will loos them I bought my ship bed for 12s
do not bye any extra clothing bring what linen you have
those articles that will pack up close such as knives spoons
matches candle sticks buy all you want before you go on
board or you will pay for them a hook pot for boiling any
thing buy it at London Wash hand basin tin teapot bring
no pots.

In other words, his brother was to buy and pack as much as possible far
more cheaply than he could do on arrival. Prudence was the key to success. One of the Wades' friends from Barford had arrived three months
earlier with £50 and was already worth at least three times that. Like
many new arrivals, Thomas could scarcely believe his good fortune.

Emigrants were constrained from imprudent exaggeration about
their opportunities and their jobs, wages, houses and social experiences
because, invariably, they had friends and acquaintances already in the
colony who were also writing home to the village. Stories could be cor-
roborated or falsified by families who shared their antipodean kin's correspondence by passing their letters around and often allowing them to
be read aloud in the village public house. Sometimes they were given to
the local press to publish. Most colonial correspondents sent news of
friends living nearby or recently arrived. Families at home passed on

Thomas Webster, *A letter from the colonies*, 1852 (Christopher Wood, *Paradise Lost: Paintings of English Country Life and Landscape 1850–1914*, Grange Books, London, 1993, p. 113. Courtesy of Christopher Wood Gallery)

information in letters to their colonial kin about what they, too, had heard of the settlement of friends' and neighbours' children in the colonies. In this way, the complex and interwoven 'crimson ties of kinship' created a network both in the colony and at home, placing at least some pressure on truthful, if sometimes emotionally loaded, accounts of settlement.

On the *Royal Sovereign*'s 136-day passage from Plymouth to Sydney in the early 1840s, one steerage emigrant, travelling with his wife and seven young children, spoke highly of the solicitous care received before boarding. Emigration authorities knew that considerate treatment was crucial to the way in which emigrants approached their first step up the gangway of the ship that was to carry them across the globe. Many had never travelled on a train, let alone a ship. At least one emigrant was far more terrified by the train on which she was to travel for the first time to Plymouth, than by the prospect of the voyage. The fastest speed most had experienced on land was the pace of a jogging horse harnessed to the cart in which many rode on the way to the quayside. Approaching a bustling port — the largest town many had ever visited — also held terrors for many emigrants. Anxiety about leaving home and family was exacerbated by the noise and confusion that they confronted at the port. Immune systems were undoubtedly at low ebb in those fraught days leading up to embarkation.

Pregnancy and birth

On the *Royal Sovereign*, there were two births. The infants were delivered with no fuss or trouble, wrote the ship's diarist, JS Prout, but one mother had not even suspected her own pregnancy, 'she does not at all understand it'.[7] The single woman had given birth during the night without disturbing anyone and declared the event, wrote Mr Prout facetiously, as entirely without cause, and 'like the lion that laid an egg, she does not at all understand it'. Having disgraced her unsuspecting family by producing an infant out of wedlock, the young woman was spurned by her mother, brother, cousin and aunt, who refused to see her. Sympathetic fellow emigrants made baby clothes out of pocket-handkerchiefs but, disowned by her family, the young single mother became ill. Uncomforted by her kin, she lingered on alone until she died. Other mothers cared for the infant until she, too, died, and 'poor little Catherine was disposed of'. Tragic stories such as this were much commented upon and discussed by emigrant diarists. Little escaped the observation of the keener chroniclers of shipboard life.

One pregnant lower-middle-class woman who expected to give birth on the *Pestonjee Bomanjee*, bound for Hobart in 1844, told her sister that 'I hope the dear little thing lives'. Her sister, too, had recently given birth at home as the ship was about to sail. Owing to the timing of her nephew's birth, Mary Anne Roberts had been unable to visit her sister before departure, but assumed that the 'dear child if he should live he will be quite a big boy'.[8] Parents (on land and at sea) did not take their infants' survival for granted in an era when, on average, 150 English infants in every thousand born failed to survive their first year of life. Moreover, the infant mortality rate was two and three times the average in some wretched urban areas, and up to four times that in the worst streets of some slum suburbs of large industrial towns, in London's black spots, and in the major cities of Ireland and Scotland.[9] Mothers understood that their infants' lives hung by the thread of fate, and usually prefaced their remarks — on shore as at sea — with 'if it survives'. Experience had taught them to consider themselves fortunate if their child reached its first birthday, and religion was their comfort.

Caroline Dorling, who sailed for South Australia on the *Princess Royal* in 1848, wrote home to her parents and parents-in-law from Bowden, a few miles from Adelaide, soon after her arrival. Like most women, her sense of delicacy prevented her from referring explicitly to her pregnancy:

> My dear Fathers and Mothers
>
> Brothers and sisters I am happy to inform you that I am still in the land of the living and with good health we are enjoying the fruits of our labour for which purpose we came so many thousands of miles. but we have no cause to

regret that we left the shores of Great Britain but as respecting the passage. as you will see in the long letter it was a very pleasant one. of which my husband has given you the full particulars. and although there are some in England who will not believe it. But I can testify with truth that it contains nothing but what is a fact. I doubt not but you have been very anxious concerning my wellfare in the situation I left home but you need not be unhappy about me for I had every attendance possible on board for both Doctor and Captain was very kind to me and my family likewise Mrs Chamberlain my friend who attended me on the evening [of the birth] moved [me] from my berth to the hospital and as you will see in the journal my trouble was soon over and I was able to get up at the weeks end to sit a short time and on Sunday the 18th we christened our Ocean born daughter Mary Sophia by the proposal of our captain who presented her with a pritty net cap and a pair of shoes likewise our doctor gave us a bottle of beautiful liquor to drink the good health of the child likewise all present. there was two other women in the hospital in the same situation as myself. I was able to leave the hospital in 15 days — so you see I done quite as well on the migthy ocean and better than I did with my former two it was not so bad on board as represented to me by [them] who had not experienced it for all the women on board had good gettings up there was 9 children born on the passage and one in port and one died on the passage 14 days old which was the only death we had the mother of which was only 16 years of age (but married). We arrived in Australia on the 15th of June the 21st I had an old friend call to see me who was by name George Driver we was very happy to meet each other in this delightfull country Where he brought an letter which I gladly received … its contents which truly dear father we have reverenced what is set forth in the hundred and seventh psalm. They that go down to the sea in ships and do business in great waters these see the mighty works of the Lord and his wonders in the deep. We had prayer meetings on board on Sunday and Thursday evenings. and now we have a chappel belonging to the Weslyiens nearly opposite our door a few yards of distance. I should be glad for father to send me the date of his and Mothers birth. I hope when you will write all will write brother William and Sarah his wife. Likewise sister Rachel we would like to see you here in Australia we hope to see brother George one day. We desire our kind love to sister Maria and her …. husband and give us the boys name, we desire to be remembered to our Icklingham friends likewise our kind love to our uncle and aunt Cotterrel and tell him his is a good Business here. our kind love to Aunt Charlotte and Mr R Jeffes and tell him we found more pleasure in crossing the mighty deep than we expected. give our kind love to brother John and sister Mary Miller and tell them we met with sister Goldsmith. I am still dear father and Mother your affectionate Daughter C. Dorling.

My kind love to Mrs Craske our neighbour and Mrs Petch dressmaker Ann Petch.[10]

Again we see a network of friends characteristic of Australia's chain migration. Caroline's delight at being brought a letter by a friend from home is palpable. Her experience of an easier birth at sea is echoed in other letters cited in the following chapters and those of women travelling to other Australasian destinations. Jessie Campbell, for example, observed on her voyage to New Zealand in 1840, that 'A Paisley woman delivered of a daughter, the women do not seem to suffer as much as at home'.[11] Twenty-six years later, Edward Allchurch wrote of his wife's confinement on board the *Atalanta* bound for South Australia, 'Anne could not have had a more favourable time than she has had, she told me it seems like a dream she cant make it out'.[12]

In 1848, the McRitchie sisters disembarked in Melbourne. Christine, aged 23, and Mary, aged 21, were Scots Presbyterian domestic servants from North Queensferry, Dunfermline, who probably arrived on the *William Stewart* on 16 May 1848 with 234 assisted emigrants.[13] On behalf of both, one sister wrote home to her father in a firm and confident hand. Their apology for not keeping a voyage diary emphasises the difficulties faced by writers in steerage owing to the lack of light. Still, countless steerage emigrants kept diaries, often written during their leisure hours on deck. 'Dear Father', they wrote:

> We are happy to inform you of our safe arrival in Melbourn on May 16th we had a good passage a good Captain a docter & officers with Temperate sailors we intended keeping a Jurnal but our part of the Ship being so dark many day we could not se their was nothing of speaking about but we caute a few Fish & Shirks [sharks] & thay passed away their time chirefully their was some children died but none of the old people died it would have been a great deal worse if there had been but the Children were never much minded there was Eight Births no marradges on board but their was two of the Children Baptized named Elizia & William Stewart. Dear Father be shure & let us know the name of our last sister that was born before we left home. I hope you received our letters from Pleamouth & we dropt one by the way, we had Church on Board every Sunday weathern permiting, we never wanted a meal of vitals all our passage, so you may consider what a passage we had, we may thank the Lord for our safe arrival.

The McRitchie sisters arrived in robust health; they were emigrating to jobs already arranged before departure, at double the wages they could expect at home. Trained domestic servants were always in demand and their references served them well. As was customary, their companions were hired before they disembarked by employers who treated their visit to the ship as if it were a hiring fair at home:

> Their was 51 Singal Woman all in our room we were very happy their was but 16 English & 35 Scotch were all

engaged on board but our-selves it was like a Fair, we went
to whom we had our letter to & thay found situations for
us & we got more wadges then was given on board, we
have good Situations & we are getting £25 the year, the
house maids have no grate to clean thay all burn wood
there is not such a thing as a grate to be seen, the work is
not so haird as it is at home nor the mistresses are not so
sassay, thay are glad to get any person to work to them.

As with many of their peers, the voyage had held no terrors for
them, and they were eager to describe the new settlement, not much
more than a decade old.

'Melbourn', they wrote, was as large as 'Dunfernline' [Dunfermline],
their Scottish hometown, and 'most of the houses are brick it is wonderful to se such a place only to be 13 years old'. They were struck by
wonder and awe at the sheer extent of the land radiating out from the
port town, and drew a picture that their father might recognise, using
their imagination to fill in the gaps in their knowledge:

it is all Buch [bush] round thousands of miles that we
would call a plantations at hom the nataivs live their &
large Sheep Stations & Bolicks [bullocks] stations their, &
the natives live like the Soldiers, thay ocopy so much
ground & thay have Kings & Chiefs & any of the rest of
them goes on one anothers ground thay fight with them.

Few emigrants failed to mention the price of food. The low prices
of meat — a luxury at home — could never go unremarked. Clothing,
tools and materials, however, were still very expensive, since they were
imported from the United Kingdom, and these prices, too, were always
included for the information of family and friends at home, especially
those considering applying for a passage:

The Beef is 2d per Pound Rice 6d per lb Bread cheep Barly
6d per lb, Clothing & Drink very high there is no Beggers
hear, Rich & poor lives all alike if people is willing to work

Single women on deck
(*Illustrated London News*,
17 August 1850)

thay can get plenty to do, the people is greate Tea Drinkers, the tea is 1/6 per lb thay have it after every meal …

Like Adelaide, though, Melbourne's infrastructure had not kept pace with its burgeoning population, and it would not be long before 'Marvellous Melbourne' became 'Marvellous Smellbourne', as the gutters ran with sewage:

> the weather has been very bad since we came & the streets is not for Femails to walk thay are in such a state thay will not let us out thay bring everything to us that we want the people are so kind that we are quite ashamed of their kindness to us for Mr and Mrs Brown thay are afull kind to us & always to make their house ~~their~~ our home at any time. be sure and tell Mr William Brown & the famely that their both well thay have three nice Children & let him know how much Obledged we are to him for his letter.

Typically, they closed their letter with salutations and

> kind love to grandmother & all friends & acqentances, that none need to be afraid to come here but for the passage for it is so long it is upwards of twenty thousand miles, we have never seen any person that we knew of as yet. Dear Father be sure & write and let us know how you are all at home. The money that we received from you that we never needed any of it so we put it in the Bank, and if you want any money be sure and let us know and we will remit it by a Bank order.

The passage must have seemed like twenty thousand miles to the McRitchie sisters, but it was seldom longer than 16 000, depending on prevailing winds. Some ships followed the winds much further south-west, approaching Rio de Janeiro before finding a south-westerly to carry them to Australia. Perhaps their vessel followed a similar route, increasing the mileage. The sisters had landed on their feet, and expected to meet friends soon: they had been employed in a manner characteristic of the chains that linked settlers in the colonies with contacts radiating in all directions.

Accidents on board occasionally accounted for emigrant deaths. Seamen received appalling injuries or died after falling from the rigging; emigrants too, suffered scalds, broken limbs from falling down ladders, and bruising during heavy weather. More unusual was the death of a woman noted by a diarist on the *William Money*, bound for Adelaide in 1848. James Menzies, a 22-year-old single man, described an event early in the voyage when many women were laid low by seasickness. With so much sickness and prostration on the steerage deck, the surgeon super-intendent relied upon the matron's assistance. In administering medicine to one of the sick women, she opened the wrong bottle and gave the patient a dose of 'chloride of zink', a disinfectant. When the doctor dis-covered the error, he gave the suffering woman an emetic, but a short time later she died, leaving five children. It was only due to sheer luck that the other seasick women were prevented from taking it.[14]

As so often happened on voyages where sham trials and debates prepared emigrants for jury service on board, the horrified emigrants took the matter into their own hands and held an inquest in the captain's cabin. The 12 men on the jury brought in a verdict of accidental death, since the two bottles looked alike. But the story had a tragic sequel. The day following the appalling accident, another woman was confined but, according to James Menzies, she was so terrified when she heard the story of the swapped medicine that she too died suddenly, leaving several children, including her newborn infant who did not long outlive her.

Worms were the cause of much fretting among children at sea, and a constant source of concern for surgeons. On this voyage, too, James Menzies noted the occurrence of worms among the children, observing the production of five worms at least eight inches long by one young sufferer. Worms over 12 inches long were described by other diarists, and it seems that medication for worms was one of the more useful drugs in the surgeon's cabinet.

Depots,
sickness and sanitation

Another Scot sailed for Sydney with 291 other emigrants (207 adults and 85 children) on the 729-ton barque *Sarah* in August 1849. Travelling with his wife Margaret, Hugh Wilson kept a letter-diary for his family on his 104-day voyage ending in Sydney on 10 December 1849. He was a 'little agitated', he apologised when he bade his family farewell, but otherwise the prospect of the journey held no fear for him, 'no tears graced our departure'.[15] Margaret had become very seasick on the coastal journey by steamer from Scotland before they even reached Deptford to prepare for their transoceanic voyage. On arrival at a private emigrant depot at Deptford — which he believed to be run by Caroline Chisholm, the champion of British and Irish emigrants to colonial Australia, with whom he had corresponded — the emigrants were given their allowance of

> dry bread and bitter coffee, boiling hot. I am sure I am not the only one who lost the skin of the roof of the mouth but I do not feel much privition [privation] as it may be better next time, but one cant expect great things wheir we are … but I was well pleased with the usage we got at Deptford our provisions were of excellent quality and we experienced great civility.

At breakfast the following day, before roll call, they were given 'good coffee, Bread and excellent butter', after which he took his turn to scrub the mess tables. It was in the depots that emigrants were acclimatised to the journey ahead. Depots were set up like ships, with messes and berths where emigrants learnt how to co-operate in cooking and cleaning routines, how to use the water closet and how to organise their berths. They were also given lessons on various ways to entertain themselves usefully on board by learning new skills such as rope making and tying, straw plaiting, bag making and basket weaving — guaranteed to be handy in the colonies.[16]

After walking into the town to top up his provisions for the voyage, Hugh and the other emigrants were ferried to their Plymouth-bound steamer. They were alarmed by a collision between their barge and another steamer, but they were 'more feard than hert'. After boarding the Irish steamer that sped them 'down Father Thames', the large crowd was restricted to the deck, which was soon swimming with the contents of their stomachs:

> men, wemon & children, crowded together, like a beggars opera, as the sea got fresh this place was everything but fresh passed Margate Ramsgate, as night came on, no beds, one woman indecent …

Hugh Wilson was disgusted by sailors and soldiers staggering about drunk, and was pained by the lack of privacy. Finding a space for Margaret in the fore cabin, he found himself a spot under a 'tawpaulin'. The bread they were given was mouldy, 'not fit to feed pigs'. But Hugh knew his rights and determined to write to the Emigration Commissioners; their address was well known to emigrants like Hugh who read the numerous periodicals published by private promoters of emigration. 'I said I would write to Park St make a noise about it'. This well-informed Scot was not going to accept any nonsense from English officialdom.

As the steamer headed for Plymouth, Hugh was not happy. Although it was a pleasant day, 'this place at the best is most sickening'. In Plymouth, itself, confusion reigned: 'no one could inform us what we are to do or where go'. But he was well pleased with the comforts at the Plymouth depot, run by the Emigration Commissioners, which was far larger than the one at Deptford, 'good meat and accommodation. I was the Capt. had to go for the meat … We had more room both inside and outside'. Visits into Plymouth were prohibited because cholera had recently arrived in the town. Emigration authorities were determined to isolate the emigrants from the risk of infection so that it would not be imported into the depot or insinuate its way up the gangplank of a government-chartered ship. Nevertheless, Hugh put himself, his wife and fellow passengers at risk by paying several visits into town on shopping expeditions. He also took meals in the town. But, he explained somewhat disingenuously:

Mess room in the emigrant depot at Birkenhead, Liverpool
(*Illustrated London News*, 10 July 1852)

this rule was more rigidly enforced towards the time
when we left, unfortunately I broke one of my lock bolts
just as they were putting the chests aboard the lighter, so
I was in a bad fix. the gate keepers would not allow me to
go out so I applied to the governor [of the depot] who
gave me leave, but being pressed for time I had enough to
do to get it on in time

Cholera had first arrived in the United Kingdom in 1832 during a
pandemic that had begun in India. It travelled through Persia to Russia,
reached Germany, and spread rapidly via shipping routes, from Hamburg
to the United Kingdom, before crossing the Atlantic, to reach New York
within months. The next pandemic travelled a similar route, reaching
Britain and Ireland in 1849. The seaboard, as usual, received and transmitted the disease trans-nationally in the age of sail, and it was to British
and Irish ports that prospective emigrants were bound.

Once the *Sarah* was ready for boarding, three lighters, or barges,
conveyed the emigrants from the quay to the ship anchored in
Plymouth Sound. Having boarded and inspected the steerage quarters,
Hugh was not at all pleased with his berth; he had hoped to be nearer
the hatchway for better light. Accepting it with good grace, 'I began to
like it'. The Irish 'were kept separate from the others' because, he wrote,
they were unclean and had unruly children. It has often been assumed
that, bearing the burdens of class, ethnicity, race, gender and religion,
Irish emigrants suffered prejudice at the hands of officials.
Unquestionably, there were some surgeon superintendents and ships'
masters who were barely able to mask their prejudice, and Irish immigrants often faced intolerance and bigotry in Australia. But the
Emigration Commissioners and their Secretary insisted that emigrants
be treated with equal fairness whatever their origin, and they champi-
oned Irish recruits at times when colonial employers criticised their
selection. Surgeons and matrons who were reported for unkindness to
Irish emigrants were summarily dismissed from the service. The
Commissioners were vigilant about combatting anti-Irish feeling and
refused to tolerate any injustice to emigrants traveling under their

auspices. Bigotry, however, often travelled below decks, where Irish emigrants were barely tolerated by their fellow travellers, not least other Celts such as the better off Scots like Hugh Wilson.

In the mid- to late 1840s, following decades of high migration out of Ireland, Irish small farmers and labourers left home in extraordinary numbers for the United States, Canada and Australia, seeking to escape from the famine that had ravaged the country since 1845. Irish emigrants were seldom from the poorest stratum of their battered economy. Nevertheless, many were physically weak, and unaccustomed to the diet and cleanliness routines on a government ship. Highland Scots, too, and many from remote English villages — had to be coaxed into discarding customary habits and adopting the rules of personal hygiene demanded on these highly regulated ships.

Just over a week after sailing from Plymouth on 28 August 1849 — although the Wilsons' journey from Scotland began ten days earlier than that — the weather was so warm that awnings were stretched over the deck:

> so we have ample shelter from the sun's rays, and all our officers seem to try all they can to promote the comfort, and preserve the health of those under their care, but all seems unavailing for the Government regulations and the disposition of the immigrants parilise the efforts of our Captain and Dr. In the first place the Government have made ~~ample allowance~~ arrangements for the Emigrants to have our ample supply of good food such as is considered suitable for English men at home, but everything but suitable for a tropical climate and the emigrants in despite of the warnings of the Doctor persist in having their full, allowance of Beef and fat pork, and at every meal they have animal food which is telling most fatally upon them, but principally upon the younger portion of us, yet death has removed 5 children and a woman of 30 years of age, the Drs orders are not complied with. Mothers are ordered not to let their children partake of animal food

puddings etc but if the children cry for any thing the not too intelligent parent almost invariably complies with the child's desire and thereby inflicts much suffering on the child, themselves, and all around.

Hugh, who had been appointed a sanitary constable, spent a great deal of time in the company of the surgeon superintendent, who gave him ammunition for his fury with parents of young children. On one occasion, after a mother had complained about her child's bowel complaint while he was 'at her side on the po', the doctor immediately examined the stools. Horrified to find that the child had evacuated undigested fat, he communicated his anger to Hugh; the infuriated Scot believed that the woman was sacrificing the child's life. He continued to rage against women who gave their children meat-fat and rich suet puddings, against the express wishes of the doctor. The children, wrote Hugh,

> are fretful and squalling, by & by they become thin and pine away, till death kindly puts a period to their sufferings, but leaves the living to the expectation of seeing much tradgedy re-enacted … there is not ten minutes of the day but ones feelings are harrowed by the crys and tears of some of our infantine companions. I may here state I think no [one] with young childern should ever come so long a voyage as this, for 'tis painfully oppressive to see their sufferings, and the parents often as helpless as themselves, nay tis almost a wanton waste of life, and our infliction of untold misery & even married people are very uncomfortable owing to being packed up along with others who have familys of small children.

As a married couple without children, it must have been a trial, both noisy and noisome, for the Wilsons to be trapped in steerage with fretful children, soiled nappies and agitated, anxious parents.

Still, life on board had its compensations, and before long he found companions of similar temperament to himself. He decided that the advantages 'counter balance' the sickness and inconvenience of the passage. Paying homage to his parents, for whom his diary was written, he tightened the ties that bound him to his Scottish home by describing his private moments:

> you have many to converse with, and on the still starry evening you can retire to some quiet corner and hold sweet converse with your own [self, and] thoughts of the past, the present & the future, flit through the mind, recalling the bright visions of our early days, the sweet content of a father's fireside the kindness & counsel of a Mother … all float past in silent saddness.

Returning to practical matters, he described the shipboard routines for his family:

> There was a school established on board after we got over our sickness, that was 8 days after leaving Plymouth it has been kept ever since but I cant say much about the efficiency of the teachers or the progress of the scholars the school is held on the quarter deck … Monitors take a few under them, and the Master roams about from place to place, the Mrs teaches the young wemon … fancy knitting which may be all well enough for girls who are to play the lady for life, but quite out of place at a workingman's fireside, it only takes up the time which should be spent at the many useful little turns which makes a home comfortable & happy. Writeing is not taught except on the slate there are a few at Arithmetic but there are no senior classes whatever. This I think is very wrong and ought to be rectified. The female teacher acts as governess over the girls, and I do think that every possible precaution is used to preserve purity of morals and I believe there are far fewer opportunities here of indulging in improper conduct than exists on shore.

Little cheered emigrants more at sea than the sight of sails. On one day, Hugh spotted several ships within the space of a few hours.

Comforting, too, were friendships made on board. As a constable, Hugh was often called upon at night to help patients into the hospital and on one occasion found that his friend Colin McLaren had taken ill after fainting twice. Hugh was worried about his friend, whose illness had come upon him suddenly:

> I called again but he was in the little house and I was not allowed to speak with him as he did not wish his wife to know he was so ill … at 7.00am he was placed in the hospital I saw him at 8.00 he looked to ill to recover I spoke to him but he did not reply, he looked at me & I cannot tell how much I grieved in one hour afterwards he was no more, and in another hour he was buried in the deep. Helen never left his bedside till his spirit had weighed its flight to a happier world. He is the eighth who has been buried, and a sympathy for her and regret for him is universally displayed, he is spoken of as the little frank Scotchman. The Captain shed tears while the funeral service was being read, and the sailors insisted on the line [with] which he was bound being of a better quality than those which were used for the others

and the sail maker, who provided the shroud, was much moved. Many male emigrants — and Colin McLaren appears to have been among them — made firm friends with the crew, from whom they learnt many new skills, and who entertained them with stories. Sailors, too, felt the loss of some emigrants, both adults and children. Hugh described Helen McLaren's bereavement:

> Helen is very ill about the loss of him … both him and her were perfectly delighted when they found that they could get a passage for £6 and were very happy indeed until disease and death stept in and blighted all their earthly hopes. He has left many mourners on board and I believe that Helen will be better looked to than if she were at home. He was seased with cramp in the stomach

and although it is denied, I think it is cholera which has
carried off many and I fear will carry off many more.

When adult emigrants died, emigrants usually contributed to a collection for the survivor, and offered emotional support. This is why
Hugh believed that Colin McLaren's widow was better off than she
would have been on shore. Hugh had, whether he knew it or not,
described exactly the symptoms and nature of cholera, which struck
suddenly, often carrying off its victims from dehydration within hours.
Like a few other ships that left Plymouth during the epidemic, his
vessel probably carried at least one barrel of contaminated water. It is
likely that the first case of cholera — which appears to be that of Colin
McLaren, in spite of Hugh's suspicion that the earlier deaths of children
could be attributed to cholera — occurred after the broaching of a
barrel that was, perhaps, carrying the bacterium *Vibrio cholerae* (which
would be isolated by Robert Koch, who also isolated *micobacterium tuberculosis*, in 1883).

Cholera is an acute diarrhoeal infection, transmitted either in
infected drinking water or by the oral-faecal route — that is, by contamination from infected faeces, usually via eating or drinking with
unwashed hands after a visit, for example, to the lavatory where cholera
bacteria had been deposited, or where an infected person, failing the test
of minimal hygiene, passed on the bacteria to others who handled items
that he had also touched. An important mode of rapid infection was
when contaminated sewage found its way into a water source, leading
to mass infection. Transmission via these routes was swift and efficient.

Symptoms leading to death include vomiting and a rapid loss of fluids, causing extreme dehydration. Many observers describe sufferers
shrinking to mere skeletons before their eyes. Fatality rates often rose as
high as 70 per cent during the great pandemics, although resistance to
infection is probably high, owing to stomach acidity. If cholera, rather
than acute diarrhoea, was responsible for the fatalities, Hugh Wilson was
one of those who appeared to have been resistant. His own complaint
was, rather, constipation, which often made him unwell. He continued:

> During the week we have had many deaths on one day
> one woman and three childern were committed to the
> deep and still a few are ailing and we will likely have many
> more. I have felt very weak and had little appetite & cos-
> tive. the Dr advised me to take no medicine as I had pas-
> sage [of his bowels] once a day my bowels became open
> and I felt much better. I feel weak or perhaps lazzy even
> yet.

The weather continued very hot, even though they had not yet reached
the equator. Hugh reported:

> More deaths last night … the grown up people and the
> most of the childern were carried off in a very few hours.
> it was striking to some [healthy fellow travellers] but on
> many it had no effect whatever and noise, jokes swearing
> and bad language were the order of the day while poor
> wretches were panting for their last breath, in an adjoin-
> ing room, indeed it seemed the same room for the hospi-
> tal is only part of our place boarded off.

Although rainwater was caught in awnings, it was used only for
washing and bathing, even though Hugh Wilson thought it tasted far
better than the drinking water 'which smells ill but we must drink it'.
Hugh's strategy was to mix bicarbonate of soda and tartaric acid —
which he had purchased at Deptford — into the water. Thus he and
Margaret managed 'to smother the smell'. In any case, he believed that
the acidic mixture prevented an attack of cholera:

> Occasionally I hold my nose and the water serves very
> well and refreshes one too but it is very little of it I use
> for I always endeavour to get an extra allowance of soup
> and I generally use it fresh so I don't require to use the
> water. Boiling the water does not alter the flavour of it for
> the taste is quite desirable when made in to tea or coffee
> but not in soups.

He remained on good terms with the cook, who gave him as much pea soup as he could consume. English porridge offended his Scottish sensibility, but 'when helped with a little Butter and sugar' even porridge was 'a treat'.

Hugh Wilson, who described his supervision of the daily holystoning, scrubbing, disinfecting and fumigation routines, found the sociability on board suited him well: 'I have not experienced any of that loneliness which I expected'. When free of his constabulary duties, he looked forward to finding himself a quiet, comfortable spot under a lifeboat to think, read and write: 'One has so much to think of, and observe, that the mind finds full employ on board and the idea of loneliness never forms a resting place on the mind'. Hugh was not one to suffer boredom, but he gives his reader no idea of what his wife Margaret thought or felt about the voyage. Time passed quickly for him, owing to the routine of meals, chores, bathing, and washing dishes and clothes on deck. The young women, he observed, were too coy to remove their clothes in bed and, in the tropics, 'melt away' all night while the young men slept naked on the decks. On some ships, however, women left decorum behind when their vessel entered the tropics, spending days and nights on deck attired only in their underclothing.

More irritating even than English porridge to Hugh Wilson's Scottish Presbyterian sensibility were the 'railing Methodists, and their noisy devotional exercises'. His opinion of the single English girls on deck sank lower and lower as the voyage progressed. As a constable, he was infuriated by what he saw as their laziness, giggling and lack of attention to their own hygiene. They were scarcely able, he reported, to wash their own clothes. But the disease on board occupied his mind rather more than the habits and manners of his companions:

> Disease and death reign around us … it is ever before our eyes, and we get hardened and hope holds out its pleasing but perhaps delusive [picture] …
>
> 16 have been dropped overboard since leaving Plymouth, this day completes one month (of 4 weeks)

which we have been at sea and if we had had health on board we would have had a degree of comfort which we never anticipated — but it is a very heartless sight to see the stout dropping so fast, and without any warning.

Although all of the dead, so far, had been carried from the married quarters (13 children, two women and one man), several of the single men and women were ailing. On the previous night, one young man developed 'cramps in the legs & vomiting and sudden sinking health and strength, this has been the symptoms in the adults who have died and I fear he will go also'. Hugh and Margaret Wilson remained in good health, but they knew that 'death's shaft fly thick'.

Of the 60 children who boarded, about one-fifth had died during the first quarter of the voyage. Hugh was dismayed:

> Our Doctor is inexperienced but I believe well meaning this is his first trip to sea and it is most unfortunate at least for the passengers, we can scarcely say that a single individual who has been really ill has recovered.

When Margaret fell down the stairs after being distracted by a spiteful comment from a male emigrant, she suffered a hysterical fit that annoyed her unsympathetic husband. Fresh air on deck, recommended by the doctor, brought her to full recovery. Although there were several disturbances among the messes over the quality of the beef rations, Hugh, a printer hailing from a 'respectable' working-class background and better off than many emigrant diarists, was more than satisfied with the diet, which allowed him to put away treats for consuming later with tea:

> independent of the beef there was ample allowance of food, at least it was more than I had been used to at home. … There was rice with butter & sugar, plum pudding, the pudding I reserved till tea time. …

Hugh also recommended the pork, although one emigrant remarked that on a previous voyage where 300 emigrants subsisted for a long period (possibly because of a too liberal distribution of rations early in the voyage causing shortages towards the end) on biscuits and tea, no one fell ill. Abstemiousness was a virtue, according to Hugh; he was not at all surprised about the numerous bowel complaints due to the high intake of fatty meat 'at all hours and in quantitys quite inconsistent with the laws of nature'.

Although further deaths — a total of 18 in 33 days — left Hugh appalled at the average of 'more than 1 death every two days', the trade winds brought high spirits among the ship's company. Moreover, one of the critically ill men had recovered, the first to do so, giving rise to hopes of more recoveries. Before long, though, another woman, the 20th emigrant to die, was 'heaved over soon after she died and there were no symptoms of regret for her, indeed her burial excited little very little attention'. He was glad that she had succumbed because 'she had lost her reason … and become idiotic'. Indifference, as usual, replaced respectful observance as the death toll rose. Several people were still ailing 'and there have been several cases of cholera acknowledged lately': Hugh continued to believe that it was responsible for all of the deaths. This, though, is by no means certain. Given that cholera was rare as a cause of death among children, their deaths possibly resulted from diarrhoea caused by gastroenteritis, but for Hugh — and the patients — the symptoms were similar and the outcome the same.

Male emigrants frequently failed to leave their wife-beating propensities at home when they set out for the colonies. One man on the *Sarah* who beat his wife, making her nose bleed, was, characteristically, placed in the coal-hole before being allowed up on deck in irons, where 'he blubbered like a fretful child'. His feet were bound and he was lashed to the stanchions for a night and a day, allowed only fluids. The emigrants petitioned the captain to keep the offender in irons since they were all afraid of him; he had earlier threatened to set fire to the ship. Keeping order could become a surgeon's nightmare.

Meanwhile, determined to keep busy, Hugh taught himself to make coarse trousers, and he acted as ship's barber. He deplored the lowest classes among the emigrants, especially their gambling, and his belief in his own moral and economic superiority got the better of him at times. Nearing the halfway point of the passage, the water continued to smell and taste ill, 'but we get $^1/2$ gill lime juice 4 times a week which helps it a little, but I don't use the water much and as for the tea it is little better', although occasionally a broached cask proved very good. The voracious meat eaters continued to suffer from cramps, and another Irishman died soon after the onset of muscular spasms, symptomatic of cholera. On the same day, the first infant to be delivered on board was born. With the ship not yet six weeks at sea, the port wine — a staple for nursing mothers — was exhausted. Before long, Hugh recorded the death of an infant, possibly the newborn child:

> Mrs King's child died last night … it only survived her by 2 days — and was committed to the deep by 7 am. It is remarkable that in almost every case when a mother died she has been followed by one or two of her youngest children, this leaving the surviving but little incumberd. … This child of Kings make 23 deaths indeed so rapidly do deaths follow that the bread bags are not emptied till they are wanted by the sailmaker to wrap up another corpse. On Monday a piece of old sailcloth was used for D. Quade … Blair informs me that when they were sewing up this lad his fingers were seen to move.

This macabre event, if it were not merely hyperbole, may have been the effects of rigor mortis. The speed with which bodies were buried during epidemics does, however, leave room for the possibility of an over-hasty burial.

A point painfully confirmed by Hugh's observations was the hazard for the youngest children when their mothers died. Even mothers in robust health were often no match against the Grim Reaper when measles, whooping cough and scarlatina were involved. Although many devoted husbands and fathers cared for their children, especially when their wives were pregnant or nursing an infant, others lost heart once their wives were no longer able to cope, or had died. Undoubtedly, in some cases, other nursing mothers were prepared to breastfeed infants whose mothers had succumbed, but nursing mothers were often not well enough to take on the nurture of another infant, and unhygienic feeding bottles were as fatal at sea as they were on land.

Little escaped Hugh Wilson's observation. The livestock brought on board for the cabin passengers — fowls, sheep and two pigs — smelled very bad and the animals suffered from poor health. Two sheep died, and Hugh believed that the fowls were killed and eaten just before the onset of natural death. He believed that the causes of the evil smells emanating from the animal stalls were likely to affect the health of the humans on board. Although the decks, including the animal quarters, were scraped clean daily and then sluiced with a force pump manned by the sailors, the animals remained odiferous. To dry the decks after cleaning, a huge swab, about a yard long, and made from soft rope yarn joined to a handle, and resembling a gigantic mop, was wielded by a person who 'wallops it from side to side and it absorbs the water, which is wrung out of it when it becomes saturated'. Hugh was so taken with this domestic tool that he provided a drawing of it for his family.

Typically, as the ship entered the rougher waters of the Southern Ocean, seasickness erupted again. Even Hugh and Margaret emptied the contents of their stomachs during the first stormy day, with Margaret failing to improve until the calm weather returned. Although the character of many of the young single women did not meet his exacting standards, Hugh was glad to see them 'skipping about' to the music of Irish fiddlers, and was glad that 'indeed all seem very contented'. He was also delighted to make profit on the handkerchiefs he had brought on board for sale. These had cost him twopence each. As a young married man with the kind of initiative and energy guaranteed to take him places in colonial life, Hugh had brought more than handkerchiefs on board in the hope of returning a yield on his investment. Altogether, he made £21 (a fortune to a working man), a mark up of 75 per cent on some articles such as shoemakers' awls and brass buttons. He was sorry that he had not brought shoelaces, moleskins, shirtings, drab black and white linen, thread, looking glasses, straw hats and pickles. Had he been

Section of the emigrant ship *Bourneuf*, 1495 tons. Double-decked vessels such as this one were rare and it is on several of these ships, in 1852 and 1853, that high mortality occurred owing to a high proportion of vulnerable children carried on ships conveying up to 1000 souls to Australia. They were no longer chartered after these episodes. (*Illustrated London News*, 10 July 1852)

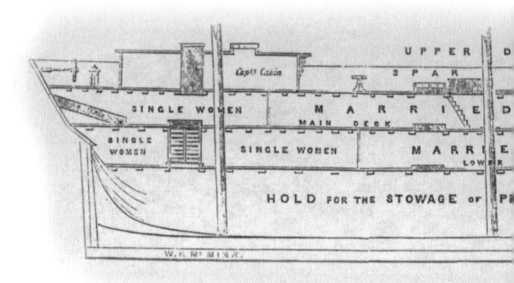

better prepared, he confessed, he would have made 'a handsome profit'. He had only to appear on deck with his bag of goods to be surrounded by eager shoppers.

Like many seafaring husbands before and after him, Hugh took responsibility for washing his own clothes, and was happiest when able to wash his shirts, stockings and underwear in rainwater. Just as bathing in seawater was irksome to some emigrants (although others found it refreshing), seawater left clothes stiff, uncomfortable and itchy, so it was a blessing when sufficient water was caught in canvas receptacles.

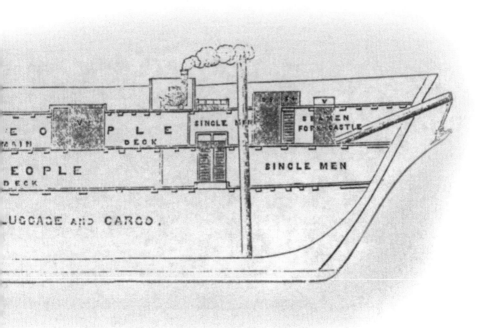

Enforcing cleanliness, however, remained a challenge for the surgeon on the *Sarah*. Before long, he again resorted to punishment to enforce cleanliness by stopping the plum pudding rations for one mess for two days owing to their failure to empty their slop pail. Although there was a deal of grumbling, Hugh did not doubt that the penalty would be effective in maintaining efficiency.

With the weather becoming ever more boisterous as the ship neared Australian waters, Hugh observed that 'the disease and death we had on board at the commencement of the voyage seem to be entirely forgot by everyone and all seem content, if not happy'. Even the rolling and pitching of the ship caused no consternation except to the surgeon, who was laid up for eight days with a bilious attack. The captain took over his spiritual duties, reading prayers and sermons in the doctor's place. Musing about his colonial future, Hugh confided to his diary that, as a printer,

> I expect to encounter many difficulties & discouragements but once they are over I hope I shall ultimately be successful, and the sooner I am embarked on my enterprise the sooner I shall attain the object which I so much desire, namely a comfortable way of living & more independence than when dependent on so fluctuating and daily … a business as the calling …

As the ship entered the colder southern climate, Hugh continued to praise the quantity and quality of the food, and the emigrants' health picked up. With the exception of the death of an infant born on board, no more deaths occurred. Still, at 24, the death toll was unusually high. With three weeks to go, Margaret became ill with toothache, and 'yesterday she had the last of the Vivald's green fresh eggs to breakfast'. This may refer to a supply of preserved fresh eggs that the Wilsons had brought on board. He recorded little about his wife's health in the diary, and left no clue as to how Margaret's toothache was alleviated, although surgeons were adept at pulling recalcitrant teeth. Toothache was a constant, painful affliction in an age before the advent of dental hygiene.

As the ship swept up the coast of Australia, passing 'Australia Felix' (Victoria) on its way to Sydney, Hugh's diary ended. His observations of the sanitary regimes, health and death confirm those of many diarists, that even under the ministrations of a conscientious, if novice, surgeon superintendent (in this case Dr DB North), the introduction of bad water or an infectious pathogen more than matched the strategies that had been put in place to minimise illness and mortality. Nevertheless, if cholera was to blame for the sudden deaths of children and adults on the *Sarah*, those strategies governing hygiene and sanitation did well to confine the deaths to 24. Given the confined space, the weather, and the weeks spent in the enervating heat of the tropics, where, if becalmed, ships were sometimes surrounded by their own detritus — sewage, slops, food scraps, soiled nappies, the discarded bedding and clothing of the dead, and so on — deaths on a cholera ship might have been far higher.

'I was never well untill after my confinement'

The 1850s

Kinship networks and advice

I n 1852, a young mother wrote home to her family from Melbourne. Lucy Hart and her husband John had arrived in South Australia on 7 April 1849, after a three-month voyage on the *David Malcolm*, which carried 236 souls to Port Adelaide, including 75 children, representing over 30 per cent of its compliment.[1] Two children died during the voyage, and six infants were born, among whom five thrived. Supervising the voyage was Dr C Meymott. Three years after reaching the colony, Lucy apologised for her long silence since arriving. Soon after disembarkation, the Harts had been seized by gold fever, made their way to Melbourne and thence, initially, to Ballarat. Her letter begins,

> Melbourne,
> Port Phillip,
> May the 3rd. [1852].
>
> My dear Mother, Brothers & sisters
>   I scarcely know how to excuse myself as how to apologise for my long silence. This is a task I have many times began but have never finished it till now. I expect you all come to the conclusion that I am dead, or have forgot you all, but it is neither the case, you must not think that because I have not wrote that I have never

thought of you, far far from that, the thoughts of my home have caused me many an unhappy hour, and more so since I have been a <u>wife</u> and <u>mother</u>. I must beg of you to forgive me. I know you will when you receive this for I well know the feelings of a mother. You will see in this letter how my time have been employed since I left England up to the present time. I cannot give but a short account of our voyage out here as it is so long ago. I will just say what I can remember. We arrived in Adelaide 3 years ago the 5 of last month after a plesent voyage of 3 months and a fortnight. We sailed from Plymouth the 4 of January 1849 with a fair wind. We had scarcely got outside of the Break-water when such a scene I never witnessed before. Out of 300 and 30 people there was not more than 6 exempt from seasickness, so it continued for the first fortnight. Neither Hart nor myself was not seasick. In about a week we reached <u>Madeira</u>. We where becalmed 24 hours close to it. No person was allowed to go on shore. It is a lovely place. We was close enough to see the cattle grazing. That is a spot I shall never forget. It was then as warm as a summer day in England.

In ten days after we left that beautiful place, we got into the <u>Bay of Biscay</u>. There we was tossed about for ten days more but not so rough as many people have found it. During the time we where tossing about there, I met with a severe accident. It was one evening the ship was rolling from side to the other. My husband had just left me for a minute or so to go to the gally for something, when the vessel gave a sudden lurch and threw down the middle hatchway. My left shoulder was put out and the leaders of my arm completely smashed. I am happy to say no bones were broke. I was in the ship hospital for three weeks and not able to move. I could not dress myself for weeks after we arrived in Adelaide. I feel the effects now and I fear I shall as long as I live. I am sorry to say my troubles did not end with that for the effects of the fall brought on a slow

fever which continued till a few days before we reached
the Port we was bound for, it made it very uncomfortable
for my husband during the voyage.

The Captain & Doctor & steward was very kind to
me. Had I been well on board, I should have got on first
rate for untill I met with the fall I used to cook for the
Cabin, and that was how they were so kind to me, but
through sickness I was not allowed the privilege, but
Providence ordained it for some good purpose in the end,
I have no doubt.

It was very hot in crossing the line, but I have found
it a great deal hotter here. We also passed the <u>Island of
Trinidada</u>.[2] I did not see it myself as I was too ill to go on
deck. We did not see any more land till we reached
<u>Kangaroo Island</u> ... about one hundred miles from
Adelaide. We reached this island on the Friday and landed at
Port Adelaide on the following Monday. You may depend all
hearts did rejoice to be expelled from our floating prison (I
termed). ... The town of Adelaide is ... a very fine large
town just another such place as Southampton with about
40 thousand inhabitants, so you can judge it is a fine place.
We was greatly surprised to find such a flourishing town.
You can get everything here the same as in England, and
many things was a great deal cheaper. I am speaking of when
we came here. Not now, for these are <u>golden days</u> now.

Well, my dear Mother, when we reached this fine
town, of course we had neither house nor home to go
to, and we could not tell where to find my husband's
brother as he had never wrote to his home since he left it.
Neither could we get a lodging, so we was obliged to go
back to the ship again, for it is the custom for emigrants
to stay on board for 14 days after they are in port till they
can get work or some place to go to. But, however, Hart's
brother lived 70 miles in the Bush and he happened to be
in the town to the Races just the very time we came, and
he saw our names in the paper, as everyone's name is

advertised that comes to these colonys, which is very convenient, and more so if you have any relations here before.

He came down to the ship directly, and you may suppose we was glad to see him. I had never seen him before, neither had I ever seen his wife. My husband went to work at <u>Clarke's Brewary</u> the same week for 25 shillings per week, and as we could not get a comfortable lodging, I stayed on board the ship till his brother went home, and then I went home with him and left my husband in town. I had been there three days when I was taken ill with a fever & dysentery. I was ill a week before I would let them send for a doctor for they had to send 16 miles, and when he came I was quite out of my mind, no one ever expected to see me recover any more. I was like that for 12 days before the fever turned. My husband was sent for you can fancy what a state of mind he was in. That bit of sickness cost us 15 pounds, and <u>that</u> was our first coming to the colony. In about a month with the help of a kind providence, I was enabled to take the journey for Adelaide where my husband had endeavoured to get a very comfortable room for me close to his work, which you may depend I was very glad to find.

My dear Mother, I was never well untill after my confinement. I have got a fine little girl, she is three years old next September. Her name is Lucy Anne. Her father would have her named after me. She is an interesting little child. She is now by my side asking all sorts of questions. When I told her I was writing to her grandmother, she directly said — She is a funny old grandmother not to come & see little Lucy sometimes! She told me to tell you if you will come here and live with us, she will dearly love you and you should always sit in her arm chair. Her father is doatingly fond of her. She has a fair complexion, light brown hair & black eyes, and very fat.

She is loved by everyone that knows her. She is so good tempered. She can say anything the same as I can, and repeat several pieces of poetry, and not three years old yet, so you may depend we are very fond of her. My dear Mother, I have had many trials and troubles since I saw you, and a great deal of sickness, but I never wanted for anything, a man [her husband] got it all, and for the first twelve months we was getting what I call — one step forward and two back. I think I told you when I was home that Hart is very saveing and fond of money which made me very uncomfortable has I could not save anything out of his wages has we had so much sickness, and of course I had many little things to buy for such a time. I could not save much you might think, but Mother, I have never been without a <u>pound</u> in my pocket since I have been <u>John Hart's wife</u>, and I think that is a great thing to say. Should I have been so well off in England? No! Work hard & be half-starved. Australia is the place to live. I would not come back to England again unless I had enough to keep me without work on no account. Neither would my husband. I am speaking now the very sentiments of our hearts, but people must be saving, industrious and persevering. We have deprieved ourselves of many things we might have had, but what was it for? All to try to do something for ourselves so that my husband should not always work under a <u>Master</u>, and happy am I to inform you that we have gained that point, he is now his own master.

My dear Mother, after I had quite recovered from my confinement and quite strong, I was determined to work to help get a living. I began to take in washing and ironing at 3 shillings per dozen, so I used to earn about 15 shillings per week, which was much as I could do with a young baby. Then we could save a pound per week for a nice house & garden. We was then getting on in the world, very rich for working people, and just got things comfortable about us when my poor husband was taken ill with a violent fever. Fevers are very prevalent here and so they are in most hot climates. It was twelve weeks before he went to work again, and the very day he went to work, we had but one shilling, but thank God we did not owe any person a penny piece. He went back to his old place to work, and you see, My dear Mother that through our own industry, it kept us from the <u>cold hand of Charity</u>. I still kept on my work all through his sickness, so you might think my hands was full enough then. I never expected him to recover, the Doctor gave me very slight hopes for him. After he got well, went to work again, we was obliged to begin afresh, and try to save a little more. That is two years ago this month. Since then we neither of us have not had a days illness, and everything have prospered.

Then in a month or two, we brought a <u>cow</u>, and she used to turn me in about 12 shillings a week, and then in a little time we brought another <u>cow</u>, and I had a lot of poultry of my own rearing. We was then doing well. I had by that time a great deal of washing, so I have not spent much idle time. I was situated exactly like that when Mr. White brought the letter to me that Stephen wrote, and we had got 50 pounds in the Bank, and all got by real hard work. I must tell you, Mother, that Hart is a very steady sober man and would not spend a shilling in waste on no account, neither would I myself.

My dear Mother, now I will tell you how we got to <u>Melbourne</u> I have no doubt you have heard of the <u>gold diggins</u> here at Port Phillip before this reaches you. The diggings broke out soon after Mr. White called on me. Well, I begged of my husband to come here and try his luck, as so many Adelaide people had been here and done well. At last he made up his mind to come and leave me in Adelaide as I could get my living without touching the little money we had saved.

He left Adelaide the 20 of October last and got here in three days with a fair wind. It is only 5 hundred miles and only three days sail with a good wind. As soon as he got to Melbourne, he started for the diggins which is about 90 miles from the town. It is called Mount Alexander. They was eight in a party from Adelaide. They all go in partys, one man alone is of no good. There is now about seventy thousand people in the diggins at this present time.

In about 5 weeks after he left, I received a letter from him containing the joyful news that he had got his own share 200 pounds worth of gold, and also to tell me to sell my things and come to Melbourne as quickly as possible, so my dear Mother, gladly did I comply with that request. I sold my things and took the first vessel bound for Melbourne. We had a very rough passage, we was ten days coming. We got to Melbourne the day after last Christmas Day, where I found my husband anxiously waiting my arrival. He was then determined that I should not work so hard any more. I have no need to now, for with the money that I brought with me, we could raise 300 pounds, and now I consider myself well off in the world, so I do nothing but my own work now.

We are living in a nice house called "Devon Cottage". We pay 16 shillings per week, and that is cheap as times are here now. There are hundreds of people living in tents on the Banks of the Yarra River, and there is not houses enough for the people as they are flocking from all parts to go to the diggins and the tradesmen will not work for any money that is offered them, they are off to the diggins. I only wish my own brothers was here, they would do something for themselves.

Now, Hart has bought 2 horses and a dray he gave a 100 & 50 pounds for them. He is now taking stores to the diggins for shopkeepers and he is making 30 pounds per week, and making money fast, but he will be off to the diggins again as soon as the rain comes, as they are obliged to wash all the earth after they dig it, to find the precious metal. I hope he will do something handsome this time.

There are many poor workingmen that I know have 3 or 4 thousand pounds and gone back to England.

Now mind, Mother, this is the real truth you may show this letter to any person in the world. This is a second <u>California</u>. Things are an awful price on account of labour being so dear, but there is a great deal of money to be got here. Just fancy, 6 pence for an egg, 3 shilling a pound of butter 1/6 for a small loaf of bread, 6 pence for a pound of flour, but what matters that if you got plenty of money to get it with 5 shillings for a small Barrel of water. I had almost forgot to say that <u>Melbourne</u> is a splendid town far before Adelaide.

My dear Mother, you can imagine my surprise when Mr. White came to my door to enquire for me and said he came from Winchester and that he had got a letter from my brother. I bid them come and made them welcome. I was glad to have a letter from Stephen although we cannot read half of it. I hope he will improve in his writing. I am very sorry to hear of George's affair. I don't think it was the boy's fault for I saw quite enough when I was home to satisfy me about Ann White. I hope he never intends to marry her, if so, I should be very angry with him.

My dear Mother, do beg of him to come out here, and William. Do, Mother, for their own welfare. I would not wish them to come on an uncertainty for they are sure to do well. Any person can do well here if they like to try. I only wish I could persuade you to come with all the children. You, Mother, should have a good home and no work to do. Why not come, Mother, there was many older women than you came out in our vessel, and are now doing well. If you wont come, do let the boys come.

Give my kind love to William Carmaker and his wife and tell them to delay no time in coming to Melbourne for he would sure to get on here, never mind the voyage, that is nothing — why not all of you come together? Should any of you come, be sure to bring a few little things with you such as a bit of Bacon & a little flour and little things to make yourselves comfortable during the voyage, although there is plenty, such as it is, on board.

Now, I shall expect some of you out here in about twelve months from this time, if not be sure to write me a letter, and a long one, as soon as you get this.

I hope dear Sister is a good girl & hope Tommy & Stephen are good boys. Should dearly like to see them. Give our kind love to them all. I expect you are nearly tired of reading my scrawl, so I will now conclude with our kindest love to all, and little Lucy sends her kind love to you and her uncles and aunt.

And believe me to be your affectionate daughter
Lucy A. Hart

direct

Mrs John Hart
Post Office Melbourne
Port Phillip

P.S. My dear Brothers, do come or be sure to write me as soon as you get this. Dear Mother my next letter shall be something inclosed to convince you of what I say. It be posted a month from this time. Let me know where my brothers are.

My dear Mother, should any of you come here, you had better come to

Devon Cottage, Moor Street
Collingwood, Melbourne

and should we not be living there, the people there might tell you where to find us but be sure to direct your letters to the post office as we shall be sure to have them then. Tell me all the news and whether any of you went to the Great Exhibition.

I have never seen Mrs. White since the week after they landed for they went out in the <u>Bush</u> to live, but I hear they are doing very well indeed. Her daughter is married — I tried to my utmost to find her son George but I cannot, since I cannot find any person that has ever seen him, but you might as well to try to find a person in London as to find them here unless you know where they live. Give my kind love to Fanny Edwards and tell her I should like to see her here very much.

My love to all at Westmeon [West Meon, east of Winchester] and tell them from me that I am not such a character as they think I am, that I am as well off as they are now. My love to my dear brother George and William, and tell them to be sure to come here.

> Goodbye, God bless you all,
> Goodbye, God bless you all,
> <u>Lucy Ann Hart</u>

Sadly, Lucy's mother never knew what had become of her daughter. She died before the long-delayed letter reached England. Treasured by her siblings in England, it was kept by Lucy's brother. Eventually, it found its way back to Australia after the First World War. A precious symbol of the family's history, it was later taken to the United States by a descendant before being returned, eventually, to the family in Victoria. Like family bibles, numerous letters travelled the oceans in this way, as cherished mementoes of ancestral history.

Another woman, Mary Marshall, who arrived in Victoria from Chipping Warden in Warwickshire with her husband James and daughter Elizabeth, also wrote home to her sister and brother three years after arrival, during which time she had given birth to three children, including twin girls who died in infancy. Her two surviving daughters were thriving at the time of writing. Again, we see the comfort brought by the presence of a brother-in-law, and friendships characteristic of chain migration. Mary Marshall's letter is typical of an intuitive writer, who spelled each word phonetically, but whose content and meaning is clear.[3] Her letter indicates that literacy is an elastic term. A woman, who might be termed illiterate by some observers, was capable of sophisticated, expressive and deeply resonant communication. A translation, in italics, follows:

Diament creek february 21 1851

Dearest sister and brothere it is with plasure I take my pen in hand to wright thes few lines to you hopping to find you all in good Health as i ham happy to say this livves us all At this presant thank god for it deare sister i have not Received but one letter from you for three heares i hope you Will rite to me hofenere as i want to her from you Deare sister i have had 3 children since i rote to you to litel girls was born the day as thomas sited this land But tha did not live long ann dide wen she was aleven Wicks old susan lived to be foremonth my litel Emmar was born november the 4 and is in good Health than god for it Elizabeth is groen a fine Girl and sends hir love to hir hant and hunkel And hall hir cosens she ofen tolk of you hall Since hir hunkel as told hir about all hir friends over the water der sistere i have been much happiere since thomas as been here with us heas been very kind to me and to the childeren james was up the counterey above a hundered and fifty Miles With the time when Emmar was born and did not reach home till she was a fortnite old tomas was at home with me he was very kind to me hall the time I was hill he is very pleas with a litel neice he and hir intended hant is to stand to hir Deare sister we have toke a pice of land on the Diment creek togathere and i hope with the blesing of God we shall be seteld for life now we have been moven about the counterey long anuf But you canot get a home in this counterey till you can by one of your hone deare sister i think i soon shall have a sistere in this counterey Now and that is what i happen have pray for tho i have not wanted fore any thing in this conterey theare as ben many lonely houre i have spent wishin i hade a friend ore a sistere to speek to this last twelve month i have been very lonley thom and jim as been spliten timbere fore to Fence with and we had to live in the bush to be handy to thare work and theare as not been a nabour within to miles of me thomas is Goen to make is hut by oures and get a wife so i shall have a companon now i hope tha will be happy togathere the place as we are liven on is to be a linland town now so wee shall have plenty of compeny soon it is nerily hall bote and not been put up for sale only one month it is foreteen miles from milbourne deare sistere we have had along drouth this sommere we have not scarcley had any rane this six months theare is plenty of the catel dien fore want of water on the planes in the interere of the Counterey

Deare sistere i have a bad acount to give you About this counterey now wee have had a dreadful fire heare this counterey is not like home it is very large you can go to sidney overe land 5 hundered miles to poret hadled 7 hundered miles it is hall alevel counterey with grass and trees the fire comences in the interere of the country and ranged over many hundered miles every thing was dry fore Want of rane the harvest was just over it reached to the cultavated land it burnt every thing before it corn stacks houses catel and hall it did not rech us the wind changed before it come with in 7 miles of were we lived theare was agreet deal of corn burnt and catel by hunderes theare was several lives lost to a woman and five childeren was burnt to deth on the same creek as i live an about aleven miles from us and hir husbon was burnt so as he dide in three days aftere Corn is risen fast on account of the fire but we had bote us plenty to last us till we can gro more thank god it did us no hurt in any way fore our catel was hall at home everything besides floure is about the same price as when i rote to you before

Now i think i have told you hall about this counterey good and bad deare sistere give my love to deare mothere and fathere i shall right to halford as i received a lettere from them last wick and from alstere i shall send one to you to send to my deare brothere and i siscerely hope as he will soon send one to me deare sistere i hope you are happy and richard and all youre deare childeren i should like to see you hall again i hofen think as i should like to see richard but i feare i nevere shall in this woreld but you must give our kind love to him and hall the childeren and receive the same youre self so no more from us this time deare sistere and and believe wee to remain your Efectonet sistere and brothere James and Mary Marshall

please to return the post as soon as you can derect james T Marshall as heare is anothere james marshall heare bareing the Bambury post stamp from Chipenworden

TRANSCRIPTION

Diamond Creek, February 21, 1851

Dearest Sister and Brother

It is with pleasure I take my pen in hand to write a few lines to you, hoping to find you all in good health as I am happy to say this leaves us all at present. Thank God for it. Dear sister I have not received but one letter from you for three years. I hope you will write to me more often as I want to hear from you. Dear sister I have had three children since I wrote to you. Two little girls were born the day that Thomas sighted this land.[4] But they did not live long. Ann died when she was eleven weeks old. Susan lived to be four months. My little Emma was born November the fourth and is in good health thank God for it. Elizabeth is grown a fine girl and sends her love to her aunt and uncle and all her cousins. She often talks of you all since her uncle has told her about all her friends over the water.

Dear sister I have been much happier since Thomas has been here with us. He has been very kind to me and to the children. James was up country above a hundred and fifty miles

away when Emma was born and did not reach home till she was a fortnight old. Thomas was at home with me. He was very kind to me all the time I was ill. He is very pleased with a little niece. He and her intended aunt will stand as her godparents.

Dear sister we have taken a piece of land on the Diamond Creek together and I hope with the blessing of God we shall be settled for life now. We have been moving about the country long enough. But you cannot get a home in this country till you can buy one of your own. Dear sister I think I soon shall have a sister in this country now and that is what I happen to have prayed for though I have not wanted for anything in this country.[5] There have been many lonely hours I have spent wishing I had a friend or a sister to speak to. These last twelve months I have been very lonely. Tom and Jim have been splitting timber for fencing and we had to live in the bush to be handy to their work and there has not been a neighbour within two miles of me. Thomas is going to make his hut by ours and get a wife so I shall have a companion now. I hope they will be happy together.

The place we are living on is an inland town now so we shall have plenty of company soon. It is nearly all bought having been for sale only one month. It is fourteen miles from Melbourne.

Dear sister we have had a long drought this summer. We have scarcely had any rain for six months. There are plenty of cattle dying for want of water on the plains in the interior of the country.

Dear sister I have a bad account to give you about this country now. We have had a dreadful fire here. This country is not like home. It is very large. You can go to Sydney overland 5 hundred miles; to Port Adelaide 7 hundred miles. It is all a level country with grass and trees. The fire commenced in the interior of the country and ranged over many hundred miles. Everything was dry for want of rain. The harvest was just over. It reached to the cultivated land. It burnt everything before it: corn stacks, houses, cattle and all. It did not reach us. The wind changed before it came within 7 miles of where we lived. There was a great deal of corn burnt, and cattle by hundreds. There were several lives lost too. A woman and five children were burnt to death on the same creek as I live and about eleven miles from us, and her husband was burnt and he died three days after.

[The price of] Corn has risen fast on account of the fire but we had bought plenty to last us till we can grow more. Thank God it did us no hurt in any way for our cattle were all at home. Everything besides flour is about the same price as when I wrote to you before.

Now I think I have told you all about this country good and bad. Dear sister, give my love to dear mother and father. I shall write to Halford[6] as I received a letter from them last week, and from Alister.[7] I shall send one to you to send to my dear brother and I sincerely hope that he will soon send one to me. Dear sister I hope you are happy and Richard and all your dear children. I should like to see you all again. I often think that I should like to see Richard but I fear I never shall in this world. But you must give kind love to him and all the children and receive the same yourself.

So no more from us this time dear sister and believe us to remain your affectionate sister and brother, James and Mary Marshall.

Please return the post as soon as you can direct to James T Marshall as there is another James Marshall nearby bearing the Banbury post stamp from Chipping Warden.

Mary Marshall's attitude is characteristic of women who saw their labour as essential components to the employment of their husbands. Their unwaged work was a crucial contribution to the family economy, and they were well aware of their worth. As another pioneering woman wrote home to her mother from Yass in 1853,

> a man with a good wife, one he could depend upon with-
> out a penny in his pocket was better off than he who had
> a thousand pounds in his purse without one, for she
> would be worth more than that to him.[8]

Storms,
sickness and misery

On the 112-day voyage of the 704-ton *Pestonjee Bomanjee*, bound for
South Australia between 17 June and 7 October 1854, carrying 308
emigrants, including 102 children — again one-third of the compliment
— the surgeon was Dr WH Motherall, supervising his first voyage. He
buried six children and four adults at sea, and delivered five infants. The
causes of death of the two adult males, two adult females, three boys and
three girls (all aged four or under) included four attributed to diarrhoea,
two to fever, one to apoplexy, one to inflammation of the brain, one to
water on the brain and one to epileptic fits.[9]

Also on board were at least two diarists. One, Malen Rumbelow,
began his journey at the Nine Elms Depot on the Thames below
London, where emigrants were housed at a daily cost of 1/3d, paid
from the colonial land fund. This new depot had replaced the Deptford
Depot months earlier. It was owned and operated by the London and
Southwest Railway Company, which, from later in 1853, was also contracted to convey the emigrants from the depot to the Southampton
docks, from where many ships sailed in mid-century. At the time of
Malen Rumbelow's voyage, however, a temporary Southampton Depot
was in operation, to which he was obliged to travel the next day from
Nine Elms, at an exorbitant cost to himself of 12 shillings, when a
steam trip from Dublin to Liverpool could be had for under one
shilling. Malen's baggage was examined on arrival at the Southampton
Depot, and he was given the mandatory ship's kit before being appointed a constable. The following day, the emigrants boarded and received
their mess utensils before the ship weighed anchor the next day. His
was a speedy departure.[10]

An infant was born on the second day of the voyage. In spite of
the fine weather, seasickness set in immediately. Within three days of
sailing, a four-year-old girl had died 'by drinking wine'. This causation
does not fit with the surgeon's report — he recorded the death as
'apoplexy'— but, as we can observe from Eliza Whicker's diary below,

Emigrant ship leaving
Southampton for Australia
(*Illustrated London News,*
28 August 1852)

fellow emigrants believed that the child had, essentially, died by misadventure.[11] With heavy weather setting in, a woman was severely injured by a piece of timber falling from the main mast, and the cook was badly scalded owing to the lurching of the ship. In spite of the weather and seasickness in the first fortnight, after three weeks at sea Malen reported 'the people much better, schooling on deck, our rations pretty good, and plenty, the people in good spirits with but little sickness'.

A fortnight later, with the weather warm, awnings were rigged on the deck. Malen Rumbelow reported that the people kept themselves and the ship clean, with the captain and surgeon regularly visiting below decks to ensure that order was kept. Following the death of a Lascar sailor, a solemn burial service was held. As the voyage progressed, singing and dancing continued in the evening; infants were born, and the regular rhythm of shipboard life continued. Malen took every opportunity to cook any flying fish that happened to land on deck. Although fresh fish must have offered a chance to vary an otherwise tedious diet, few emigrants attempted to catch fish for their own consumption. For Malen Rumbelow, the voyage continued pleasantly; he observed that in the tropics the emigrants discarded clothing and lay naked on deck at night, relishing their extra rations of lime juice and porter and, when becalmed, bathed in the sea.

The vessel encountered boisterous weather on the run down towards Capetown; upon rounding the Cape, the tremendous seas were terrifying. Malen described the scene:

> No breakfast until 10 o'clock, no dinner at all, and but half the quantity of water for tea, the sea pouring down the hatchways by pailfuls, women and children all in bed, one of the crew had his fingers much hurt by another letting go a rope. Ship going 7 or 8 knots under a fair wind, which died away at night, leaving a heavy swell which caused the ship to roll most frightfully, removing everything that was not made fast, and at 10 o'clock at night there was a pretty sight, pots, pannikins, tins, spoons, knives and forks, rice, coffee, pepper, biscuits, oatmeal,

baskets, shoes, boxes and salt-water, with sundry other things all jumbled together and flying too and fro the ship, many of the people much frightened, the child Fredk. very ill with thrush.

The following morning was spent clearing up the mess, and during the afternoon the doctor was called to the child, who was given a warm bath and brandy with water, which seemed to revive him. With a freshening gale, accompanied by thunder and lightning, the pitching and rolling of the ship caused one of the constables to be 'thrown down and his head cut'. As a constable in charge of the ailing child, Malen gave him 'three powders' and, as the man responsible for slaughtering the live animals on board for the cabin passengers, he killed another sheep. Within days, the well-fed cabin passengers were fed freshly killed pork. Another constable was hurt by falling debris, and the sickly child continued to improve with doses of port wine.

At the end of August, well over two months into the voyage, many of the emigrants, Malen included, succumbed to diarrhoea. With the emigrants continuing ill, one 16-month-old child, who had been constantly bathed to relieve his distress, died and was buried the same day, at sunset, and 'another had a narrow escape of being smothered, by being rolled up in bed by mistake'. Within hours of the burial of the 16-month-old boy, his mother gave birth; her distress presumably hastened a premature delivery. Malen's interests were eclectic; in the same brief entry he noted that 'the provisions are getting bad, biscuits mould, butter rank, eggs rotten'. This could, of course, account for the diarrhoea. One 60-year-old man, having been taken to the hospital suffering from acute diarrhoea, died — exactly a month before arrival — 'although the surgeon was unremitting in his attentions'.

The *Pestonjee Bomanjee* endured storms and gales all the way to Australia. Whereas many emigrants reported fair weather sailing for the whole of their passage, this vessel was beset with intensely cold and frightening conditions. With tremendous waves breaking over the ship and pouring down the hatchways as the captain sought the Southern Ocean's roaring forties for an easterly run, people were 'tumbling about and hurting themselves much, several still ill'. The fever and diarrhoea continued, and, to add to the distress, a fire in the bakehouse caused consternation one night. With the wind blowing 'enough to tear the masts out of the ship', and with violent squalls of rain, hail and sleet, a five-month-old child died, and was buried at the same time that a married woman succumbed to fever, leaving a husband and baby. She also was buried during the storm. The terrifying hurricanes continued; on one night, Malen Rumbelow estimated that about two tons of water crashed down the hatchway, completely drenching four families in their beds, 'and carrying every moveable thing before it [and] stoving in the pig pen'. As the vessel neared its destination, the weather had not abated, and a married 32-year-old woman who died in the early morning was buried at noon,

> leaving a husband and 2 children one of which was born on board aged 9 weeks, in the afternoon a child died in a fit aged 2 years … many of the people still ill of Fever, and all becoming very impatient for the termination of our passage which we expect in 5 or 6 days as we have about 1000 miles more to go, in the evening the wind arose almost to an hurricane accompanied with vivid flashes of lightning.

The woman's nine-week-old son survived the voyage, probably nursed by another breastfeeding mother. With seven days to go, the ship at last met moderate weather. But with many still ill, 'we are all becoming tired of hard biscuits and salt meat and much require some vegetables'. Like most emigrants, Malen had been very happy with the diet, but with fresh supplies dwindling as they neared shore, the emigrants' health was at serious risk. Two days before landing, another eight-month-old child died, and was buried in the late afternoon, 'the friends singing a hymn'. In spite of the despondency following the infant's death within sight of Port Adelaide, the emigrants were greeted by 'splendid warm weather'.

As the ship approached Port Adelaide, letters were sent ashore on the mail steamer, and a steam tug towed it 'over the bar and to within 2 or 3 miles of the port where we dropped anchor at 5 o'clock, the tug leaving us to fetch fresh provisions for the cabin'. In the evening, they were towed into the dock and visitors were allowed on board:

> the people [were] receiving their friends some bringing green peas, lettuces, spring onions, etc. drinking and making merry the whole of the day, some of the crew obtain leave to go on shore but none of the people owing to our not having been mustered by the Doctor from the shore, the day was spent in the utmost confusion, the police on board to preserve order and protect the people, no prayers read today.

Colonists well understood the enthusiasm with which fresh fruit and vegetables, and treats like gingerbread, would be greeted on arrival. They also knew, from their own experience, that fresh food was essential for the health of people about to face a new kind of hardship on shore. On the following day,

> At 10 we were mustered by Dr Duncan the immigration agent who interrogated us as to our treatment etc. on the passage and if we were satisfactory we were then liberated to go on shore and thus ended our passage of 112 days from London to Adelaide.

Malen Rumbelow survived the tempestuous voyage to found a dynasty on the south coast of South Australia, where he was a landowning ratepayer by 1857.[12]

Sharing his rough passage was Eliza Whicker, who had emigrated from Guernsey with other Channel Islanders, for whom prayers were spoken daily in French.[13] She, too, noted the death early in the passage of the four-year-old who, she reported, was given wine dosed with opium without the knowledge of her parents. Having fallen asleep after taking the medicine, she had failed to awaken. This observation may confirm that the surgeon's recording of the child's cause of death as apoplexy was somewhat evasive. The child, however, may well have been given a sedative in wine for acute diarrhoea. Perhaps she was overdosed, or perhaps the surgeon administered the dosage in the belief that the child was, in any case, dying. Eliza Whicker voluntarily nursed in the hospital during most of the voyage, often at night, and was able to observe the surgeon's movements at close hand.

Eliza Whicker also noted the birth of a stillborn boy to a woman 'in a very critical situation'. This may have been the mother whom Malen Rumbelow described as having been prematurely delivered to save her life. The birth of the stillborn infant was an event not recorded by the surgeon superintendent, Dr Motherall. Although many surgeons did not fail to record stillbirths, there seems to have been no consensus about whether stillbirths ought to have been recorded as deaths, as we noted on page 59. Significantly, the 'Nosological Index' compiled by William Henry Archer, the Registrar-General of Victoria, which was an adaptation of the index compiled by the United Kingdom's Registrar-General, William Farr, offers 'premature birth' as a cause of death, but not 'stillbirth'. There was, on land as at sea, no category under which a stillbirth could be officially recorded. Deaths were recorded only for infants who had drawn breath, in which case both life events — the birth and the death — were recorded.[14] Therefore, those surgeons who recorded a stillbirth often did so because the dead infant's mother also died, thus indicating that her death occurred during, or immediately after, childbirth. In such cases, the stillbirth represented, as it were, the cause of death. Sometimes surgeons recorded a stillbirth merely as a matter of interest on their official reports, as information additional to the summary of births and deaths.

When Eliza Whicker's daughter became ill, the solicitous surgeon sent special meals from the cabin for her. Besides watching over her own family's health, Eliza kept a close observation of her fellow travellers. The heads of one family, which were infested with 'vermin', were cropped and washed. Their beds and bedding were thrown overboard, and the family was moved to an isolated part of the ship. Eliza, too, was alarmed by the epidemic of diarrhoea and noted that the feverish people were treated with blistering. Fire, always a momentous occasion, also alarmed her, and she noted that the platform under the bakehouse burst into flames three times, and was put out by 'throwing water about'. She believed that the fever on board was 'ship fever' (and therefore possibly typhus).

Unlike Malen Rumbelow, Eliza Whicker did not dwell on the turbulent weather. A matter-of-fact practical woman, she noted, on arrival in the colony, that her daughter was better 'but she cannot walk about & I fear she will be an idiot'. Her son had scalded his foot 'so to begin we have the two most likely children laid up with fever'. Eschewing sentimentality, she set her face towards the challenges ahead and, having paid 12 shillings a week for a house 'which is neither wind nor water tight', she contemplated her future. Meanwhile, Surgeon Superintendent Motherall's performance was vehemently criticised by the Immigration Agent. Dr Duncan believed that the surgeon's laxity and inexperience had contributed to the ten deaths on board. In an attempt to impress upon him the solemn responsibilities of the position of surgeon superintendent, Dr Motherall was deprived of his return passage money. Needless to say, he did not again supervise a ship bound for South Australia.[15]

Wild weather did not always contribute to a higher death toll among the emigrants. The 1285-ton *Hornet* carried 448 emigrants, including 95 children, from Southampton to Victoria on a 102-day voyage between 23 May and 2 September 1857. Dr JH Brownfield superintended a boisterous passage that was not marred by deaths although, as was common in stormy seas, a 16-year-old sailor fell from the main yard. As well, four infants were born on board. From the beginning of the voyage, one diarist, TB Atkinson, noted 'sickness, sickness, sickness: Sickness and misery'.[16] Storms and gales accompanied the ship nearly all the way to Australia. Among other discomforts, TB Atkinson found that the marine soap was of no use in cold water; he warmed the water for his child's bath: 'Washed the baby in seawater this morning — Elizabeth still too weak for exertion. The Doctor too much on his hands to give attention to individual cases'. Like numerous husbands, he cared for his children and took turns at cooking during his wife's indisposition.

For the Atkinson family, squalls, hail and rain made a misery of their 103 days at sea 'in what the Times calls our "nautical prison"'. Such voyages were also a challenge to surgeons faced with far more accidents than on a calm passage, and with seasickness continuing throughout the voyage. TB Atkinson was very happy to find his brother waiting for them at the port in Melbourne where, forbidden to board the ship before formalities were completed, he handed up a parcel of ginger-bread for the family, who eagerly accepted their 'rare treat'.

Stormy passages placed crew members at high risk and several diarists recorded the deaths of sailors — not merely from falling off the rigging, but through freak accidents such as long boats wrenched from their lashings by a sudden lurch, crushing a crew member, as happened on the *Invincible* in 1856. On this vessel, the usual infestation of lice was dealt with by the first mate, who, Thomas Lyons noted, threw overboard blankets 'that were rather thickly inhabited with a certain small creature peculiar to dirty people'.[17] Besides the sailor's death, violent accidents were rife on this vessel. On one occasion, another emigrant's hand was crushed in a block while he was helping the crew with ropes. Thomas Lyons held the injured hand steady while the surgeon amputated three fingers and sewed the skin over the stumps after dosing his patient with a glass of brandy.

A fine passage, 1853

Another anonymous settler, signing herself only 'Mary Anne', had set her sights on prosperity in New South Wales. Writing home to her 'dear Mama' in November 1853, she reported that she and her husband Thomas, a miller, had 'put in at no port during our voyage and the Captain would not permit any letters to be forwarded by homeward bounders that we met'.[18] She and her husband 'landed in excellent spirits and health' under 'auspicious circumstances'. Mary Anne implied that it had been an uneventful and pleasant voyage. She recorded the frustration of the emigrants when, in sight of land, the captain of the *Isabella* was forced to tack up and down the coast in search of his bearings and a favourable wind to take them into port. As usual, the pilot 'a thick set man with terror in his countenance' arrived with his stern question directed gruffly at the surgeon 'have you any sickness on board'. She continued,

Now we had one or two of the sailors laid up and likewise two or three of the passengers in a delicate state of health from being so long on sea provisions and the doctor being a young man and unaccustomed to deal with such a peremptorary customer hesitated a moment. So the old fellow shouts out 'you are on your oath', answer me immediately or I will put you in quarantine'. 'Have you any contagious disease on board'. 'No', says the doctor. 'Very well', said he, 'why could you not say so before'.

Fearful of epidemic disease arriving on ships, it is understandable that port authorities were stern.

Mary Anne, an intermediate, or third-class, passenger whose surname is unknown, was delighted with her first view of Sydney Harbour. Writing to her mother after a short period in the colony, she observed the lay of the land, the housing, the social life, prices of furniture, and so forth. Rent was expensive; her husband made forays from the vessel, and was

fortunate in obtaining apartments after some little trouble about three miles from Sydney at a place called Chippendale. It is a small cottage with two rooms one up and one down. You have water for fetching a few doors off, that is for washing water. For drinking water you must buy so much a load. Thomas tells me there is nothing but the two bare rooms and no stove in either of them (that is another article that is very little used here for you may go into fifty houses and not see one, the reason is they burn all wood, therefore a hearth suits better) without even a wash-house belonging to us. It has a yard large enough to dry a shirt in and for this we shall have to pay sixteen shillings a week, paying a week in advance, and we have plenty on board who would jump at that as there are several going to pay that for one room in Sydney.

The arrival of the famous SS *Great Britain*, the fastest, most innovative and revolutionary of the auxiliary (steam and sail) vessels of its day, was heralded by a burst of canon fire from its ten guns. Its entry into the harbour created great excitement, although its contribution to Sydney life was by no means all positive, since the demand for goods by its emigrants and those from other vessels that arrived on the same day,

> considerably enhanced the prices of everything. Bread is fourteen pence the four pound loaf, meat that used to be three half pence and two pence a pound is now raised to three pence, legs of mutton four pence a pound, potatoes four pence and those half bad, cabbages without any hearts to them, in fact such as you would give pigs to eat, eight pence each, onions three for two shillings and these small and dwindling; tub butter two shillings a pound, fresh half a crown and three shillings. Peas three to five shillings a peck, ale two shillings a quart, porter three, milk four, rum three shillings a wine bottle, cheese very bad one shilling a pound, oranges four for sixpence (large ones), peaches the same price.[19]

However, Mary Anne was not forced to pay Sydney prices. Before leaving the ship, Thomas was approached by an employer from Yass who offered

> one hundred and four pounds a year with rations sufficient for [a couple] and likewise a house to live in. The news seemed really too good to be true. I could hardly bring my mind to believe it. Fortune actually coming out of Sydney to meet us. I could not sleep a wink for thinking.

They were able to forgo their expensive lodgings in Chippendale, and head instead for Yass, a town about 200 miles from Sydney, where 'board, lodging, and firing found us'. Travelling by stagecoach and dray, at their employer's expense, Mary Anne was nervous:

> I feel very timid at the thoughts of going up the country such a distance particularly there having been a most brutal murder just committed there which you have doubtless heard of in the papers. The man now lies in Goulburn

Jail awaiting his trial. However, there was no alternative so
made up my mind to it in the best way I could.

Recalling her first day ashore, she told her mother that

> I stepped upon shore for the first time I may say after 4
> months imprisonment, pleased enough to bid farewell to
> old "Isabella". I had as many good byes and as many
> requests to be sure and write as I had upon leaving Old
> England, everyone congratulating us upon our unrivalled
> success.

Shops and inns, Mary Anne assured her mother, were fitted up
exactly the same as in England, although around Yass, she thought, there
were rather more Irish than English:

> You see written up at the public houses 'Real Alton Ale',
> 'Fine Devonshire Cider', and good 'London Porter'. At other
> shops you see 'Goods of the first quality as cheap as any
> house in London'. 'What can be more thoroughly English'.

The sight of handsome houses spoilt by unsightly annexes discon-
certed Mary Anne, and she was unimpressed with the unkempt roads
and causeways. The omnibuses were totally without comfort, their
clumsy structure 'constructed without the slightest regard to comfort,
convenience or appearance, I thought the Jersey ones bad but they are
perfection in comparison to these'. Nor was she complimentary of
Australians and their

> most forbidding countenances which is easily accounted
> for, their being chiefly the descendants of convicts, conse-
> quently crime is indelibly stamped upon them and no
> doubt will be for several generations to come without
> there is some alteration for the better in the class of emi-
> grants hereafter sent out.

Many of the females, Mary Anne considered were 'loose, reprobate characters'. She, herself, a respectable miller's wife, took no prisoners in her assessment of her adopted countrymen and women.

Mary Anne described her journey to Yass by stagecoach in vivid detail, relishing the hot suppers, at two shillings a head, taken (as was customary) with vast quantities of tea. Their repasts along the way were sumptuous. At one stop, 'a leg of boiled mutton, a joint of roast beef, a dish of mutton chops, a boiled duck, green peas, greens and baked potatoes formed the sum total'. After their meal, Mary Anne and Thomas wandered down to the overgrown churchyard, which they found enveloped in wild roses and other flowers,

> We read upon its weather-beaten stones the name of many a one whom it specified had emigrated from England and ultimately found a shelter from the storm of life beneath the verdant turf of a foreign church yard. I read upon many a stone that well known favourite old epitaph 'Application sore long time I bore'.

Her stroll in the churchyard reminded Mary Anne of the many times that she and her mother had 'trod together the paths' of their local cemetery at home, at Bearsted, near Maidstone in Kent. The couple endured a terrifying journey over potholed roads, made worse by the traffic heading for the diggings. On the way, she heard of numerous fatal accidents on the roads caused by overturning drays crushing their occupants. The cottage was not at all what they expected; Mary Anne was horrified. It was worse than the worst house in their street at home and upon first sight of it she 'shed a silent tear'. But, determined to succeed, her enterprising husband set to work improving it and, in the pioneering spirit that she was determined to foster, she resolved to lower her standards:

> There are no backdoors in Australia to creep out as you must take everything as it comes when you get here. You may tell anybody you know coming out that emigrating to Australia claims some affinity to matrimony; it is for

better for worse, for richer for poorer; you must taste bitters as well as sweets. Do not let them come out with an idea that they can have the comforts England has afforded them. For if they do they will most assuredly be disappointed. We have no society but each others but I do not much care about as no one can be more happy and comfortable with themselves than we are. All I have to say on this subject is that Thomas proved a man of his word.

Exhorting her mother to remember them to all their friends and relatives in and around Bearsted and Maidstone, and in Jersey, Mary Anne completed her long description of settlement:

I think you had better shew this letter round to all the family as I cannot write such letters as these to everyone. Besides it comes very expensive. A letter under half an ounce costs five pence from where we live to England; two pence from Yass to Sydney, and three pence from there to London. And now accept my kindest love, wishing you health and a long life to receive many such letters as these, so that when our wanderings shall be completed we may yet enjoy that felicity of meeting once more this side of the grave but should Fate will her desires otherwise we yet have a hope that fadeth not of one day being united in that eternal home when all our earthly wanderings are o'er, and now farewell, farewell, God bless you.

Mary Anne failed to notice the irony of postage costing twopence for a 200-mile journey by dray, and threepence for a 12 000-mile journey by ship. Hers, though, was a fairly typical story of a woman who knew her value as a wife, and who appreciated the efforts of her husband to make her comfortable.

'Them as are not clean have no dinner till they are'

The 1850s

Looking forward to land

A 25-year-old miller from Preston, Lancashire, who arrived on his own to pioneer the emigration of his wife and family in 1853, was one of many male emigrants to emphasise the importance of their wives. Joseph Metcalf arrived on the Fox Line's 741-ton *Ann Holzberg* in August 1853 with 202 other emigrants. He had paid his own way — at a passage cost of £30 — arriving safe after a fine but tedious passage during which the vessel was becalmed for five weeks. Three emigrants were buried at sea, and seven infants were born on board. Writing to his wife Mary, he described his first days in the colony and his reunion with a cousin. As for Mary,

> I am glad you did not come for most of the women were very
> sea sick but except that we had very little sickness on board.
> My dear Mary I hope that day is not very far distant
> when I shall again clasp you in my arms I already feel my loss
> very much and should like you to have come very much but
> for the length and disadvantages of so long a voyage.[1]

Exhorting her to give his love to their numerous relations and to their own children, he ended by enclosing a summary diary of the voyage.

He had had to put his finger down his throat to induce vomiting during the Bay of Biscay when so many were sick, 'If you had come you would have wished your-self home again'. Sharing his cabin with a farmer, a doctor and other 'very nice men, we live first rate we have $2\frac{1}{2}$ cheeses and 6 hams beside bacon and other things we share alike but I cannot eat the beef and pork yet'. The passage passed uneventfully, sighting the usual landmarks, accompanied by whales and porpoises, and suffering the usual squalls. Joseph often dreamed of home: 'I suppose by this time you will have berry pie I would very much like to join you with a pint of sweet milk but this cannot be but I hope you will get plenty'. Exchanging ham for eggs relieved the tedium of his diet, and he made the occasional rice pudding. As the voyage progressed, Joseph's earlier good spirits began to wane:

> I shall be very glad when I put feet on land again we had a little new bread to day they make yeast from hops alone and very nice bread it makes but is very rare to get a bit I would give anything if I could but know how you and my father all of you are but I must wait a little longer. I hope you are all in good health I shave myself 3 times a week the water is awful bad it stinks like a sink I cannot drink it at all. I never thought I should have to drink such filth as it is.

With so many emigrants complaining about brackish water, it is remarkable that ships like Joseph's were not beset by serious illness.

The hygiene, social and religious routines on board emulated those on government-sponsored ships. The women, wrote Joseph, dressed in their best silks and satins for Divine Service on Sundays, and 'there was a child christened to day she was called Ann Holzberg Smith the captain stood as godfather and more than a present of five pounds they called it after the ship'.[2] Naming the newborn child for the ship or the captain was a common practice. The report of one conscientious schoolmaster and religious instructor, who arranged a school on board the *Whitby* bound for Port Phillip in 1849, noted another example. As well as teaching adults and children in separate classes by age and gender (the women were far more enthusiastic pupils than the men), Mr Sherlock took regular services at which he preached. He also 'got up a choir of hymn and psalm singers', and oversaw the distribution of sewing materials for the amusement of young women, who were 'anxious to be taught fancy work'. His spiritual duties included christening and burial services.

Writing home to the committee of the Emigrants' School Fund (a philanthropic organisation that was, in effect, an arm of the Society for the Propagation of the Gospel, which funded the salaries of religious instructors and schoolmasters on emigrant ships), he wrote on 13 March 1849, a month after departure, that

> Early this morning there was quite an excitement on board. One of the emigrants brought us a boy babe, the first addition to our large family. The Captain is to be one of the godfathers, and has already named the child after himself and the vessel. An allowance of grog was given to the people to drink the boy's health: the men wished there might be a new baby every day of the voyage.[3]

Six days later, however, he reported that

> We have had sorrow amongst us during the last few days. The poor mother of the babe abovementioned died early on the morning of the 16th. She came on board in a very weak state. Our medical gentleman [Dr AJ Gunning] says she died of exhaustion and diarrhoea. He was very desirous of opening the body, but finding that the feelings of emigrants generally revolted at the idea of the opera- tion, I persuaded him to give up his intention. It devolved on me to read the service for the funeral of those who die at sea. The body was sewn up in a new canvas, covered with a flag, and committed to the deep. The sailors all attended, and were neatly attired, and most of the emigrants wore some token of mourning. The service appeared to be very impressive. I felt its solemn beauty, as a strong testimony was borne to the departed having had an experimental knowledge of the Gospel. The poor little babe is doing well as yet: it has been committed to the care of a young woman who lately brought up her baby-

sister by hand. Yesterday (Sunday) I preached from the words "And the sea gave up the dead which were in it".[4]

This mother's death was one of only two deaths reported by the surgeon superintendent, both adults. The child, reared 'by hand' by the passenger, probably on a traditional mixture of milk — in this case preserved — and pap (bread or biscuit crumbled into milk), appears to have thrived.

Post-mortems were occasionally carried out on board, but the emigrants' repugnance to the procedure on this occasion is another reminder that their feelings were taken into account by surgeons, who understood the depth and delicacy of emotion aroused by the idea of medical interference with a recently deceased body, especially that of a woman who died following childbirth. For the emigrants familiar with death during, or after, childbirth, there was no mystery to be solved, and the procedure was merely a gratuitous one, heightening the tragedy of a tragic moment for her husband, family and friends on board.

Meanwhile, Joseph Metcalf, on the *Ann Holzberg*, could see the coast of Brazil quite clearly as the vessel tacked close to land in preparation for its south-easterly run. After rounding the Cape and running into the higher latitudes, the boat encountered hail and snow, 'the waves rise higher than I have ever seen them yet but they are beautiful it is bitter cold here and we have no fires'. Nearing Adelaide, he reported that

> We had another death to day it was a woman she died of childbirth she had never been well since she came on board and before she came she had never had a days sickness for 22 yrs. She has left her husband with 7 children they were all on board.

The tragic death of Elizabeth Payne during childbirth on the *Ann Holzberg*, just days before landing, was a severe blow to her husband, forty-two year old well-educated yeoman farmer George Payne, known as 'Migrant George' to his descendants. Having buried at sea his wife of twenty years – the mother of his seven surviving children, aged two to eighteen – the widowed farmer from Leicestershire faced, with pluck and

199

energy, an uncertain future that he had expected to share with Elizabeth, who was no stranger to farming or hard work. Buffered by an inheritance, and ably assisted by his older children, themselves suffering distress and shock having left behind their extended family and having endured their mother's death and burial, he soon took up an eighty-acre holding near Keyneton, where he lived until his death in 1889, aged seventy-eight. This robust pioneering widower (and erstwhile gold prospector and land investor) managed, in spite of his bereavement, to raise his family and forge an identity as a leading pioneer in his district.[5]

Richard Murphy, a schoolmaster who had been sponsored by the Emigrants' School Fund as religious instructor on the *Blonde* bound for Sydney in 1849, was delayed in sending his report of his classes on board because, he wrote from Chippendale, Sydney, 'Having buried my wife at Gravesend, and my youngest child at sea, the charge of six still devolves upon me; all of whom, with myself, have been ill, more or less, since arrival here'.[6]

Richard Murphy's life on board had begun miserably, yet he maintained his classes throughout the voyage while caring for his remaining six children. At sea, undoubtedly, fellow emigrants gave him sympathetic help. Life could be bleak, however, for immigrants who arrived having buried their wives at sea, and with no friends or relatives to help support their families, or who lacked the resourcefulness of their more successful peers. For single women and widows, the trials were even more severe.[7] In the absence of a Poor Law in Australia, widowed or destitute emigrants who arrived friendless usually had no option but to seek the equally cold charity of an amalgam of philanthropic and government-funded agencies, including the Destitute Board in South Australia, various benevolent societies in the other colonies, as well as immigrant homes, public hospitals and a range of benevolent asylums for the impotent poor.[8]

Despatches from colonial governors occasionally voiced complaints about the quality of immigrants arriving, and insisted that the Emigration Commissioners advise their shipping agents to attend to rules 'prescribed for their guidance on the selection of Emigrants'.[9] By

way of illustrating his grievance on one occasion, the Governor of
South Australia named an emigrant who arrived on the *Santipore* in
October 1848, who was 'likely to remain a burthen on the Colony'. The
man and his wife were both aged 48 at a time when the maximum age
for an assisted passage was regulated by the South Australian legislature
at 40. This man, argued Governor Young, was in so debilitated a condition that he was unable to support his family, including three children
aged 12, eight and five. Not only that but, unusually, he was illiterate,
another mark against him. The South Australian legislature was, quite
rightly, worried about the arrival of people likely to burden the infant
colony's welfare arrangements. Vigilance such as Governor Young's,
however, minimised the importation of unsuitable recruits. That immigrants incapable of supporting themselves were named individually in
these reports suggests that, on the whole, emigrants were capable of self-
sufficiency. It was inevitable that some would suffer the slings and arrows
of misfortune and require state or charitable assistance.

In the meantime, schoolmaster Richard Murphy's Anglican connections probably meant that he was able to seek employment, assistance or
charity from a range of evangelical organisations in Sydney. Church-run
immigrant homes, where friendless arrivals could lodge while seeking
work and a permanent home, were also set up. Thomas Lyons, for example, 'bid farewell' to the *Invincible* on 25 December 1856, and 'took lodgings at the Wesleyan Emigrants home for the present'.[10]

Meanwhile, in 1853 Joseph Metcalf was delighted to be met by his
cousin John, with whom he maintained close and supportive relations.
Anticipating his wife's arrival once he had established himself, he found
work immediately. Joseph found, on landing, that labourers could earn
between seven and ten shillings daily, and buy a two-pound loaf of bread
for a penny. The following month, again signing himself 'your affectionate husband', he wrote again about how pleased he was with the colony:
'I am in very good health and spirits I never felt better in health and can
eat my meals like a thrasher I like the country very well it is a very nice
and healthy place'.[11] Having walked to the diggings 'near Adelaide' with
three friends during the first week after landing, Joseph spent only a few

days there before returning to find work as a gardener in an orchard where 'Oranges lemons apricots figs almonds plums olives and vines or grapes and almost every other sort of trees' were in blossom. He was astonished by the wages offered. He could earn seven shillings for working from 8 am until 5 pm, even on days when it rained — something unheard of at home. A chapel-going man, he eagerly described the sermons and described his prospects:

> the place is stocked with every sort off goods new almost and even over stocked there is plenty off money nobody is without that I see there is a great deal of drinking too the women drink a deal some off them and the men more ... it will be a fine place in a little time I intend to be as careful as I can and get a little money and see if I cannot doo some thing farming is paying well and a steady person might doo well at but you know it wants money for that as well as anything else.

Thomas painted a picture that he hoped might induce his wife to follow:

> I can hardly tell about you coming as yet you know I have not been here long but I think it very likely you will have too come and I hope you will do your best and I will do mine be as careful as you can for there is no telling you see I am not quite settled for I keep on the look out too mend myself as soon as I can a woman can do well here clothes are four shilling a dozen washing and I know two parties that cannot get there shirts washed at all that came out with us at least they have not yet but my cousin got my [mine] washed servants can get from 9/- to 12/- a week board and lodging.

Undoubtedly, Mary Metcalf's passage would have been far more comfortable had she emigrated on the same ship with Joseph, rather than face the prospect of a voyage on her own with the children, especially as he had already prepared her for the probability of debilitating seasickness. Women, who faced far worse seasickness than their male

Table 8

Provisions, stores etc. to be found by the owners of emigrant
ships chartered by the Emigration Commissioners, 1854

Rations, according to the following Scale, are to be issued during the voyage
to each Male and Female Passenger of 14 years of age and upwards; Children
between 10 and 14 are to receive two-thirds; and Children between two and ten
years of age, one half of such rations:–

DIETARY SCALE

	Biscuit.	Beef.	Pork.	Preserved Meat.	Flour.	Oatmeal.	Raisins.	Suet.	Peas.	Rice.	Preserved Potatoes.	Tea.	Coffee, weight when ground.	Sugar.	Treacle.	Butter.	Water.
	oz.	oz.	oz.	oz.	oz.	oz.	oz.	oz.	Pint.	oz.	oz.	oz.	oz.	oz.	oz.	oz.	Quarts.
Sunday	8	–	–	8	6	3	2	1¹/₂	–	–	4	¹/₄	–	–	2	–	3
Monday	8	–	6	–	6	3	–	–	¹/₄	–	–	–	¹/₂	4	–	2	3
Tuesday	8	–	–	8	6	3	2	1¹/₂	–	4	–	¹/₄	–	–	2	–	3
Wednesday	8	–	6	–	6	3	–	–	¹/₄	–	–	–	¹/₂	4	–	–	3
Thursday	8	–	–	8	6	3	2	1¹/₂	–	–	4	¹/₄	–	–	2	–	3
Friday	8	–	6	–	6	3	–	–	¹/₄	–	–	–	¹/₂	4	–	2	3
Saturday	8	6	–	–	6	3	2	1¹/₂	–	4	–	¹/₄	–	–	2	–	3

Weekly
Mixed Pickles - - - One gill
Salt - - - Two ounces
Mustard - - - - Half an ounce
Pepper - - - Half an ounce

NOTES Children between four months and two years old are to be allowed 3 pints of water, and a quarter
of a pint of milk daily; also 3 oz. of preserved soup, and one egg, every alternate day, and 12 oz. of biscuit, 4 oz. of oatmeal, 8 oz. of flour, 4 oz. of rice, and 10 oz. of sugar, weekly. To infants under four
months old, the surgeon may issue such nutriment as he may, in any case, think necessary, with any
quantity of water, not exceeding one quart, daily. He may also, if he thinks fit, issue three times a week,
to children between two and seven years of age, 4 oz. of rice or 3 oz. of sago, and one egg, in lieu of
salt meat.
SOURCE Select Committee on Emigrant Ships, *BPP*, 1854, vol. XIII.

relatives, depended on their husbands or other kin in those first few weeks. However, he concluded, having urged her to keep him informed of their financial situation,

> Accept my best love yourself and keep up your spirits for I hope we shall soon meet I assure you I am very anxious to see you and I hope the day is not very fare distant when we shall meet again if you are to come here I don't think you will ever repent it if you were here we might doo very well but I will see into things a little more before you come I think it is as well that you did not come at first and I hope you are willing or will be willing to come if I should every want you but if you are not to come at all which I hope I shall soon be able to see it is very likely I shall come back but mind you I shall not come back if I see that we can do well here and I don't see why we should not so you must not be surprised if I should send for there is no great danger or at least I saw none in coming over so don't be afraid of that if I should send.

Assuring Mary that he was as lonely for her as she was for him, he reminded her 'to do your best for I am sure you will'. He could not end before enticing her with an account of his daily meals:

> I have just had my dinner and a very good one had roast leg of mutton and plum pudding it is the only novelty I have had I have had it every Sunday at my cousin John Sand I am with him now but where I live we have plenty of meat we [have] meat to every meal either hot or cold and I assure you I doo justice to it every time and I am very glad I can for I cannot go and get a piece of pie or anything of that sort I must eat what comes and there is nothing comed wrong yet I can eat cabbage like a Britten.

Apologising for his spelling 'blunders', he closed with 'I am dear Mary, Your affectionate Husband, Joseph Metcalf'. Mary, who was two years older than Joseph, treasured the letters and brought them with her when she followed him. Seven more children were born in South Australia between 1856 and 1869. Two died in early childhood, and of the other five, one died aged 61, one in his 70s, two in their 80s, and one lived to be 98. Joseph, himself, who described himself as a miller and a storekeeper in colonial records, resided at various towns in the mid-north of South Australia, and lived to be 81. Mary died aged 73. Undoubtedly, their own longevity and the successful raising of a large, long-lived family, places them among the most successful of settlers.

Health and diet

Another emigrant who delighted in the food on board her ship, the 1037-ton *James Fernie*, bound from Southampton to Moreton Bay in 1855 with 409 other emigrants, including her husband and six children, aged two to 15 years, was 36-year-old Julia Cross. Writing home to her family in Ely, Cambridgeshire, she told them, accurately, that there had been one death and six births on board the ship, which departed Southampton on 24 October 1855 and arrived in Moreton Bay on 24 January 1856, following a 92-day passage.[12] On behalf of the New South Wales government, the Emigration Commissioners had paid a contract price of £12.18.6 for each adult supervised by Dr WJ Rowland. Among the 410 emigrants, were 105 children, representing a quarter of those travelling in steerage. With so many children on board, one death was a triumph by any standards, representing a loss rate of 0.2 per cent.

The Cross family, although registered as agricultural labourers, were better off than most. Leaving Ely by train, Julia told her mother 'I can enter into all your feelings when you was at the train — I can see your worn stricken face even now, never shall I forget it'. In spite of her own distress at leaving her mother, Julia was pleased with the well-lit Southampton depot, where they were served plenty of bread, beef and potatoes before going before the doctor, 'to show that we had been vaccinated he looked at our arms'. On board, she was equally pleased with the quantity of tea, sugar, butter, coffee, 'flower', bread, biscuits, 'plumbs', 'we make our own puddings — baked or boiled'. She enjoyed the salt beef, salt pork, oatmeal, tinned preserved beef, rice, preserved milk for the children — half of one pint daily and one egg each morning. Pregnant women were allowed a pint of porter daily and two eggs, and as much sugar, arrowroot or tapioca as they could eat.

Despite, the many 'huzzah's on leaving Southampton, with tremendous cheering and a loud rendition of 'Three Cheers for the Red, White and Blue' and other songs, Julia's heart 'was full … only think, my dear Mother, sixteen thousand miles of sea between you and me'. The vessel was so large, Julia reported, that 'you can't see one end t'other', and the noise was sometimes intolerable. Her older daughters slept in the single women's quarters. (Until 1854, adolescents aged 14 and over were deemed by the Passenger Acts to be statute adults, and the government was charged an adult fare for them; thereafter, children aged 12 and over were counted as adults.) They all found their quarters very comfortable with everything in its proper place.

While the family experienced the usual rough weather and seasickness in the Bay of Biscay, they enjoyed the fiddles, flutes and dancing on deck by moonlight. The younger Cross children romped on deck, and quarrelled endlessly, as the ship forged its way under favourably strong winds towards Australia. Although one of her daughters fell down the hatchway ladder and was badly bruised, Julia reported that the voyage was 'most beautiful … our Ship is like a fair from morning till night'. She baked twice a week, made pies from leftover meat and potatoes, and washed daily in seawater. Over a month into the voyage, she wrote that 'All my children look uncommon well considering the voyage — as yet — we cannot tell what might occur … Many who boarded then [thin?] are fat now'. Were she to do it again, she stressed, she would bring pickle, and pickled onion, and apples.

Julia was indignant that so many of the emigrants rushed to the surgeon to complain about short-weighted rations, causing him to admonish the steward, when in the heavy swell the steward did his best,

> for tis impossible with the roll of the ship to be correct in an ounce or so … For it is quite wrong to be dissatisfied about a trifle when there is plenty, for the Doctor will see that we have our full rations.

Julia sent numerous recommendations for relations and friends wishing to follow, mentioning the excellent treatment at the depots at Nine Elms and Southampton, and she gave them directions to secure their passage. 'We have not had anyone die yet', she explained, but 'the doctor is so particular' about cleanliness, that he refused to allow emigrants to

> have any dinner till there places are all cleaned and every
> bed took on deck and then he makes us all go upon deck
> all ways before dinner and inspects the ship every day and
> if the places are clean we go down to dinner and them as
> are not clean have no dinner till they are and so with the
> Blessing of God and the Doctor's care we have been kept
> in good health as yet.

The food continued excellent: roast beef and pudding and potatoes. The tinned beef in jelly Julia found to be very good, especially with mashed potatoes, made from dried potatoes to which boiling water was added. She was allowed far more tea and coffee than she was accustomed to, and was pleased to be able to consume as much oatmeal, tapioca and sago as she wanted. Ship's biscuit (double-baked bread brought on board) and fresh bread were given on alternate days. This was a prudent measure — stretching out the flour rations — given that many ships ran out of flour within weeks of landing, creating great hardship for emigrants who were then expected to consume the ship's biscuit. Not only were they unaccustomed to it and despised it after fresh bread, but it was distributed at a time when children, who found it unpalatable, were weakening after three months at sea.

On the *James Fernie*, too, the ship's oven caught fire when the slate beneath it overheated, causing the boards beneath to smoulder. Catastrophe was only averted by the intervention of an Irish woman, lying in a berth beneath the bakehouse, who observed the smouldering boards and alerted the crew. After much drama, the fire was put out, but Julia was terrified. During the entire passage, she was far more frightened of fire than of tempests. Julia, a mother of six, chatted with the other women, and noted that

Government emigrant depot at Birkenhead, Liverpool
(*Illustrated London News*,
10 July 1852)

> All the women that are likely to have a young one are
> wishing that it may happen here for if they have got no
> clothing for their young one here is bags full on board the
> ship and two nurses and every attention paid them and
> they have wine gruel — and the Best of everything
> 3 glasses of sherry or port wine every morning and night
> and all fare wonderfull well in the ship.

Julia prepared 'plumb pudding' three times weekly; like so many of her peers, she wished she had brought supplies of bicarbonate and baking soda, but found the spice she had brought on board very useful.

The *James Fernie* was one of many teetotal ships that carried emigrants to Australia. Although no alcohol was allowed, plenty of lemonade was offered. The 90-day voyage went very fast for Julia, who was busy caring for her large family. She allowed herself, though, moments of contemplation. Reminding herself that she was now 'far away from the sea girt isle', she assured her mother that she had left England

> with a Mournful heart, where the Beaming Eye and the
> heartless smile saw the emigrant depart, how I am hoping
> and trusting you will get this letter. Be sure to answer it
> directly you get it, 3 months after you get this I shall expect
> one from you … be sure to let Mary Clark read this.

Julia composed for her parents a typical blend of lament and eager anticipation. She owed it to them to mourn their parting and the great distance now between them, while simultaneously asserting her family's determination to fulfil their hopes and aspirations in the colony. As the ship sailed along the coast towards their anchorage in Moreton Bay (Brisbane), Julia compared the views of the shore from deck with the hills around Cambridge. A curious comparison; perhaps it was an appeasing gesture to parents living in Ely, near Cambridge, whom she knew would continue to mourn her departure, meant to convince them that she remained connected to her home and family.

After the usual arrival formalities, Julia and her husband George, who was unwell, were permitted to stay on board for 14 days, during which time fresh beef and mutton, and fresh bread, were brought daily from Brisbane: 'I wish you had now the meat that we and many more are oblidged to fling overboard for we really cannot eat it all'.

Once they were discharged from the ship after the 14 lay days, the family lodged at the government depot for three weeks with 800 other immigrants. Julia turned down an offer of three shillings weekly for one of her daughters to become a nursemaid because she wanted her to recuperate at leisure after being cooped up on the ship. Her oldest son travelled to Ipswich, 25 miles away, in search of a job and her husband was delighted to find that they were not obliged to pay £12 for their son's passage as they had been led to believe. It transpired that anyone who was hired immediately, was granted a free (rather than an assisted) passage: 'There is no mistake about it I can tell you the Captain had word sent him to the ship. But none of us could believe it till we came to the depot and found it true so that has cleared us of 24 pounds'.

Again, the family was delighted with the food at the immigrant depot, where plentiful beef ('4 pound and a half for my family alone every day'), potatoes, fruit and much else, including half a pound of sugar daily, was offered. Moreover, they were allowed to stay as long as they liked, but were obliged to leave once employment was found. Mosquitoes, as usual, were a trial. She explained that the 'musketers' were like gnats at home, and until one had secured a home of one's own with windows covered with gauze, 'they bite you dreadful': 'Face and flesh look like smallpox after they've bitten you all night some people have festered faces exactly like the smallpox'.

Where Julia had scratched her leg following an irritating bite, she had an abscess: 'you might put a pea in the hole'. Tropical ulcers were an ever-present danger in the heat and humidity, as they battled the cruel attention of the ubiquitous insects. At the depot, Julia smoked out the maddening creatures with smouldering cow dung, and they were forced to sleep in gloves although the temperature had reached 95 degrees Fahrenheit. Attempting to save her children from bites, she sewed them into their nightgowns, enclosing their arms and feet, and tied handkerchiefs around their faces, leaving slits for their nose and mouth. They were, she claimed, the least bitten inmates of the depot. Besides bites, one of her daughters was ill with dysentery, 'a complaint that is prevalent here'. She had taken nothing but wine and water 'to get her strength up'. With her daughter wasting, Julia told her mother, 'I hope and pray she will get well'.

Before long, George Cross was offered a job at the government gardens (possibly the Botanical Gardens) at 30 shillings weekly. Julia took in washing at five shillings per day, and the older children also earned wages. Hence, the combined income of the family was substantial.

The Cross family thrived and prospered in Queensland. Owing to the availability of cheap food, George immediately gained weight, as did their eldest son, aged 15, who was apprenticed to a butcher. Another son became a shepherd, and the entire family moved to Ipswich, where George worked for a farmer. They eventually bought land and built their own house. Writing home, soon after settlement, Julia marvelled at their good fortune:

> Do you think we could better this at home, 50 pounds a year, we don't eat so much flower as we did at home, we have more meat and almost vituals enough for the family, a place to live in all the firing we like to burn … next month I am going to have a cow and a calf, butter is 2s6d a pound. I can run as many cows as I like and cost me noghting, as much garden as we like to cultivate and I mean to have some fowl eggs are 2s a dozen … I make my own barm and bake my bread in a camp oven and have as good bread as I had at home. How you learn things by going out and about! … Tis a nice place where we are in the bush, there is some fishponds where we live free for anybody. George catched an eel weighed three pounds on Sunday, plenty of birds of all sorts.

Julia and George were able to gather mushrooms, fish for freshwater shrimps and eels and, if they wished, shoot animals and birds. Like many of their predecessors, they were astonished at their freedom to do so. Julia bottled food as fast as her family could bring it to her, marvelling at its abundance. She envied the gloss that a local washerwoman hailing from London was able to iron into shirtfronts and asked her family for a starch recipe that would teach her to produce the same sought-after shine. Toughened by hard work in the freezing, windy and damp fens of Cambridgeshire, Julia did not let Moreton Bay's searing heat, humidity and mosquitoes dent her enthusiasm for colonial life. Nor did these inconveniences interfere with the sheer determination that she required to establish a large family in one of Queensland's frontier towns.

Life and death on the frontier

Another emigrant, who established himself successfully on a farm near Gawler north of Adelaide, was William Wingate, who emigrated with his wife Fanny and their children from Birdham, near Chichester in Sussex, in 1850. Five years later, he wrote from 'Birdham Farm' on the Gawler River to his brother Joseph and his wife. They were living at Itchenor, a village in a parish adjoining Birdham. In this, the first of a number of failed attempts to persuade them to follow, William Wingate offered to pay the deposit and associated costs for their assisted passages:

> we do still more rejoice to here that you are inclined to come to see us in Australla now as you say you do not now know to get here there is noughting that will give me more plesure than to send for you this I will do by paing your passage so that you shall have no defecuty in coming and when you come I can find you plenty of work.[13]

Enjoining Joseph to bring farming tools and a variety of seeds, William reminded his brother that his own family of six children, the eldest of whom was 20, farmed 200 acres

> and we have as good a house as anny on Gawler River and kitchen and store room and a very good Garden we have horses and bucklocks [bullocks] to work in fact we have every thing heart can witch for but come and see then you will be able to judge your self now I am happy to tell you that fanny is in good health to at present.

Anxious to smooth the way for his brother's emigration, William Wingate organised bank drafts and guided Joseph through the application process, concluding, characteristically with, 'good by god bless you and if we do not meet on earth may we meet in heaven Amen Amen'.

Months later, William, who valued his independence above all else but his religion, tried again. Having sent a second bank draft, he reminded his brother that

> I have roate to you before as to your coming to this collinny and I have paid your passage and your wife and child and I have also sent you five pounds in money witch you will be abell to gett at the bank of London when you present this note … now I trust my brother & sister that you will lose no time in coming be not afraid to brake up your housekeeping I now it will seem hard to you at first but my Dear brother if you new what I now nough you would not stopped in England so long where now you might have been independent the same as I am thank god I can say I am independent of the world for I work when I like and I play if I like this is a comfort to be highly prized blessed be good [God] I can that that this is truth god being my wittness but dear brother and sister you will believe for yourself when you come to see us for seeing is believing my Dear brother I would not lead you astray if posable I should be very sorry to try to get you out here if I thought it would hurt you I would rather say farwell for every in this world but not dismaid you will be far better of when you come than we was when we came for we had no frend here to speak to much more to lend us assetence now Dear brother and sister as soon as ever you get this letter make all things reday and send us word in what ship you are coming in then we shall know when the ship comes in to the port we will be there directly to take you away.

Joseph Wingate, however, stayed put in Itchenor for the rest of his life. Although he received the bank drafts enabling him to emigrate, the Rector of his parish dissuaded him from applying for an assisted passage.[14] Nevertheless, William kept in touch with his brother and, in 1862, seven years after his first letter, he conveyed some sad news:

> My dear brother and sister I now take the opportunetty to tell you of my loss you will think me very unkind because I have not told you of it before but I can assure you that it is as much as ever I can do now I have lost my dear Fanny her was ill altogether for a twelvemounth but her kept her bed for nearly four mounths her illness was the Liver complaint I thought I should have lost her four years ago but the Lord spared her till last April the 16th although her kept her bed so long there was never a murmer come from her lips you may readelly ask what was it kep her so peacefull I can tell you what it was it was the Love of Christ shed abroad in her heart by the holy ghost witch was given unto her and if ever you saw a person dy happier her did I used to be with [her] by day and night the hole time her kept her bed I watcht her every night myself but part of two nights praps you will think this impossible but I can assure you it is the truth her did not like any body else to be with her but the person that watcht her part of the nights I spoke of was Mrs Sparshott from Sidelsum [Sidlesham, also near Chichester] John parhams sister I new them home very well I live now close by them and have done for this 12 years now.[15]

Fanny Wingate had been unwell for several years, although she appears to have been healthy during her first few years in the colony. The sheer hard grind of clearing and working land in the harsh, dry climate had almost certainly taken their toll on the wife and mother, upon whom devolved the responsibilities of keeping house for a husband and six children. William's life, too, was foreshortened in spite of his phenomenal success as a farmer in an abrasive environment far removed from that of his homeland. Whereas the adventurous and enterprising William lived to the age of 68, dying at his home near Gawler in 1881, his brother Joseph — eight years his junior — remained in his Sussex village and outlived his antipodean brother by 22 years, dying at the age of 82 in 1903. William sorely missed his wife Fanny, and life was never the same again. After describing the days leading up to her death in vivid and moving detail, he told his brother that with her dying breath, she

> said we speak of the realms of the blest that country so bright and so fair and oft are its glorys confest but what must it be to be there and then her sweeting fell asleep in Jesus what a blessed thing a Christian dy in the Lord my dear Brother and Sister although I have Lost her for atime thanks be to god I now where she is am sure while her body lys in Stone Hill Chappel yard her soul is at rest in Christ but if ever a man mist his wife I can assure you I have mist mine for a better wife never was for her stood by me all mytryals and asspecelly when we came in this Collenny at first we had to pass through manny trialls I can assure you but wee labord on and with Carefullness and indstray thanks god wee where just got cum-forttable ever thing we could witch for thank god we had I can assure [you] I have as good a Trap to ride in as even Mr. Gibbs had praps you may dought this but I can assure you it is the truth and noughting but the truth but I still feel I have lost my dear Fanny but I no if I am faithfull to the grave witch god has given me I shall one day see her again in heaven where hurting will be no more where day without night we shall feast in his sight and eternetty seem as a Day …

William Wingate's letters, like those of many chapel-going immigrants, resonate with snatches from hymns, prayers and the Scriptures. He knew that his brother would respond to these allusions. Like numerous emigrants, many of them autodidacts who had been immersed in the Scriptures from their youngest days at Sunday School, William's deep faith in God, and in his own determination to succeed, allowed him to see his dearly loved wife's death as a blessing. He placed his pride in his successful bid to gain independence, and his freedom from the constraints placed upon the labouring classes in England (where an agricultural labourer was expected to know his place), squarely at the feet of his wife. Without her, he could never have even aspired towards his goal, let alone reached it. The close proximity of friends from his home village had also been a comfort, especially during Fanny's final illness, testifying again to the importance of familial networks that emigrants developed to shield each other from despair and loneliness.

As a testament to Fanny's significance in his life, William promised to send his brother her 'likeness' very soon, along with one of his own. Again exhorting Joseph to follow him to South Australia — twelve years after his own arrival — William hoped that his brother had placed his trust

> in the presious blood of Christ if you do now this there is an inward voice speaks to your soul and without this exper-ramenttle knowledge of your exceptance with Christ you have neither part not lot in this matter for the man that feareth god and noweth righteousness is excepted of him I bless god I can truly say I have an intrest in the attoneing sacrafice of Jesus Christ I have been a member of the Wesleyan Society for Twenty years and I have been a Class leader for same I suppose you no what that is but if you do not ask some person that is a Wesleyan they will tell you.

William was excited to read that South Australian wheat and flour had 'got the first prize at the great exabition in England that's a very great Laurell for the south Australians is int it now'. Believing himself a contributor to this triumph at the Great Exhibition, he told his brother that he cut ten acres of wheat per day by machine drawn by six horses. As an emigrant made good, he owned the farm, the wheat, the machine and the horses, and employed the farm hands, whereas at home he would have been one of the hired hands himself. Moreover, he had a very good vegetable garden, 'and last year I made a 100 and 20 gallons of wine and a half of pint would make you tipsay but I suppose you will never come and taste it will you'. William was giving up hope of his brother joining him.

Although he lived for another 20 years after Fanny's death, the last few years of William Wingate's life were sorrowful. Apart from physical weakness and general debility, 'his mind was very bad at times and his reason seemed gone'. Succumbing to a sore throat caught from one of his 38 surviving grandchildren (eight had died in childhood), he died leaving four daughters and two sons, all married to emigrants and farming successfully near his original home. He maintained his Sunday chapel observance until his death, and was buried at the Wesleyan Church following a 'very large funeral' where his daughter counted 49 buggies and carts.[16]

Leaving hunger behind

Another optimistic and hardworking autodidact's testimony echoes William Wingate's. Forty-one-year-old Jacob Baker, from Chiseldon in Wiltshire, also settled on a farm north of Adelaide in the Lyndoch Valley with his wife Charlotte, aged 43, and their nine children, aged one to 23 years. The family was subsidised by Lord Bruce's Wiltshire Emigration Society to travel on an Emigration Commission ship, the 464-ton *Navarino*, in 1851.[17] The composition of the family — two parents in the prime of life, accompanied by five children capable of working at farm or domestic labour, with younger children capable of work in the near future — was ideal in terms of the colony's requirements for importing working families.[18] Their 88-day passage, with 209 other assisted emigrants, ended on 25 September 1851, when the vessel reached its anchorage at Port Adelaide, having buried one adult and one child at sea. The voyage, superintended by Dr J Hannan, held no terrors for Jacob Baker. On board, he composed a poem, the spelling of which has been tidied up by its transcriber:

The Voyage to South Australia
from England
on Board the Naverino

'twas on the 29[th.] of June, from Plymouth we set sail,
On board the "Naverino" with fair and pleasant gale.
Our captains name was Mr. Page, though not a man of a great age.
Yet he's well taught in every notion, how to sail and plough the ocean.

Our ship, she is well manned, and the captain's full of craft;
Some of the sailors are down below, and others are aloft.
Our ship, she is fifty yards in height, likewise ten yards in width,
She is forty yards in length my boys, likewise well built for strength.

She is tight and sailed and managed. Strong and swiftly do we glide along,
With storms and gales we do contend, in hopes to shortly reach the end.
The weather's been hot enough, sweat we did enough,
Sometimes we took a pipe, sometimes a pinch of snuff.
Off we go to Adelaide as fast as we are able,
Beef and mutton we expect to see upon the table.

The 14th. night of August there was great alarm,
And in the morn when we arose, there was a baby born.
The 27th. of August death to our vessel ran,
On one he laid his icy hands, and she a victim fell.

The burial service it was read, and many tears were shed.
She was committed to the deep, and left her friends behind to weep.
Death was not satisfied, she gave us now the second call,
She took an infant from the breast, into his Saviour's arms to rest.

The sailors and the lads my boys, to face the stormy weather,
While they are clothed from top to toe, in mackintosh and leather,
With their broad hats, and hearts so tight they never fear the heat nor cold
And when the work with them begin, the song they sing is "Chilly Men".

All the children who are on board are taught to read the Sacred Words,
They are taught to figure, and to write with their pen,
He taught them how to fear the Lord and shun the path of sin.

And when at Adelaide we arrive we will our fortunes strive to win,
For in my head there is a notion, that we shall safely cross the ocean.

The "Naverino" safely landed all her passengers but two,
Though wind and waves blew hard upon us,
Yet safe the Lord has brought us through.

Here's to the "Naverino", likewise to her noble crew.
Here's to the "Naverino", that crossed the ocean through.
Success to her rudder, likewise her rudder bands,
Good luck to the "Naverino" that Captain Page commands.[19]

It is little wonder that Jacob Baker looked forward to beef and mutton on the table. He and his family had lived all their lives in one of the lowest paid regions in England, in a county where farmers were among the most prosperous, but where excess labour held wages down: the repeal of the protective Corn Laws had created tension and animosity in landed Wiltshire circles. Jacob's family was caught up in this cycle. Their diet was fairly typical of the daily food intake of labourers throughout the south-west of England, from where a high proportion of Australia's immigrants were drawn. One national survey found, in 1851, that a labouring family living on an average wage of about seven shillings weekly, lived upon the diet shown in Table 9.

Table 9

Diet of Wiltshire labourer, 1851

Breakfast   Water broth, bread and butter, or sop, bread, and sometimes butter.
Lunch   Husband and children have bacon (sometimes), or cabbage, bread and butter.
Supper   Potatoes or rice, or onions, bread, butter or cheese.

SOURCE Extracted from a contemporary survey by John Burnett, *Plenty and Want: A social history of food in England from 1815 to the Present Day*, London, 1985, p. 139.

On a weekly wage of eight shillings — at the top of the wage range — one surveyor found that a farm labourer's weekly expenses for a family of six living in Taunton, Wiltshire were as shown in Table 10.

Table 10

Weekly budget of a Wiltshire labourer, 1840s

Rent on a two room cottage (rent of 2s. shared with a lodger)	1s.0d
Potatoes (4s. per bag)	1s.3d
Bread (6 loaves @ eight pence each, made with second flour)	4s.0d.
Salt, 4 oz. candles, 4 oz. soap and 6 herrings	1s.9d.
Total expenditure	8s.0d

SOURCE Extracted from a contemporary survey by John Burnett, *Plenty and Want: A social history of food in England from 1815 to the Present Day*, London, 1985, p. 139.

In the prosperous counties north of, and including parts of Lincolnshire, Leicestershire and Shropshire, farm labourers' wages were far higher, even double that of their peers in the south, and their diets and weekly expenditure reflected their relative affluence although they, too, lived mainly on bread, but with larger quantities of cheese and milk, bacon and vegetables. Farmers in the midlands and northern counties were compelled to retain traditional annual hiring and other customs related to farm labour, and to pay higher wages, by the fear of losing labour to the higher-wage industrial mill towns and northern conurbations of industrialising Britain. The proximity of the northern ports, from which ships departed regularly for America, taking with them disaffected workers, also impelled farmers to offer fair wages and conditions.[20]

In the year before Jacob Baker's family of 11 headed for South Australia, protectionist farmers in Wiltshire were calling meetings to protest against further relaxation of barriers to the importation of grain from abroad. After years of agitation and the fall of a protectionist conservative government, the Corn Laws had been suspended in 1846, during the second year of the Great Irish Famine, allowing imports of grain from the United States and elsewhere into Britain and Ireland. In 1851, Wiltshire's conservative farmers were particularly vociferous in calling for the reimplementation of heavy protective duties. During one of these meetings near his home, Jacob Baker, a self-taught lay preacher, had unsuccessfully sought permission to make a speech protesting against an announcement that local wages were to be reduced even further. Denied a public voice, the assertive farm labourer sent his prepared speech to his local newspaper, the *Devizes and Wiltshire Gazette*, which printed it, having tidied up the spelling and syntax. The non-conformist autodidact pleaded for work for himself and his sons during the winter lay-off, emphasising the versatility of his skills as a rough carpenter, pig slaughterer, well-sinker, road-maker and gardener. First and foremost, he could plough, sow, thrash and mow, and could make ladders, gates and common buildings. He mended his own children's clothes and shoes and could turn his hand to anything. He even occasionally earned sixpence from drawing teeth. 'Now gentlemen', he concluded, 'is not this a shame that I should be out of work and in this distress? and I defy any man to bring any charge against me for dishonesty, drunkenness, or idleness'. He had, he said, 'not half victuals enough, I am come here to know how I can get some more'.[21]

Although the editor claimed that Jacob had sent the speech to him for publication, it is evident, given its inclusion of sophisticated statistics on the national budget in one paragraph and other interpolations, that the editor freely and heavy-handedly used the article for his own purposes to promote free trade by pumping it up with his own rhetoric. It is also clear when comparing Jacob's second letter (see below), that the spelling in his speech was heavily edited, as was its composition, although his voice through most of the speech is recognisable.

Disappointed with his unsuccessful attempts to improve his family's lot in Wiltshire, Jacob and his family grasped the opportunity to take up the Wiltshire Emigration Society's offer to pay their deposit and clothing expenses on a government-assisted passage to Australia. Five months after arriving, he wrote home to his family, epitomising the confidence, determination, enthusiasm and enterprising spirit shown by other non-conformist emigrants of his era. Because of his earlier public stance against the farmers, his letter was picked up again by the local newspaper, the *Devizes and Wiltshire Gazette*, to whom it was sent by one of Jacob's former employers in Hodson, Thomas Dyke, with whom he remained in touch. It was reproduced in other newspapers, including the *Scotsman*. This time, the local paper did not tidy up his spelling, but printed the letter verbatim, as part of a longer article entitled 'Farming in Australia by the Wiltshire Labourers: Well done the Wilts Emigration Society, Earl Bruce, &c.' An accompanying letter to the editor from Thomas Dyke was also printed. Jacob, he wrote, 'is a capital labourer who work'd for me the last 10 years, principally in the winter as a woodman'.[22]

Besides Jacob's prodigious skills, his former employer reported he 'has a wonderful memory and is a fine active, handsome fellow, full of nerve, capital constitution ... He talk'd often about going for years before he went, and had a very hard matter to persuade his wife to start'.

Following this testimony, Jacob's letter, phonetically spelled, was printed in full. Read aloud, it resonates with his Wiltshire accent. Its emphasis on the freedom to hunt food, the liberality of wages and rations, and his easy relations with his colonial employer, ought not be underestimated as symbols of his successful relocation to an imperial destination where his skills were in demand. A transcription is given, in italics, below:

Dear Friends and Naibers, 15 February 1852

This comes with all our kind love to you, hoping to find you all in good health, as it leaves us at present, thank God for it. We had a very good pasage, and all of us got owr quit safe in 13 weeks. We had two deaths and one birth in the ship. We landed at port Adelhed, 8 miles from the town, and we stoped there one week. We went to work in a gentleman's garden. Timothy and Fred and me, for 10 shillings per day. Mary entered into 4 weeks good serves in a gentleman's hous on the foorst day we got there, at 15 pounds per year, and then a farmer cane down out of the bush and hired us — Jacob 10, Timothy 9, Fred 7, and James 5 shillins per week, with raishens which is 40 pounds of flour, 40 ditto of meet, beef or mutton, and 1 pound of tea and 4 pounds of sugger, with hous rent and firrin free, so we have no miler or bucher for to pay. Ann can get 1 shilen a day and her grub with her nidel; we have hired ourselves for a grat deel to lit-tel monney. But we plased master very much in doing the moing, so he gave Tim and me a wery nice cow and calf over our wages: he had not got a cottag large enofe for us, so he found me the timber and sent two men for to dig some stones and paid me for bilding the house. Day men get twelve shillins per week and raishens. I could not think how it was for labren men to get a farm, but now I can see how it is. I can save monney enofe in one week to buy one aker of land so, if plase God, we have got our health, by the time this year is out I think of getting a littel land; if I do not buy some, I can reant some at 5s per aker, and by it for one pound ditto. I am about taking 20 akers of land. I have for to thank God for the means which brought us out hear. Please for to tell Mr Croydy, Mr John Brown, Mr Meyrick, Mr Dyke, that I will rite to them after a wile. Master is very well plased with the boys and have promised for to give Tim and Fred a young ox a pice after harnvest. If George Robson et aney one else ould like for to com they can do well, and the larger the famley the better they can do. All my children can make thiear own forting if I should di tomorro. Mary and Ann have got the refues of 2 young farmers now, and their is another farmer and his wif who have got a farm of thier own and ondley one daughter, and this daughtter and her mother is very much strock over our Fred, and all they have got is for the daughter. This is the contrey, my boys. I have borte a dog for shuting. Tim and me can take our guns and dog, and go out and shut all we can without licences; we have plenty of buteful parets and wil turckes, and ducks and other birds. Our master is a man of a grat deal of biseness, and is out three or four days at a time; and I have for to look after all the men, and the cear of all the cattel when he is out from home. I sent out a letter and foaund my brother. Him about 500 miles from us, and there is great deal of gold digin going on there, and master and Tim is going to make a trial. Some have been and have go 100 pounds a week for six or seven weeks together and praps we shall get a prise. I have seen Elen and Lucea and John Tucker, and they are all weel. Timothy ould like for Robert Besely and Richard Osmon and Joh, or aney one else to com; they can get 12 shillins per week in to house. Poor pipel in Hodson do not know what good living is. We have got a goint of fresh meat on our table every day, and littel Bill sayes I

want to give Tom Weston some. Thomas Archer can do
well if he likes to come. Crismus Day is about the midel
of harvest with us. We do not take out a beet of bread
and chees into the feeld with us, but all come home to
a good hot diner everey day. Barley moing is 4s per aker
and raishens, and hay mouing ditto, and weat ripenge 12s
per arker and raishens. Best weat, 4 shillins per bushel;
barley 2s per bushel. Butter 9 pence per pound; best beef
and mutton 2 [and halfpence] per pound; a good fat
sheep for 6s. Suger, 2 pence per pound; tea, 2s a pound;
we do not put in tea in the pot with a tea spouan, but
with the hand. Job is into house, 3s per week.

Spritul afaiers. When I forst com hear, the pipel did not
go to church or chapel, and I asked them the resen why
they did not go. It is eight miles there and eight back; so
I tould them we ould have a chapel under that lorg tree
next Sunday. So I went and preached Christ to them and
the next Lord's day, from this text: 'Awake to righteousness and sin not, for some have not the knowledge of
God'. And I sun got a house for to preach in; so the pipel
com and hear the word with gladness, and the cry is, com
over and help us; and it is no smal task for me to meet
the seam congregation every Sunday. So I pray, brethren,
pray for me, that the word may still run and be gloryfied.
Bless God, our meetings have not been in vain.

So no more at present from your old friend,

Jacob Baker.

Please for to tel our gentelmen I will send them som
nusepapers.

Direct to me, Jacob Baker, Lyndock Valey, near Goaler
sound, Port Adelhed, South Austrilea.[23]

Dear Friend and Neighbours 15 February 1852

This comes with all our kind love to you, hoping to find you all in good health, as it leaves us at present, thank God for it. We had a very good passage, and all of us got over quite safe in 13 weeks. We had two deaths and one birth in the ship. We landed at Port Adelaide, 8 miles from the town [of Adelaide], and we stopped there for one week. We went to work in a gentleman's garden. Timothy [aged 23] and Fred [aged 18] and me, for 10 shillings per day. Mary entered into 4 weeks' good service in a gentleman's house on the first day we got there, at 15 pounds per year, and then a farmer came down out of the bush and hired us — Jacob, for 10 shillings, Timothy, for 9 shillings, Fred for 7 shillings and James [aged 14] for 5 shillings per week, with rations which is 40 pounds of flour, 40 pounds of meat: beef or mutton, and 1 pound of tea and 4 pounds of sugar, with house rent and firing free, so we have no miller or butcher to pay.

Ann [aged 16] can get one shilling a day and her food with her needle; we have hired ourselves for between a great deal, and a little, money. But we pleased our master very much in doing the mowing, so he gave Tim and me each a very nice cow and calf over our wages: he had not got a cottage large enough for us, so he found me some timber and sent two men to dig some stones and paid me for building the house. Day men get twelve shillings per week and rations.

I could not think how labouring men could get a farm, but now I can see how it is. I can save enough money in one week to buy one acre of land so, if please God we have got our health, by the time this year is over I think of getting a little land; if I do not buy some, I can rent some at 5 shillings per acre, and buy it for one pound per acre. I am thinking of taking 20 acres of land.

I have to thank God for the means which brought us out here. Please tell Mr Croydy, Mr John Brown, Mr Meyrick, and Mr

Dyke [his former employer] that I will write to them after a while.

*Master is very well pleased with the boys and has prom-
ised to give Tim and Fred a young ox apiece after harvest. If
George Robson and anyone else would like to come they can do
well, and the larger the family the better they can do. All my own
children can make their own fortune if I should die tomorrow.
Mary [aged 20] and Ann [are being pursued by] two young
farmers now, and there is another farmer and his wife who have
got a farm of their own and only one daughter, and this daughter and her mother are very much struck over our Fred, and [the
daughter is to inherit] all they own.*

*This is the country my boys. I have bought a dog for
shooting. Tim and me can take our guns and dog, and go out and
shoot all we can without licences; we have plenty of beautiful par-
rots and wild turkeys, and ducks and other birds.*

*Our master is a man of a great deal of business, and is
out three or four days at a time; and I have to look after all the
men, and care for the cattle when he is away from home. I sent
a letter and found my brother. He lives about 500 miles from us,
and there is a great deal of gold digging going on there, and master and Tim will be going there [to try their luck]. Some have
been and have got 100 pounds a week for six or seven weeks
together, so perhaps they shall get a prize.*

*Timothy would like Robert Besely and Richard Osmon
and Joh, or anyone else to come; they can get 12 shillings per
week [as an in-house farm servant]. Poor people in Hodson do
not know what good living is. We have got a joint of fresh meat
on our table every day, and little Bill [aged 5] says I want to give
Tom Weston some. Thomas Archer can do well if he likes to come.*

*Christmas Day is about the middle of harvest with us.
We do not take out a bit of bread and cheese into the field with
us, but we all come home to a good hot dinner every day. Barley
mowing is 4 shillings per acre plus rations, and hay mowing is
the same, and wheat reaping is 12 shillings per acre plus rations.
Best wheat sells for 4 shillings per bushel; barley is 2 shillings*

per bushel. Butter is 9 pence per pound; best beef and mutton 2¹/₂ pence per pound; a good fat sheep costs 6 shillings. Sugar is 2 pence per pound, tea is 2 shillings per pound: we do not put tea in the pot with a teaspoon, but with the hand. Job [aged ten] is working as a servant in the house for three shillings per week.

Spiritual affairs: When I first came here, the people did not go to church or chapel, and I asked them for the reason why they did not go. It is eight miles there and eight back; so I told them we would have a chapel under a large tree next Sunday. So I went and preached Christ to them and the next Lord's day, from this text: 'Awake to righteousness and sin not, for some have not the knowledge of God'. And I soon got a house to preach in, so the people come and hear the word with gladness, and the cry now is, 'Come over and help us', and it is no small task for me to meet the same congregation every Sunday. So I pray Brethren, pray for me, that the word may still run and be glorified. Bless God, our meetings have not been in vain.

So no more at present from your old friend,

Jacob Baker

Please tell our gentlemen that I will send them some newspapers. Write direct to me, Jacob Baker, Lyndoch Valley, near Gawler Sound, Port Adelaide, South Australia.

Like most letter writers and diarists, Jacob emphasised both the quality and the quantity of provisions in Australia. So high were his family's antipodean wages, and so generous the rations, that he could throw a handful, rather than teaspoonfuls, of tea into the pot. Meat three times a day was undoubtedly bad for digestion for those unused to unlimited animal protein. But, for poorer emigrants like the Baker family, its abundance was a mark of a new-found status in a country where prosperity was within their grasp. Undoubtedly, many emigrants regaled their friends at home with exaggerated stories of unfettered upward mobility. However, for numerous emigrants represented by earnest lay

preachers like Jacob Baker and William Wingate, whose communications could easily be checked against those of numerous other
correspondents among their fellow settlers who hailed from the same
regions, their letters provided information for those who followed,
while transmitting a vivid picture of the rewards attainable to those with
the spirit and adventure to follow in their wake. Jacob lived for almost
40 years after arriving in Australia. On his death, aged 80, he left a
few acres of land and a small sum of money, 'a forting' for a Wiltshire
day labourer.

'He never knew
One yet that died
from seasickness'

The 1860s

Corporal punishment
at sea and
its consequences

B y the 1860s, with the aid of numerous suggestions and exhortations from colonial Immigration Agents, supported by their own intelligence-gathering over the past two decades, the Emigration Commission had instituted all of the sanitary and hygiene routines that they believed had dramatically improved life-saving procedures on board ships bound for the colonies. They had also improved cooking and baking facilities, and introduced new dietary regimes for infants and young children. The risk of death for adults was no higher at sea than on land, and the health of older children at sea had improved. However, ships sailing after 1860 occasionally suffered horrendous mortality in spite of these improvements. Moreover, from 1861, Moreton Bay had discarded its provincial status. The new government of Queensland — the colony that attracted the vast majority of assisted emigrants after 1860 — thereafter assumed responsibility for its own recruitment and mobilisation of emigrants by appointing an Agent General in London. Its determination to control its own immigration policy led initially to a relaxation of the rules that had proved so efficacious on Emigration Commission ships. Before long — after several unacceptably high mortality voyages — the Queensland legislature turned temporarily to the Emigration Commission for assistance on regulating its own procedures.

But it was never to remunerate its surgeons as generously as the other colonies, leading, perhaps, to inferior management of its ships.[1]

Nor, since the Queensland government made its own arrangements with various shipping lines, did the Emigration Commission have jurisdiction over these ships. The Commission chartered just 27 ships between 1860 and 1866 on behalf of the Queensland government, over which it was able to exert its authority. On these vessels, as we can see from Table 2 on page 30, 9112 assisted emigrants embarked in England, among whom 124 deaths were recorded, registering a percentage loss rate over that period of 1.4 per cent. Of the 124 deaths on the 27 ships, 69 were of children under the age of four, and a further 15 were under the age of 20. On these 27 passages, 97 infants were born, among whom ten died, a loss rate among infants born on board of 10 per cent.[2] On ships chartered directly by the Queensland Agent General, though, Woolcock found that the survival rate of infants was higher than that of one-year-old toddlers. She argued that breastfeeding afforded infants immunity to shipboard infection against which recently weaned infants had no protection. Moreover, she found that adventurous toddlers lacked the kind of parental care necessary in such confined spaces. Contributing to the higher mortality of very young children, Woolcock maintained, were the 'pressures of pregnancy, child-rearing, nursing, and child care, in addition to the ordinary adjustments to maritime conditions'. These stresses, 'took their toll on married women, particularly in the 24–44 year group', who suffered higher rates of mortality than their husbands, and 'were reflected in the high mortality among the little children and infants'.[3]

As we have seen, at sea as on land, the mother's mediation of her infant or young child's environment was crucial for the survival of the youngest children: frail or ailing mothers augured very badly for their offspring. We can see evidence of this terrible wastage of the youngest lives in 1862, when William Kirk set sail for Brisbane from Queenstown (Cork) on the *Chatsworth*, upon which he noted a birth, a death and a marriage on one day. Although he enjoyed the passage, during which he cheerfully scrubbed berths and decks twice weekly, he was troubled by the deaths on board of 12 children from whooping cough and measles.[4] Quarantined on arrival, 18 more children, two men and a woman died. William Kirk arrived during a period when the vast majority of all ships docking in Brisbane carried emigrants assisted by the Queensland legislature. On the week that he stepped ashore, 2000 people, he claimed, had arrived and, with Brisbane overcrowded, most were sent to country towns where their labour was in demand.

Another male witness of lives lost on board was Albert Barrett. On 12 October 1865, he set sail from Plymouth on the SS *Great Victoria*. On 31 December, his vessel anchored in Moreton Bay after an 11-week passage for which he had paid £40 for his fare and outfit. Before reaching Plymouth, he had set out by rail from Richhill Station, in Armagh, and boarded a steamer from Belfast to London for a sightseeing tour of the capital before making his way to Plymouth. There, he also arranged his land order to be redeemed on arrival for a specified acreage. Emigrants with enough capital to pay their passage to Queensland were given a credit in land to compensate them for funding their own passage. On this steamship, besides a near-fatal accident when a child fell into the furnace (a menace that emerged only as coal-fired steamships began to sail regularly with emigrants to Australia), children began dying three weeks after departure. By the time the vessel reached Moreton Bay, 16 emigrants had been buried at sea, all but one of them children, two of whom died as the ship reached its destination. Although the beef had been so bad and stinking that the emigrants had revolted, the children were undoubtedly victims of an infection brought on board. Single men like Albert Barrett seldom recorded — or perhaps even witnessed — the drama of life between decks, apart from briefly noting yet another fatality.

Twenty-three-year-old Mary Anne Bedford, from Stockport in Cheshire, sailed from Liverpool on a private ship, the *Champion of the Seas*, landing in Melbourne in November 1864, after a 98-day voyage. Waiting for her on the wharf was her fiancé. They were married five days later in the home that he had built himself.[5] Travelling as an intermediate-class passenger, this pious young woman, who preferred prayers and hymns to dancing, observed the young Irish women on board. On this ship, the matron's boisterous and frenetic behaviour attracted the captain's attention: 'Today there was some bother with the matron and the head mate brought the irons down to put on her but she promised not to say any more so they did not put them on'.

Mary Anne was one of the few emigrants who reported eating fish caught at sea. She reluctantly tried shark caught for the sailors' mess, but loathed it. The sailors, she noted, had been swimming in the sea and managed to scramble aboard when the shark arrived on the scene. Accidents on the *Champion of the Seas* kept the surgeon busy. One young man broke his arm, and scalds occurred frequently as people fell, or slipped, on the steps carrying boiling water from the cookhouse to the steerage quarters. The harrassed surgeon on this ship, though, was soon to find himself in very hot water. Corporal punishment by surgeons was forbidden; surgeons sailed no more on government ships if reported for striking an emigrant. Mary Anne recorded such an incident when the surgeon on the *Champion of the Seas* was imprisoned on board for behaviour that later earned his dismissal from the service. After he had 'hit one of the Irish girls … the priest made a bother about it and had him locked up in irons for 24 hours'. That he was punished immediately after the priest's complaint to the master, without waiting for an official enquiry, gives some indication of the strictures introduced for the protection of single women during their voyage to Australia. Many single women demanded proof of such protection before boarding. Rather than an oppressive system designed to crush the will of female emigrants by intimidating them at every turn, superintendence was designed to protect them.

In spite of the doctor's punishment, Mary Anne later described both him and the captain as kind men, who walked around the ship at 10 pm each night, to see that all was well, saying 'Goodnight Ladies'. Perhaps the doctor had learnt his lesson from that early confrontation. But the matron proved herself a harridan. She quarrelled with the single women all day, took a brush to one, and had to be constrained by emigrants during other rows. One girl threw water over her, and then several girls, egged on by the sailors, beat her. The captain refused to take sides, though. Mary Anne insisted, 'She is such a bad woman'. Whenever the crew became querulous, however, they were threatened with irons.

Although emigrants seldom mentioned rats, on this ship they were irksome. As it was a private vessel, it is possible that the cleaning routines on board were less than efficacious; however, the emigrants were refused permission to disembark before Melbourne's health authorities interviewed them. Mary Anne Bedford thrived in the colony, dying at the age of 67 in the home her husband had built for her. She outlived him by 14 years.

Dr Sanger and the Atalanta, 1866

One male emigrant who wrote extensively about family life below decks was Edward Allchurch, who arrived in South Australia with his wife Ann and children on board the 930-ton *Atalanta* on 15 April 1866, after an 82-day voyage from Plymouth. The surgeon was Dr JC Sanger, a veteran of 17 voyages since 1849. He had also superintended three coolie (Indian indentured servants) vessels to Demerara and Jamaica.[6] His career as a maritime surgeon had not been uneventful. Among the 17 vessels was the *Marion*, which foundered off the coast of South Australia in 1851 with no lives lost from shipwreck, although on shore a woman was crushed by a cart carrying salvaged baggage up a cliff path, and an infant died from exposure. Six emigrants had, however, died before reaching landfall. After investigating the disaster, the Immigration Agent reported that 'I cannot, in justice to Dr Sanger, surgeon-superintendent of the Marion, conclude this notice without bearing the strongest testimony in my power to his great kindness and zeal for the welfare of the people'.[7]

Dr Sanger also supervised the *Morning Star* in 1862, upon which an epidemic of measles and scarlatina carried off 26 of 452 emigrants, and he was one of two surgeons on the ill-fated double-decked fever vessel *Ticonderoga* on which 165 of 795 emigrants, or 21 per cent, died in 1852 en route to Victoria. Twenty of 377 emigrants also died on the *David McIver*, bound for New South Wales in 1854 under his supervision.

However, if we omit those epidemic ships from his record, the loss rate on the other 14 vessels — 56 deaths among 5014 souls — reveals an average loss rate on (non-epidemic) ships supervised by Dr Sanger of 1.1 per cent. This is the precise average of vessels during the period 1855–69 for South Australia and New South Wales, as we can see from Table 2 on page 30, or an average of four deaths per passage. Dr Sanger recorded no deaths on the 972-ton *Chance* to New South Wales in 1860, and on several passages there were three deaths or less. On the *Atalanta*, however, there were nine deaths and eight births.

Two infant girls among the six girls and two boys born on board lived for only 16 and 26 days respectively before being buried at sea. Among the other seven deaths, all were of children aged three years or under. Hence, on the *Atalanta*, the loss rate of 1.8 per cent was higher than the average for the 14 non-epidemic ships that Dr Sanger supervised to Australia. The loss rate for adults on the *Atalanta*, though, was zero, and the proportion of children who died in transit was 8.3 per cent. For all voyages to South Australia in 1866, the equivalent loss rates were 0.9 per cent (all), 0.1 per cent (adults), and 4.9 per cent (children), with the number of deaths per ship averaging 3.5 on vessels averaging 387 emigrants per voyage.

On this voyage, with double the average number of deaths for 1866, and nearly double the average child mortality percentage loss rate, something had gone amiss, although the immigration agent was not unduly concerned. Alarm was always greater if numerous adults died. Their labour was lost to the colony, as was the substantial cost of their passage funded by the colonial legislature. In the case of the *Atalanta*, the contracted passage cost for each adult was £12.6.9, representing over £4300 in passage money for 308 adults and 83 children (who represented 21 per cent of the emigrants on board).

Apart from the costs of chartering the *Atalanta*, other sums were paid at the end of the voyage. Owing to the Immigration Agent's satisfaction with the state of the vessel upon arrival, Dr Sanger was paid £1 for each emigrant landed alive, a total of £390 for his 20th voyage. Typically, besides the surgeon superintendent's own considerable gratuity, the master — in addition to his contracted wage — was paid two shillings for each emigrant landed alive (£39). Similarly, the first and third mates were each paid an additional one shilling (£19.10.0), and the volunteer schoolmaster and the matron — who also reported to the British Ladies' Female Emigration Committee — were each paid a total of £5. The sub-matrons appointed by the matron were paid £2 each, the cook received a gratuity of £5, and his assistant received £3. The 'man in charge of the Distilling Apparatus', a voluntary constable, was paid a £5 gratuity, as was the 'Water-closet constable'. The volunteer hospital assistants received £3 each, and the ordinary constables, including Edward Allchurch, each received a £2 gratuity.

The surgeon, too, had found the passage satisfactory in spite of the deaths of children on board. He reported that the ship's accommodation was 'generally well adapted' for this 'good fast sailing ship', but that it was 'imperfectly ventilated' at each end of steerage, and 'too deeply laden by 1 foot 6 in.' He also found the arrangements for the hospitals and the water closets inconvenient. The emigrants' behaviour was 'generally very good', and the provisions and water were 'ample and good' and he had served out extra water rations in the tropics. The medical comforts, too, were 'ample and good, with the exception of Mutton and Chicken broth, about a third of each being bad'. Although the medicines were 'Good and generally ample', he reported that 'Chlorodyne would be a desirable addition' and double the quantity of citric acid ought to have been included. As for the state of health of the people,

> The emigrants were generally in good health on arrival. Before and after Embarkation the weather was very boisterous at Plymouth giving rise to many cases of Bronchial, Catarrhal and Bowel complaints, especially amongst the younger children, many of whom were ill the whole of the voyage, and 5 of whom died soon after coming suddenly into cold damp weather out of the tropics.[8]

Although Dr Sanger's summary report gives no clue as to how he used the chlorodyne, perhaps this anodyne — a preparation containing chloroform and morphine — had been administered to ease pain during or after the nine deliveries, leaving Dr Sanger short owing to the fecundity on board this ship. Chloroform had only come into vogue in the previous decade for relief during childbirth, especially after it had been administered to Queen Victoria, and it is possible that maritime surgeons used it liberally. Given Anne Allchurch's astonishment about her easy delivery, described below, it is likely that she had benefited from Dr Sanger's medicine chest, although, curiously, his list of medicines, supplied by the Society of Apothecaries for each ship, indicates that Dr Sanger arrived with the same quantity of '*Morphiae Hydrochlor*' that he had begun with, and that he had only used half of the chloroform. His comments on the insufficiency of chlorodyne suggest that his stocktaking at the end of a busy voyage was faulty.

Surgeons were specifically asked to report on the conduct of the emigrants, and 'especially that of the single females', and in response to this question on the pro-forma report, Dr Sanger commented that the conduct was 'Generally very good. A few of the single women, mostly Irish (which is not usual) were unruly and insubordinate.' As instructed, he went on to name the 'cases of serious misconduct'. The regulations, he reported, were 'generally well observed' and the school was 'Tolerably well attended by children and Adults with fair results'. With respect to water on board, he was very pleased with 'Normandy's distilling apparatus, which consumed $3\frac{1}{2}$ cwt. of coals and produced 300 gallons of pure water daily except Sundays'.

On the subject of ventilation, Dr Sanger recommended, as instructed to do should he have any suggestions,

> in addition to Dr Edmonds ventilating apparatus, cowl-headed ventilators both on the Quarters (well aft) and on the forecastle (well foreward), as a great deal of hot fetid air collects forward and aft, especially in ships having no stern ports between decks.
>
> The hospitals were found to be insufficient to the demands for room, several births occurring in rapid succession. Other patients suffering severely from protracted

List of medicines for emigrants on the *Atalanta* (SRSA, GRG 35/48/1866)

LIST OF MEDICINES, &c. FOR* *350* EMIGRANTS

AS SUPPLIED BY THE SOCIETY OF APOTHECARIES, LONDON.

	Quantity put on Board.	Quantity issued.	Quantity remaining at the end of the Voyage.		Quantity put on Board.	Quantity issued.	Quantity remaining at the end of the Voyage.
	lb. oz.	lb. oz.	lb. oz.		lb. oz.	lb. oz.	lb. oz.
Acid Acetic ...	1-12	1-0	12	Glycerine	1-12	1-10	2
„ Citric ...	7	7	- -	Hydrarg. Ammoniat.	7	4	3
„ Gallic ...	3½	0	3½	„ c. Cretâ	3½	2	1½
„ Hydrocyanic. Dil. Ph.	3½	1	3½	Iodum	3½	4	3½
Brit. plainly marked				Liniment. Saponis	3-8	2-8	1-0
"POISON." ...				Liquor Ammoniæ	1-12	1-0	-12
„ Hydrochlor.] Carefully	7	3	4	„ Plumbi Subacet.	14	4	10
„ Nitric Fort. } packed in	7	0	7	„ Potassæ	7	6	1
„ „ Dil. { small case,	-7	3	4	Magnesiæ Sulph.	70-0	30-0	40-0
„ Sulphur Dil.] with sand.	1-12	4	1-8	„ Carb.	4½	8	6
„ Tartaric (Pulv.)	7-0	3-0	4-0	Morphiæ Hydrochlor.	7½		7½
Ammon. Carb. ...	1-12	4	1-8	Ol. Lini	1-12	1-0	12
„ Hydrochlor.	1-12	2	1-10	„ Menth. Pip.	3½	½	3
Amylum ...	3-8	3-0	8	„ Anethi	1½	½	1½
Antimon. Tartra.	3½	½	3½	„ Anisi	1½	½	1½
Argenti Nitras	1½	½	1½	„ Olivæ	7-0	6-0	1-0
Borax (Pulv.)	3½	1½	2	„ Ricini	14-0	12-0	2-0
Calomelas ...	7	3	4	„ Terebinth	1-12	1-0	12
Calx (Recens.)	1-12	12	1-0	„ Croton	7½	½	7½
Camphor ...	1-5	5	1-0	„ Morrhuæ	14-0	14-0	
Chloroform ...	7	3	4	Oxymel Scillæ	3-8	3-8	
Conf. Sennæ ...	1-12	4	1-8	Pil. Hydrarg.	10½	1	9½
Copaibæ ...	1-12	12	1-0	„ Calomel Comp.	1½		1½
Creosotum ...	1½	½	½	Plumbi Acetas	7		7
Cretæ præp. ...	7-0	2-0	5-0	Potassæ Bicarbonas (Pulv.)	14	12	2
Cupri Sulph.	3½		3½	Potassii Iodidum	7	3	4
Ergotæ (Pulv.)	3½		3½	Pulv. Acaciæ Gummi	3-8	8	3-0
Emplast. Cantharid.	14		14	„ Aluminis	1-12	12	1-0
„ Lythargyri	14		14	„ Antimonialis	3½	½	3½
„ Resinæ	14		14	„ Aromat.	7	4	3
Ext. Aloes ...	1½		1½	„ Catechu Comp.	3½		3½
„ Belladonnæ ...	3½		3½	„ Cretæ Aromat.	7		7
„ Coloc. Comp. ...	14	10	4	„ Ipecac.	14	4	10
„ Conii ...	1½		1½	„ „ c. Opio	10½	6	4½
„ Hyoscyam.	1½	½	1½	Jalapæ	1-5	5	1-0
„ Opii ...	1½		1½	„ Kino c. Opio ...	10½		10½
Ferri Sulph. ...		2	5	„ Opii ...	3½	½	3
Gentianæ incis. ...	1-12	1-0	12	„ Potassæ Nitrat.	1-12	8	4

* This blank and the blanks in the columns "Quantity put on Board" are to be filled in from the printed List placed in the Medicine Chest by the Apothecaries' Company.

238

4

—	Quantity put on Board. lb. oz.	Quantity issued. lb. oz.	Quantity remaining at the end of the Voyage. lb. oz.
Pulv. Potassæ Tartras. Acid.	1-12	1-4	8
„ Rhei	1-12	12	1-0
„ Scammonii Comp. ...	2¼	1½	¾
„ Zingiberis	14	7	7
Quinæ Sulph.	3½	1¼	2¼
Saponis Dur.	1¾	1	¾
Santonine	1¾		1¾
Sennæ Fol.	2-10	2-0	10
Sodæ Bicarbonas (Pulv.) ...	10-8	4-0	6-8
„ et Potassæ Tart. (Pulv.)	1-12		1-12
Sp. Ætheris	1-5	4	1-1
„ „ Nitrosi	1-12	1-10	2
„ Ammon. Arom. ...	1-12	12	1-0
„ Tenuior	1-12	1-12	
Sulphur Sublim.	3-8	1-0	2-8
Tinct. Camph. c. Opio. ...	14	14	
„ Card. Comp. ...	3-8	12	2-12
„ Catechu.	2-10	-	2-10
„ Digitalis	7	1	6
„ Ferri Perchloridi ...	7	4	3
„ Hyoscyam.	14	2	12
„ Kino	14		14
„ Opii	1-12	12	1-0
„ Rhei	3-8	2-8	1-0
„ Scillæ	14	13	1
„ Sennæ	3-8	2-8	1-0
„ Valerianæ Ammoniat.	14		14
Unguent. Calaminæ	1-12	4	1-8
„ Cetacei	3-8	8	3-0
„ Hydrarg.	14	4	10
„ Hyd. Nit.	3½	2	1½
„ „ Oxidi Rubri	7	3	4
„ Resinæ	1-12	6	1-6
„ Sulphur.	7-0	3-0	4-0
„ Zinci Oxid. ...	7	4	3
Vini Colchici	14	2	12
„ Ipecac.	1-12	1-12	
Zinci Sulphat.	7	2	5
Lard	3-8		3-8
Linseed Meal	30-0	24-0	6-0
Lint, Best	3-3	3-0	3
Tow, Common	7-0	6-0	1-0
„ Fine	7-0	6-0	1-0
Chloride of Zinc ... Galls.	7		
Chloride of Lime	196		
Disinfecting Powder ...	196		
Alkaline Permanganatis (Condy's preparation.) Galls.	7		

—	Quantity put on board. lb. oz.	Quantity issued. lb. oz.	Quantity remaining at the end of the Voyage. lb. oz.
Emp. Resinæ ... ... Yds.	7	1½	5½
Male Syringes (one glass) No.	7	2	5
Female ditto	3	1	2
2 oz. graduated Glass Measure	3		3×
Minim Glass ... ... No.	2		2×
Bolus Knives ... „	2		2×
Assorted green flat Phials Doz.	12	9	3
Phial Corks ... ... Gross	2	1½	½
Flannel ... ... Yds.	12	12	
Calico ... ... „	24	24	
Sponges ... ... No.	12	12	
Bed Pans ... ... „	2		2×
Paper of Pins	2	1	1
Pieces Filleting, for Bandages, Bleeding, &c. ... No.	4	2	2
Trusses, for Hernia, Right and Left ... ... No.	4	1	3
Papers of Pill Boxes „	4	2	2
Gallipots (assorted) Doz.	72	60	12
Paper, for putting up Medicines ... ... Quires	4	2	2
Blank Adhesive Labels No.	1000	200	800
—			
India Rubber Cloth ... Yds.	1½	1½	
Yard of Oiled Silk ... „	½	½	
Water Cushion (Hooper's) No.	1		1
Square yard of Markwick's Spongio Piline	½	½	
Complete Set of Cline's Splints.	1		1
Double-action Enema Apparatus ... ... No.	1		1×
Bleeding Porringer ... „	1		1×
4-oz. Syringe ... „	1		1×
Set of Copper Scales and Weights, ¼ lb. to ½ oz. No.	1		1×
Box of small Scales and Weights	1		1×
Wedgwood Mortars and Pestles	2		2×
„ Funnel ... No.	1		1×
Iron Mortar and Pestle „	1		1×
Pair of Scissors ... „	1	1	
Skins of Leather ... „	2	1	1
Pill Tile ... ... „	1		1×
Tin Bath	1		1×
Saucepans of different sizes, for the exclusive use of the Hospital ... ... No.	4		4×

The articles marked (×) have been in [illegible]

gastric irritation were much annoyed by the propinquity of the general female water-closets, which in my opinion ought never to be placed in the neighbourhood of the hospitals. On the whole I consider the arrangement of hospitals and water-closets observed at Liverpool to be far preferable to the London method.

There do not appear to have been any spare Mess utensils put on board consequently much inconvenience was occasionally experienced where articles were accidentally lost or broken, and quarrelling frequently occurred over the ownership of those remaining. The charcoal was nearly all used before the embarkation of the passengers. Clean efficient fires in the swing stoves could not be obtained for the want of this article.

Taking his cue from the surgeon's report and from his interview with Dr Sanger, 'a familiar face … late of the Morning Star', the *Advertiser's* shipping reporter wrote that

The system of electing gentlemen of experience evidently works well, for it almost invariably produces a degree of co-operation highly necessary in promoting the well-being of the persons on board. With regard to the sick list, the cases entered on the hospital record are by no means important; some few children and persons in delicate health being the principal patients treated, and even those cases were partly attributable to inclement weather experienced while in the depot at Plymouth. The mortality on board was one less than the increase by births, the former being young children and infants — two of the latter and one of the former having succumbed to the damp cold weather experienced while running down the easting in the Southern latitudes. The general appearance of the people was prepossessing in the extreme, indeed, rather more so than some batches of importations; and it is extremely pleasant to add the Surgeon's testimony to a course of good conduct during the voyage. The only disagreement was some *fracas* between the feminine portion of the population, which, however, ended in nothing. … Of the recently introduced ventilating trunkways, his opinion is decidedly opposite, and he remorselessly condemns the whole affair as calculated only to monopolise valuable space without corresponding good result.[9]

The voyage of the Atalanta: *an emigrant's perspective*

In spite of the nine deaths, the Immigration Agent was impressed with the ship and the health of the immigrants, and the local press had eulogised the surgeon and his guardianship of his charges. We now turn to the testimony of an observant eyewitness on board. Edward Allchurch was born at Deptford, Kent, in 1828 and his wife Anne was born at Beachy Head, Brighton, in 1835. The couple, aged 38 and 31, boarded the *Atalanta* laying at anchor in Plymouth Sound on 23 January 1866, with their three children aged seven, five and four.[10] Leaving his job as a policeman, Edward and his family made their way to the Plymouth Depot, where they remained for a few days, enjoying the sightseeing before departure. For well-off working-class people like the Allchurch family, being herded together in the depot, while receiving instruction on the discipline and expectations on board, was something of a fall in status and dignity. Others saw the opportunity of three good meals and the availability of baths and medical attendance as a rise in social standing. For Edward, his first taste of the depot on Tuesday 9 January, literally made him spit:

> The ship has not arrived yet through the heavy weather. Of all the filth that ever you tasted our drink for breakfast and tea beats all. This afternoon was allowed off, went for a walk and then to a coffee shop and had tea and we did enjoy it. We retired to bed. The noise in the Depot is fearful. This night a poor woman was confined here, but such

a place to be confined in. The bed and bolster like wood.
In the evening the minister preached so as they all paid
good attention to what he said.

On the following day, things had not improved:

> Wednesday has gone on the same as yesterday — the same
> breakfast, the same dinner, the same noise and confusion,
> been out to tea the same, and now going back to Depot.
> I believe the ship has not arrived yet. We dread going back
> to the Depot.

Nor on the next:

> Had breakfast, the same stinking stuff for breakfast, the
> same noise and confusion. The weather so cold we can
> scarcely sit with all our things on. It's dinner time, we are
> all waiting like hungry wolves. Poor Cooper is in a awful
> state his messmates are all Irish they eat up everything
> they can get hold of. ... Been out to tea again.

The weather failed to improve; the bitter cold had made the children poorly and many children in the depot were already ill with colds.
In this case, the weather was undoubtedly responsible, as the surgeon
had reported, for an inauspicious beginning to the voyage. Although
Edward's diary is rather coy on the subject, his wife Anne was not only
coping with the cold and her husband's misery over the depot and
weather, as well as the children's ailing health, but she was seven months
pregnant with her fourth child.

Within a few days, with the heavy weather continuing, the emigrants were given the order to embark and Edward approached the surgeon about a position as constable on board. As a policeman, he was an
ideal candidate. After being ferried by a steamer to the *Atalanta*
anchored in Plymouth Sound,

> As soon as we got on board [a] lot [of] women was sick
> and some men. Anne very ill. One great fellow said he felt

very ill and shortly was fearful sick. The day has passed
with a deal of sickness on board. I took my turn watching
from 4 bells. Am appointed Constable. Anne very ill.

On the following day, the weather remained rough, and

> Anne very ill, quite afraid of [for] her, got her to lie down.
> Have to attend to the single girls mess. tis shocking to see
> the sick women. This morning a poor woman was taken
> in labour, [I] was on watch. Got some hot water, was con-
> fined of a daughter, I made some tea for her. Our ship a
> fine craft, two thousand tons burthen, was 14 days com-
> ing from East India docks [London], had awful weather
> coming down the channel.

The emigrants remained at anchor, wallowing in the heavy seas for
a few more days. After a night of violent weather, Edward reported that
'the fumes from a condensing apparatus came through our next neighbour's berth and they had to turn out. Poor Anne is very ill'. Despite
these poisonous fumes and their consequences at the beginning of the
voyage, the surgeon eulogised the distilling apparatus in his report. The
man 'attending the distilling apparatus' must have fixed it.

With the squalls abating, the women began to recover, enabling
Edward and Anne to contemplate their departure as they stood on deck
looking towards the lights of Plymouth:

> Anne and me has been thinking of old times as we ...
> look over the land that we shall not see much longer. Tis
> a beautiful night, the moon shining on the sea the same as
> Brighton, the light from the end of the Breakwater looks
> very pretty, the poor girl a little better as she looks over
> the sea this morning she said if she could only get on the
> land they would not catch her on board again.

Unbothered by seasickness, Edward Allchurch went about his duties
keeping order in the single women's quarters, and relishing his meals,
'we have good living, fresh meat and potatoes'. He appreciated the local

preacher's sermons and enjoyed the hymn singing on deck as the ship floundered at anchor waiting for a favourable wind. Determined to fulfil his duties, he busied himself helping distribute rations while the sailors prepared to weigh anchor five days after they boarded. Edward described the establishment of a routine that he, as much as the surgeon, was anxious to maintain:

> A great many is on deck, some smoking, minding children, some fishing, some at work. All trying to amuse themselves the best way they can, there's one or two sails in the distance, the chief Mate is on the quarter deck and a man at the wheel. We are all longing for a nice breeze, this morning I got up, washed and see to the single women then got our own Breakfast. Poor Anne could not get up, so had to wash and do what I could for the poor children, they are all hearty and well and don't seem to feel any effects worth mentioning of sea sickness. We have plenty to eat at present and they seem very kind, this morning the Doctor gave the children oranges which I thought very kind. I think Harry and me must get on down for we are getting very cold.

The usual round of pumping water, preparing meals, scraping and cleaning the decks, and settlement of disputes continued as the emigrants acclimatised themselves to maritime life. With Anne recovering temporarily from her seasickness, she spent time with Edward and the children on the quarterdeck. Negotiating the gangways in her advanced state of pregnancy was dangerous both for her and their unborn child, but she began to enjoy her food on deck, 'plum duff today with salt pork, plenty to eat and drink first rate allowance'. The table manners of some of his messmates did not impress Edward, but he found the surgeon 'a nice fellow, last Saturday he gave all the constables a good drop of Brandy each'. Edward got on the right side of the third mate who served out the provisions, 'got a nice drop of Brandy for Anne, poor girl I got her a drop of wine this morning but she could not keep it down

... The children had milk every day besides a mixture of rice, sago, etc.'

Yet even Edward began to feel poorly, as he witnessed the terrible sickness among the single women to whom he was ministering. Back in the married quarters,

> Our dinner table is a melancholy sight, the women sitting with their heads hanging down, Babys crying etc., such a scene, very rough night had to turn out, the children very sick, the ship rolling very heavily, every now and then a smash of tin whare, can scarcely stand.

Two days later, having dished out dinner for the single girls, 'consisting of Pork and pea soup', he remarked that

> it would not suit the stomach of a person on shore to see the dinner served out. Though good, a very few wanted dinner today, the ship was rolling and pitching very much, the pea soup flying in all directions. One soul was sitting scraping it off Him with a Knife. He had it from head to feet, shoes and all covered with it, and down below a dish upset on the deck by our table. Wherever you went was pea soup, one lurch sent all our treacle off the shelves on to the deck ... We set to and made some duff and this Evening some one called from the opposite side, I went over and there found two of our mess mates in their Bunks. One said Mr. Allchurch, do let me have a bit of your pudding, I have nothing all day and over Him in another bunk was our long friend most awful bad. We took them both some.

With the vessel sailing at a cracking pace, ten days after leaving stormy Plymouth, the *Atalanta* was in sight of the Canary Isles: ''Tis a beautiful day, fair wind, had a capital Breakfast, got a little preserved milk and put in the teapot and Beautiful it was, preserved meat again today, don't want any ... the doctor gives us a drop of grog every Saturday ...' Anne's health was improving 'first rate' and, although Edward despised the preserved meat, he looked forward to the salt pork, pea soup and suet duff: 'We still have plenty to eat'. With the calmer weather raising their spirits, and the sight of Tenerife giving them a greater sense of miles passing, Edward reported 'a splendid day, a library has been opened and a school for children, they had to have their seats lather to keep them falling off'. With the sun shining, the temperature rising and a fair wind, he spent his quiet moments 'on the Bulwark' writing his diary and observing the ways in which his fellow emigrants spent their spare time, 'amusing themselves in many ways, they wash their clothes and dry them', and could come and go between steerage and the deck whenever they liked.

Having overcome her seasickness, Anne had come down with 'a severe cold and a sore mouth', compounding her misery. The children, well and happy, had friends on board, but Harry, the eldest, had been hurt falling down the main hatchway steps. Nevertheless, with the onset of the fine, warm weather, 'All is got jolly aboard ship now except two or three that is bodily ill, the doctor said the other night He had been 30 years in his profession and that all sick people said they could die but He never knew One yet that died from seasickness.' However much Dr Sanger believed this to be true, four other surgeons recorded deaths from seasickness in their reports.[11]

With the weather keeping fine, boxes were brought up on deck. One single woman's box revealed a number of burst porter bottles, 'which caused a deal of amusement'. A pudding that Anne Allchurch had packed — a gift from a relative — had gone mouldy and spoilt Edward's best jacket, but a rescued cake was found to be 'first rate'. Within days, though, the fine warm weather had become insufferably hot. Anne and the other women were suffering dreadfully, spending the day on deck resting under the awnings. She also slept on deck at night, suffering with great discomfort the last few weeks of her pregnancy. Dressed in a nightshirt and a big hat, she spent her days on deck sending the children to her husband with messages: 'Poor Harry just come down crying. His mother sent him down for a book and the School master caught him and beat him for going away'.

Within three weeks of departure, the American-built *Atalanta* was sailing in equatorial waters. Fair winds and currents, good hull design and an experienced master, who had also commanded the *Omega* on a recent voyage to South Australia, combined to set a bracing pace before reaching the tropical calms close to the equator: 'we are supposed to be about 200 miles from the coast of Africa and about 3,000 miles from Home'. Although the food remained plentiful, Edward despised the preserved meat and the salt beef, preferring only to consume the pork, cold. Sailing slowly through the tropics with very little breeze, he remarked that 'we have lime juice every day which is very nice'. He was amused by the 'lads' who jumped into the tubs of water before washing down the decks every day, and 'The men has a wash in tubs of a morning on the forecastle, disagreeable Bill washed this morning and looked for all the world like a full blown porpoise'. As the heat intensified, all dignity was subsumed by the desire to keep cool:

> in the evening the deck was all alive persons washing in all sort of wear and after dark, men stripped running about the deck and women almost naked doing the same formed a novel sight. I was on duty till 10 from 6, it was so hot we did not know what to do, or rather some did, it doesn't affect me much, poor Anne laid on a spot alongside of me about naked and as she laid she sweat fearfully. I had a hard job to get her below when I was done but I feel very tired every night and have no trouble to sleep when I get the chance.

Anne, who could not stand the heat below, however, took to the deck, and Edward brought her meals 'and we enjoy it in the open air'. Edward, meanwhile, was caring for their three children: 'give all the children a bath this morning. Harry, I put in a tub and give a good dousing, afterwards got buckets of water and poured on him. He stood it first rate'. Continuing their meals on deck, they enjoyed breakfast of 'soaked biscuit baked coffee, first rate'. Edward snatched the odd moment from his constabulary duties to observe the scene: 'Anne is sitting below me in her white chemise and petticoat and round hat, at work'. Little Anne and Emmie (their daughters, aged five and four) were playing with other children while barefooted Harry, aged seven, attended the open-air school.

> Over their heads is the ships boats covered with beds etc. airing with an awning over all, the quarter deck is covered as usual with girls at work … Oh for a photograph of the scene on deck at the present moment, they do all they can for the passenger's comfort, theres about the finest body of men and children that ever I saw.

Anne's discomfort was increasing. Searching for a breath of air, 'she sat up from 12 o'clock the bottom of the main hatchway, the heat is very great'. Meanwhile, exactly a month after departure, 'A child was born this morning, the mother one of the single girls, a shocking affair'. Again the single mother had been able to conceal her pregnancy, otherwise she would not have been permitted to board; the birth was clearly a surprise to her fellow emigrants.

Edward bathed his children every day in salt water and washed their clothes: 'People are washing in all directions and lines of clothes hang in all directions'. Meanwhile, having recovered her equanimity, Anne Allchurch returned to pudding and pastry making, 'out of salt pork, a potato and onion that we have begged', and before long Edward was taking his turn in preparing the puddings, but he was to sorely miss her expertise during her month in the hospital following her confinement. Most of all, they enjoyed the days when soft bread was issued, which they consumed with the treacle they brought on board, 'for a treat'. Meanwhile, he reported, 'a child this morning brought up a worm just like a garden worm 9 inches in length, the child has been very ill for a long time, several has been the same'.

After five weeks at sea, Edward became troubled about his daughter Anne, who had been ailing during the tropics: 'poor little Anne seems very poorly, we afraid that she is going to have the whooping cough as a great many has it on board.' In an attempt to give comfort to his wife and daughter, he prepared gruel for them, 'for they cant eat the hard

Biscuit'. Although the next day he reported the children 'healthy and well', he remained convinced that they would soon come down with whooping cough: 'The Doctor is at his Evening Amusement again throwing nuts to the Children, it has a double purpose it amuses the Children, and likewise musters them together so the Surgeon can see them and judge their health'. A few days later, Edward commented that, having bathed the children, they 'are all healthy we are wonderful free from sickness. We can now see the Southern Cross very plain'. After putting the children to bed, Anne and Edward strolled or sat on deck in the moonlight, listening to the single girls singing on the poop deck.

During the heat, emigrants ate their meals on deck. They took advantage of the breeze whenever they could, and after tea on Sundays, a church service was conducted. On one occasion, Edward described the service on the poop deck:

> it was a beautiful evening, we was going about 8 Knotts an hour. We had, too this evening a beautiful sunset. I was sitting aft where I could see it beautiful, I called Anne to see it, the scene was very impressive, it was a scene worthy of an artist, in front of the poop hung a lamp and another on the poop, while Cooper holds one for the Minister to see by, the surgeon reads the sermon with a clear distinct voice and sings admirable, both sides of him stands the girls, close to him stands the school master and his mate, the surgeons clerk and our preacher forms the choir while in front of the galley sits the rest of the congregation.

Apart from his responsibilities in ensuring that the single women's quarters remained clean, and that they were served each of their meals and were supplied regularly with fresh clothing from their boxes, Edward reserved ample time for reflection: 'The sea looks beautiful this afternoon. It's a wonderful thing to Keep sailing day after day through this Body of Water and no land in sight. It shows the wonderful power and wisdom of God'. For nursing and pregnant mothers, though, the scene was not so divine. One of their fellow emigrants sat

nursing the Child. She looks a most pittable Object. She
has scarcely any Clothes nothing on her feet but an old
pair of shoes loosely laced across showing her naked flesh
an old petticoat and body [bodice] of dress with no
sleeves or tucked up. ... On the Poop stands the Doctor
having a look round.

The heat, far from diminishing, was intensifying:

I have felt it more today I think than I have done yet. ...
We fare well and are treated with every kindness but Anne
cant do what she would wish to do, in Her position. She
can not Poor Girl. She does her best but our food wants
seeming, as we can Cook or Bake anything we like if one
can only make them. Biscuit puddings out of Biscuits
soaked with flower and suet and a few plums, pasties out
of Salt pork potations and an onion if you can get one, are
very nice. Soaked Biscuit Baked and many other things
might be made, which is a nice change.

Anne's problem was probably constipation, owing both to her pregnancy and to the diet of pork, puddings and pastries. With her troubles
increasing, the children's coughs worsened. Moreover, 'the Beef is now
very Hard, and very salt and so is the pork the preserve potatoes we cant
likewise eat, no more can we the preserved meat so its rather short com-
mons with us yet we ought to be thankful for what we can get to eat'.
Edward's early enthusiasm for the rations was waning with the journey
only half over. Moreover, he wrote, 'it requires all our wits to get water
enough'. Nevertheless, Edward repeatedly reported that all 'the passengers are enjoying themselves again as usual, tis lovely
weather, I enjoy it very much', but his wife did not enjoy his comfort:

Anne says I seem to care for nothing, neither for sickness
or heat, the fact of it is I sweat very much and expect
to do so here near the line so make the best of it, but its
different with poor Anne. She is differently situated. I

wonder how she bears it as she does but there are some that is not situated as she is [that is, not pregnant] that makes quite as much fuss as she does or more so … Anne was determined not to sleep in the oven as she called it, so of course had her own way and slept in the midship part of the ship below the main hatchway, its laughable [that is, amusing] for see the scene every night every one is trying to get the coolest place to sleep in. We had another dispute about sleeping till at last I gave in. We got the bed out on deck and tried to sleep, I myself can sleep anywhere. I awoke about 12, half on deck and half on the bed for you must understand my wife is a good size and in the bunk we cant roll off the bed but its different on deck, so found myself as stated on deck sticking to the pitch, it would not do so after grumbling went on deck tried to have a bath but people were lying and sleeping in all directions and snoring like pigs, on the forecastle was the same.

Meanwhile, their children slept in their bunks below, and Edward's responsibilities were, in reality, only just beginning. He welcomed the squalls, which could be seen approaching, and the rain they brought with them, but many emigrants preferred their chances 'of getting wet to the certainty of breathing the Impure Atmosphere below'. On rough evenings, though, the sailors and the constables were given a drop of grog. With the ship picking up the squally breezes as they left the tropics behind, three babies were born in quick succession within three days. Seven weeks after departure, on 8 March 1866,

in the evening Anne was taken very poorly got worse. She said she knew that she should be confined before morning. After getting the Children to bed, She managed to come on deck to me. She sit for a short time with me till she cant stop no longer. I went and told the Doctor how she was. I could not see him at first, but He came down to Her, She was rather bad then He went away again, but sent for me, and asked concerning Her, and said He would come down and see Her the last thing. She got much worse but did not wish to go to the Hospital till the last thing in the Evening. When we was coming down we met a woman named Mutton going to the Hospital and two Others were bad with the same complaint.

We sit together for Hours after all had retired to rest poor Girl she begged of me to go to bed but to no purpose. She was very tired and tried twice to get in the Bunk but was obliged to get out being in such pain while sitting. Mrs Mutton's Nurse came and told us she was confined of a Boy. We still sit the ship rocking and pitching very much. When I went to see the Doctor it was dark. We sit till poor Girl she could sit no longer, the sea twice came down the Main Hatchway while sitting together. At two or three I went for the Nurse and poor Girl she could hardly get to the Hospital. We tried to get through the Female place but the Matron had not the Key, so had to go up the After Hatchway and in the Galley Way. Poor Girl I kissed Her and left Her to Her fate. I looked at the sea, it was very quiet except the noise of the wind and waves. The sea was running very high and white as a sheet all round the Vessel. I walk up and down. The Doctor was called He gave me a glass of grog, I afterwards went below. Anne [his daughter] coughed a deal, I sat and dosed but at last got up.

While Edward was washing the next morning, the surgeon's assistant

run down with the news that All was over, it appears the poor Girl was better after getting in the Hospital and the Doctor went to Bed but between 4 and 5 they called Him and she was confined about 20 minutes after 5. ...

I went and see Her this morning and she was quite comfortable, the Children All see Her. Emma is delighted with the Baby and Harry says He has had enough of

Children. The Doctor is put to His Wits how to provide room for them all there is 3 woman that is confined and 3 or four more that expects. He is having the place altered. Anne could not have had a more favourable time than she has had, she told me it seems like a dream, she cant make it out and the weather is getting quite cool. It's a great fat girl with Dark Hair [named Atalanta Hope, for the ship]. I shall not forget yesterday Evening in a hurry the poor Girl and the sitting Below sea roaring and dashing over the Bulwark down the main Hatchway, the going for the doctor and having to be very careful the rolling so.

The birth of her fourth child, so different from her earlier experiences when she was unlikely to have been attended by a doctor during a home delivery, suggests that Anne's confidence was increased by the surgeon's presence and his anaesthetics.

With the winds freshening and squalls increasing as they neared the Cape of Good Hope, Edward worried about Anne's comfort in the hospital and her susceptibility to catch cold owing to her draughty berth. He was afraid, too, for his daughters: 'Little Anne has the Hooping Cough but not very bad as yet. She is a dear little girl She slept with me in the lower Bunk and Harry and Emmie in the upper'. His anxiety about his wife, who was 'doing nicely' in the hospital although beset by the noise and draughts, was overtaken by his concern for the children: 'Went to bed early poor little Anne was very poorly she has the Hooping cough and I am affraid Emma has it too'. In spite of their highly infectious illness, Edward bathed and dressed the children and took them to see their mother and sister again. As he had expected, Anne developed a cold in the draughty hospital. Edward's commentary supports the surgeon's complaints about the insufficiency of the hospital accommodation.

The children's coughing at night increased his anxiety, but he was comforted by the surgeons' sermons: 'I dearly like to hear our Doctor'. He disapproved, though, of a pig being killed on a Sunday, 'there is no respect for the Sabbath here', but undoubtedly enjoyed the fresh pork in the following days. Edward's anxiety increased as his newborn

SURGEON'S REPORT OF ARRIVAL.

To be sent to England by the first opportunity. A duplicate to be lodged with the
Colonial Secretary.

Place _Adelaide_

Date _28th April_ 186_6_

SIR,

SUBJOINED is a Classified Summary of the Principal events which occurred on board the Ship _Atalanta_, and of the observations which I have to bring under the notice of the Commissioners.

Port of Final Departure	Date of Final Departure	Date of Arrival	No. of Souls Embarked	No. of Births on the Voyage	No. of Deaths		Total Number of Souls landed
					Adults	Children	
Plymouth	23rd Jan 1866	15th April 1866	391	9		9	390

Nominal List of Deaths on the Voyage.*

Name	Age	Date of Death	Cause of Death
		1866	
Atalanta McCormick	Infant	13th March	Debility
Maria Tucker	1 year	20th March	Diarrhœa
Francis Grant	1 year	25th March	Marasmus
James Mason	3 years	26th March	do
Thomas Green	1 year	27th March	do
Infant daughter of John & Mary Hawke	26 days	2nd April	Debility
Infant daughter of Alexander & Eliza McDonald		13th April	Inflammation of Umbilicus resulting in Mortification
J..... Th.....	1 year	24 April	.....
James Fraser	2 years	30 April	Marasmus

* The Deaths in Quarantine (if any) should also be given, where it can be done without delaying this Report.

Births on Board.

Mother's Name	Date of Birth	Sex of Child
Rebecca Johnstone	February 14th 1866	Female
Jessie Calder	23rd	Male
Mary Hawke	March 7th	Female
Mary Mutton	8th	Male
Ann Allchurch	9th	Female
Ann Grant	25th	do
Eliza McDonald	27th	do
Sarah Green	April 14th	do

S. WALCOTT, Esq.,
8, Park Street, Westminster, London, S.W.

daughter, too, caught cold. He implored the doctor to shift his wife to another berth as the draughts worsened with the rolling and pitching of the ship as they raced through the southern latitudes:

> People are fallen in all directions its dangerous to walk the deck. While I am writing this I am obliged to sit and put my feet on the Keg that holds our water that is lashed to an upright piece of wood to save me from falling off. The sea is a sight to behold it has never been like this since we started.

With his wife ailing from her cold, and the draughts bad enough 'to Kill her', Edward reported that

> A poor little Child died last night and this morning I went to see Anne and the girls said they were going to throw it overboard but I thought they would be sure to read prayers over but not so they opend the [Surgeon's] Cabin Windows and threw it out.

As usual, children slipped through the surgeon's porthole during storms were committed 'Very respectful'.

To alleviate his own wife's discomfort from draughts, Edward nailed an old sheet around her bunk, which served her well. By the next day, 'She was quite jolly and the Baby too'; she had made friends with the young single woman who served as the hospital attendant and who cared for her tenderly. Anne was 'doing first rate in health but Her poor Bones are sore with the motion of the vessel and she feels it so at the After part so'.

With his children continuing poorly, he remained anxious about his family's future.

> It almost frightens me though when I think of Landing in the Colonies with 4 children, but I know the same God

Left: Surgeon's report of arrival
on the *Atalanta*, 28 April 1866
(SRSA, GRG 35/48/1866)

that can take us so many miles across the Deep can maintain us when we arrive there. … I stood and lookd at the Awful Granduer of the scene, and thought how little there was between us and death, and yet somehow although I knew it I could not fully realise the danger as soon as you turn your head you feel in comparative safety.

Falls were rife as the pitching vessel surged through the Southern Ocean, and whooping cough had many children in its grip. His wife and newborn daughter, though, were 'doing first rate'. With about three weeks to go before landing, his other daughters' health caused him severe unease. Moreover, distressing squabbles were breaking out among the emigrants over the subject of lice, and the allocation of blame: 'to use plain language we are all getting lousy, try all we can to prevent it. One little Child has some fever and is very ill. They fumigated the place below this morning'.

Edward found Anne 'crying with weakness' in the hospital, where she was now obliged to sleep in a top berth 'with the other Lying in woman', and distressed by the noise from the single women's quarters. Nevertheless, with the epidemic raging below, he was in no hurry for her to return with their vulnerable infant. His children were rapidly declining. Edward spent his nights dealing with their vomiting and coughing. Again he was distressed to learn that during the storm another child, aged 18 months, was 'buried privately out of the Cabin Window'. 'I have another cause for anxiety', Edward wrote, 'Anne has very little milk what I have feard would be the Case. The Child is a beautiful fat Child and Anne is doing first rate only very anxious concerning the children'. Nevertheless, either Anne's milk improved or she was able to successfully hand-rear her daughter, who landed safely and thrived in South Australia to become the matriarch of a large family.

Edward Allchurch had cause to be fearful for the children's health. Seven-year-old Harry was now very ill. 'He cant keep anything on his stomache', Edward reported, 'I was almost drove crazy it was a fearful rough day'. The nurse he had eventually found to help him with his children was sick, and the hospital nurse was so busy that his newborn daughter was not washed for a day and a half, but, he wrote, 'I done what I could for Her'. With his daughters suffering severely from whooping cough, and Harry ill with 'what they call Gastrick Irritation', Edward lamented 'I don't know what to do with them. I have been obliged to get another woman to assist me'.

Although the weather was now cold but 'mild and pleasant', Edward's nights were miserable: 'I had a light last night in front of the Berth but the night before I had to carry the poor Children about in the dark or feel their Heads with a Bowl. I thought sometimes I could not bear the worry.' In spite of spending his nights holding bowls for the sick children, or cleaning up after sick-bowls had been upset over the berths, Edward cleaned his boots each evening before retiring.

Although Anne remained weak, 'the little dear round face darling is doing first rate it is the largest of the 3 in Hospital'. In spite of the vicissitudes of fatherhood, Edward described the setting below decks by lamplight one evening as 'A charming scene worthy of Hogarth or Crookshank'.[12] Still, the children struggled with their coughs, and in quiet moments while they slept, he stole moments with the engineer (his shipboard companion Andrew Cooper, the 'man in charge of the distilling apparatus' who was paid a £5 gratuity), who gave him coffee after which he found a quiet spot to write: 'The ship is very quiete only we two are moving about the only noise is the [distiller's] Engine and the Sailors Hauling and the Creaking of the Vessel as she goes through the water'.

Caring for his sick children absorbed this weary father's energy. One night, he recorded, 'after putting them to bed I made a Pot of Gruel for I was very hungry, it wants a deal of sceming to get enough to eat for one cant live constantly on Salt provision and biscuit'. The following morning, after a restless night, he bathed as usual and 'made two cakes in 2 plates soaked biscuit and pork, and we done very well'. But, in spite of his innovative recipes, he was sadly grieved 'to hear the poor Children asking for bread and nothing but hard biscuit for them, the poor little children seem to suffer the most on board, another little Child is not expected to live'. Feeling wretched about his wife and daughter, suffering from draughts 'enough to Kill a dog', he fretted about his older children:

> The poor Children worry me so I don't Know what to
> do, this Evening a dear little Child Died opposite our
> Bunk it was pretty little dear it has been ill some time, it
> was painful to see the Father mourning for Him, a mob
> of persons stood round watching Him as he lay dying. It
> died about 6 o clock and directly after the Breath was out
> of his Body He was taken away and this morning Tuesday
> committed to the deep, the Children are dropped out of
> the Doctors Cabin Window Very Respectful.

Dr Sanger also reported the cause of death of this three-year-old boy as marasmus. Had more flour been available for the daily baking of soft bread, or far more semolina, sago, ground rice or tapioca been available for soft puddings or sweetened gruel, this boy's health may not have deteriorated fatally. Edward was distressed that some married men continued to play cards and dominoes in front of the bereaved parents: 'no respect was paid' as it ought to have been.

After a night when all three children suffered vomiting and diarrhoea, Edward — with two more weeks to go before reaching port — was dispirited. Another seriously ill child was dying, 'and several grown up persons are poorly the sooner we get ashore the Better'. Respect was again paid as the dead one-year-old child, Thomas Green, was lowered from the surgeon's cabin window, 'God Knows who will be next … They are going to fumigate the Vessel.' As the child was being buried, another was born. With the ship nearing port, concerts were planned, and Edward responded to an invitation to perform by borrowing a concertina from the boatswain, and entertaining the emigrants with their favourite tunes, from 'Annie Laurie' to 'Auld Lang Syne', with 'Still so gently over the stealing' in between.

To Edward's relief, Anne began responding to the treats he brought her, including fresh mutton chops and gruel, and the children began to improve. He was always delighted when he could secure some fresh bread or gruel for the children: 'Tea time got a bit of Soft Bread and we enjoyed our tea. Sick of Biscuit, not half enough Soft Bread, Children will not eat [the biscuit], don't know what to get for them …

so I have to sceme and continue to get something for them'. On the penultimate Sunday at sea, exactly 21 days after his daughter was born, he was elated:

> This has been an Happy day for me. This afternoon Anne for the first time came out. She got just outside of the Culley [the Cuddy or the Galley] and was soon surrounded by Friends, The news was soon spread, I was too pleased not to circulate the news and very soon their was beside her female friends the Engineer Long Tom the Cook Bob the Butcher and lots other shaking hands and welcoming Her again.

So overcome was Anne Allchurch by this reception that she returned to the hospital exhausted, 'sat on a seat and cried'. The Engineer provided a drop of brandy with water, which revived her spirits, while Long Tom the cook provided a pot of strong tea. In the afternoon, she returned to the deck again with their daughter, but Edward refused to let her bring Atalanta below decks owing to the whooping cough. On the following day, an infant girl, born two days before Atlanta Allchurch, died of debility — she had failed to thrive. Two days before arriving at Port Adelaide, another 16-day-old infant girl was to succumb to a septic umbilical cord.

With the killing of another sheep, Edward was able to secure mutton chops for Anne's breakfast 'or rather the shadow of them for the poor sheep has got as thin as possible, mere skeletons, but Skeleton or Shadow poor Girl She enjoyed it and it does Her good'. He planned to provide her with as much of the fresh meat as possible. Almost in sight of land, the sailors cleaned the paintwork, but still it was

> nothing but hard Biscuit but I don't care for myself. I manage somehow for the Children and Anne gets a bit of soft Bread in the Hospital and she is out of the rows and noise (below decks) and there she shall stop if possible and as long as I can manage to keep her there.

Edward rightly remained adamant that his wife and daughter were not to face the hazards below decks, and this undoubtedly contributed to the thriving health of their infant.

They could not reach land soon enough for Edward, who expected to sight the coast at any minute, but their distress was compounded by the loss of a sailor who fell overboard, with the sea running high and the ship coasting at 13 knots. All of the male emigrants ran to help lower the boats and do what they could, but, with high seas, the boat was unable to find the man overboard. With the rolling and surging caused by the sudden tack, the ship was in uproar, with terrified emigrants staggering about. Having helped to haul the lifeboat up in the heavy seas, Edward lamented the young man, who had a mother and sister in Plymouth. He had missed his footing on the ropes as the ship lurched: 'It made us all Very unhappy for He was a nice young man much respected on Board'. Once the ship put about, Edward estimated that they were 60 miles from shore, but his enthusiasm for dry land was overcome by his grief:

> All this Day is grievous to see the Gloom cast over the Ship by the loss of the poor fellow Groups are here and there all over the Ship talking about Him. I went to the Engine House and met several sailors some went in the Boat to endeavour to save Him One stood leaning with His Back against the Boiler. At first they could not speak afraid to speak their own thoughts but at last they one and all greatly blamed the Captain. It appears a Dutchman was at the wheel or He might have been saved for no life buoy was thrown to Him, and the Sailors blamed the Captain very much. … In the Hospital All were in tears Concerning Him. … All [on board] was engaged in serious conversation concerning him.

Typically, there was far more grief over the loss of a seaman than for the children lost on board. In an era when the Grim Reaper stalked children and infants on land as at sea, their deaths were expected, but the accidental deaths of adult emigrants or sailors always provoked great stirrings of emotion. The following day, the usual pre-disembarkation cleaning rituals kept Edward busy, 'ready for the Commissioners to see when we arrive', but 'All are still very dull concerning the poor lost seaman'. Anne too, went below to help Edward prepare the beds:

> If any one wants to Know the value of a Wife come to Australia with a family like mine and be situated like I have been and you will likewise Know what a woman has to do with a family of Children and you that wish you wives to go out to work will be quite satisfied that they have enough to do at Home without doing anything else.

He believed that there was no other man on board 'that has a greater Responsibility than I have, 4 children under 7 years of age but I don't fear'. He had done extremely well to care for three ailing children, the youngest only three — a vulnerable age at sea — and his experience had taught him to appreciate his wife's domestic workload.

With a few days to go while traversing the Great Australian Bight, the emigrants were praying for a good strong wind. After his manifold anxieties during the voyage, he summed up his experience: 'The Voyage seems like a dream tis been a splendid one. We don't know what a Storm or Gale of Wind is yet'. Undoubtedly, he had heard stories at sea, perhaps from Dr Sanger and the sailors, regarding a voyage beset by terrible storms. On this 82-day passage, the winds were thought merely to be agreeably strong. Yet, with land in sight, Edward's penultimate entry reflects the apprehension that had shadowed his enjoyment of the voyage:

> Our Children are still very poorly Little Anne is very low, Harry is in a parlous way. A great many children has Death in their faces, the sooner we get to land the better.

His last entry reads: 'Been a very busy day'. In spite of his fears, his four children thrived in the colony, yet he was probably right to believe that, had the voyage lasted for another fortnight, the death toll — which was to rise by two more with the deaths of a one-year-old and a two-year-old during the lay days — would have been higher.

The absence of a complaint by the surgeon about the insufficiency of cereals on board, or of flour for more frequent bread making, is in explicable. However, a blue-collar worker like Edward Allchurch was likely to have been far more critical of the food than a labourer for whom even preserved meat was a luxury. Nevertheless, it is clear from the reports of other surgeons and emigrants that, on some ships, a concerted effort was made to ensure that children received generous daily helpings of cooked soft cereals. The inadequacy of these foods — relished by the Allchurch children — could have led to further fatalities on this vessel had it not travelled so fast. Depriving infants and young children of cereals had provoked an angry outburst from the Immigration Agent, Dr Duncan, a decade earlier. However, on this occasion, no emigrants appear to have complained, and the deficiency went unremarked.

The Allchurch family settled at Glenelg, a coastal town on the shores of Holdfast Bay, eight miles from Adelaide, where Edward followed his calling as a policeman, rising within two years to the position of Constable in Charge of the Glenelg police station. Four more children were born between 1868 and 1876, and Edward, whose hopes, prayers and dreams had been realised, died aged 88 in 1917.

A new maritime era

Among the 25 000 immigrants that the famous SS *Great Britain* (whose first voyage of 83 days was one day slower than the superbly designed *Atalanta's*) is said to have brought to Australia between 1852 and 1876 was a Scottish gentlewoman who travelled from Liverpool to Melbourne in 1869. Rosamund Amelia D'Ouseley, who was initially employed by a Melbourne doctor as a governess, later married and lived in Queensland.[13] The 3773-ton auxiliary steamship, wrote Rosamund, was 333 feet in length, 51 feet wide, and 40 feet deep, capable of 1000 tons of cargo and accommodation for 600 passengers. The SS *Great Britain's* water tanks held 200 tons of fresh water, provided by two condensers capable of distilling over 1500 gallons of water daily. There were enough stores for 740 people and, with a generous poop and hurricane deck, a promenade nearly the length of the vessel was available for passengers.

Heralding a new era in maritime comfort, the vessel's facilities included a saloon, a surgery, a mess room, a pantry, a bar, three kitchens, a carpenters' and joiners' workshop, a butcher's shop, a cowhouse, and accommodation for 160 sheep, 40 pigs and 100 dozen poultry. No one was going to starve on this revolutionary vessel. The passengers, wrote Rosamund, were housed in saloon, second and third cabins, but the steerage emigrants, she wrote, emphasising her own gentility, were 'exceedingly dirty and ill-favoured in countenance'. Upon boarding, they 'were mustered and passed the inspection of a Doctor and Immigration Officer', and the usual sermon, which Rosamund found very affecting — 'Be reconciled to God' — created the usual melancholy reaction.

Sharing her cabin with three others, including an elderly Scotswoman going out to marry 'an old beau', and a travelling companion, Rosamund did not take kindly to the Irish emigrants. As a saloon passenger, she was served roast beef and trimmings, boiled and roast mutton, potatoes, plum pudding, with pancakes and tartlets for dinner twice weekly. Baths, however, could be problematic. They were constructed on deck behind screens, and 'Caroline and I were up before six a.m. to take a shower-bath, but there were too many gentlemen about — in future we intend trying it before 5 a.m.' For women, modesty often overcame their determination to maintain their standards of personal hygiene. Water closets, too, if unprotected by screens, created embarrassment for women.

Rosamund adapted to shipboard life with enthusiasm. Although the food supplied was far more substantial, luxurious and fresh than that provided for steerage emigrants, 'we are so savagely hungry these meals do not half satisfy us … so we have an extra tea at 4 o'clock pm. & supper at 9 p.m. of our own providing or we should not be alive'. On Rosamund's fairly uneventful passage, the three-year-old son of a saloon passenger died from scarlatina, and the doctor put an Irishman in irons for six hours for being drunk and disorderly. As usual, a collection was taken for a newborn child whose parents adopted 'Britain' for his second name, and a sum of £10 presented to the parents.

Departure of the SS *Great Britain* from Liverpool for Australia
(*Illustrated London News*, 28 August 1852)

On this auxiliary steamer, the engine propelled the vessel through calm waters while sails were hoist in the brisker regions, either on their own or, at times, in conjunction with the engine. Rosamund described the alarming experience when the engines stopped, the screws were retracted and the sails trimmed. As soon as the wind failed, the engines were started again. During her passage through the Great Australian Bight, which was as rough as usual, Rosamund revealed that her eight weeks at sea had seemed 'like 8 days since we left our friends'. After the freezing ice and snow of the southern regions, the passengers were delighted by the warmth of Australian waters, and their high spirits were raised even further by a banquet including

> roast boiled mutton, pastries & puddings, in abundance, raisins & nuts, & 2 decanters of sherry & 1 port at each table, the latter was indifferent, the former very hot, but it was thankfully received by us starving beggars who have been fed 5 times a week on salt meat & twice on fresh and that not 'ad libitium'.

Scouring the horizon for land, on the day before arriving in Melbourne, they 'passed the spot where the ship "Hurricane" sank, its masts appeared above water and on one was a bright light to serve as a beacon'. Before long the pilot ship arrived and, having negotiated the danger,

> We came into Hobson's Bay with flying colours and full steam, cast anchor and a government inspector & a doctor came on board from the shore in the custom house, which was a very shabby one: the warrant passengers were mustered & passed before them.

Rosamund watched as boats came and went, taking emigrants and luggage to shore, but stayed on board for another night, expecting to travel on to Sydney where she was expected by an uncle. However, in the characteristic style of kinship networks typical of Australian immigration irrespective of class, a cousin from South Yarra whisked her off for a six-week social visit before she headed towards her responsibilities in Sydney.

From 1852, the P&O's 690-ton SS *Chusan* pioneered the carriage of mail and a few cabin passengers to Australia on sailing ships equipped with an auxiliary steam engine. In August 1853, the owners of the SS *Victoria* were the first to claim the £500 premium offered by the South Australian government to any mail steamer making the voyage within 68 days, after the vessel's passage of 56 days — the fastest ever to Port Adelaide.[14] But the 3443-ton SS *Great Britain* was the revolutionary harbinger of a new generation of sleek, spacious and comfortable high-tonnage transoceanic emigrant ships, each carrying a vast amount of canvas, and sometimes fitted with an auxiliary steam engine.[15] Nevertheless, a colossal fleet of increasingly large vessels driven by sail alone remained dominant until the 1880s. Canvas would, over the next 20 years, be replaced gradually by steam. It was on these larger, faster ships — powered by wind, or by wind and steam, until technological innovation introduced efficient, cost-effective engines in the last two decades of the 19th century — that less-crowded emigrants travelled in comparative comfort; we turn to them in the next chapter.

'What a splendid passage we had'

The closing decades

lthough steamers carried mail and merchandise to Australia from the 1850s, the SS *Great Britain* was the only steam vessel designed specifically for passengers on the Australian route until 1875. The first steamship from which emigrants disembarked in South Australia was the Orient Line's SS *Cuzco* in 1877 (a 'short ship' carrying less than 50 emigrants at a contract price of £15 each), loaded with merchandise. The first to New South Wales was the SS *Abergeldie* in 1879. However, very few steamships carried emigrants on the long antipodean run until the 1880s. In 1884, the New South Wales government negotiated with the Orient Line of steamers for exclusive rights thereafter.[1]

The Queensland government, too, used steamships continuously from 1881. Between 1860 and 1870, the Black Ball Line carried all government-assisted immigrants to Moreton Bay on its famous fast sailing vessels, with the exception of 27 ships mobilised by the Colonial Land and Emigration Commission in the early 1860s. From 1870, the British India Line was given a virtual monopoly to carry emigrants to Queensland, and between 1881 and 1914, its steamships sailed through the Suez Canal and the Torres Straight directly to Brisbane. Only about 25 per cent of British steamships carrying passengers to Australia used the Suez route in that year, the majority preferring to sail the old route via the Cape of Good Hope.[2] By 1914, only the P&O and Orient lines sailed via the Suez, a route that was, paradoxically, only 900 nautical miles shorter than the route around the Cape of Good Hope. Reasons for using the Suez had more to do with trade and mail delivery than with saving time and distance. The greatest saving in terms of distance, time and fuel was for ships sailing to India. By steaming through the Suez Canal, India- and Ceylon (Sri Lanka)-bound vessels lopped about 4400 miles off the previous route around the Cape of Good Hope to Colombo and points east.[3]

After the Second World War, migrant ships bringing 'ten pound poms' to Australia followed the Suez and Indian Ocean route direct to Fremantle, near Perth, the first port of call in Australia.[4] Another consequence of the introduction of steamships, which required constant refuelling, was the gradual reassignment of third class to tourist class on ships carrying assisted emigrants. From the 1880s, emigrants, too, saw themselves as tourists, sightseeing at every opportunity after leaving home. They were financially better off than their predecessors three or four decades earlier, and had loose change to spend at the numerous ports of call. Many saw the trip as a chance to visit exotic locations in the Mediterranean and Indian Oceans that they were not likely to see again. For others, it was an educational tour as well as an enjoyable vacation. The focus on vessels carrying subsidised emigrants in the early to mid-20th century changed little in so far as guarding the health and well-being of the emigrants is concerned, but enhanced facilities, space and modern technology on 20th-century vessels brought luxuries undreamed of a century earlier.

There was little change in the cost of steerage fares between 1860 and 1914, with adult passages averaging between £12 and £16. Under the special contracts organised by each colony's Agent General, the cost to government was about £1 to £3 less, depending on demand in specific years. Cabin fares were still too high for the vast majority of travellers. Although various classes of cabin accommodation were introduced in the last third of the century, the proportion of cabin passengers remained extremely low. In 1912 and 1913, for example, 90 per cent of passengers from the United Kingdom to Australia travelled third-class, the equivalent of steerage.[5] Passage length, though, had diminished markedly from an average of 94 days in the 1860s, to 85 in the 1870s and 77 in the 1880s. Steamers to New South Wales in the 1890s covered the distance in 45 to 52 days. In the 1900s, the passage time had reduced to as little as 40 days, about the same as a voyage after the Second World War.[6]

New technology, new expectations

The 2138-ton *Lady Jocelyn*, commanded by Captain G Jenkins and supervised by Dr William Dyas, was one of five sailing ships to carry assisted immigrants to Port Adelaide in 1875.[7] The *Lady Jocelyn* had begun life as a sailing ship with an auxiliary engine in 1852, but, by the 1870s, the uneconomical engine (with its characteristically insatiable appetite for coal) had been removed, and the vessel was fully rigged as a barque. On board as the *Lady Jocelyn* sailed from Plymouth in October 1875 (having begun its journey seven days earlier at Deptford) were 508 souls, including 89 children, who were carried at a contract price of around £13 per statute adult. During the 70-day passage, two infants were born, and two emigrants were buried at sea, a nine-year-old boy from bowel inflammation, and an 11-year-old girl from chronic diarrhoea and exhaustion. Among the emigrants was a 31-year-old diarist, George Dodson, and his wife Mary Ann Ester (called Polly), both of Oxford, and their four daughters and two sons under the age of 11, all of whom landed alive. More than eight years later, two colonial-born sons increased the family, both of whom failed to survive infancy.

A clerk in the Locomotive Department of the Great Western Railways in Oxford before his departure, George Dodson gained employment on arrival as a storekeeper with the government railways in South Australia. He remained in that position for eight years before a promotion took him to Port Augusta. There, two years later, he lost his life in a boating accident while fishing in the Gulf of St Vincent, aged 41, barely ten years after arriving, and just two weeks before he and his wife were to return to England on a long-promised visit to his parents. Polly Dodson remained in Port Augusta, where she ran a dairy while her daughters conducted a dressmaking business. Their eldest son, aged 21, took over his father's job at the railways. Once several of her children were married, Polly and her younger daughters sought their fortunes in the West Australian goldfields, where marriage networks saw Dodson descendants settling from Fremantle to Coolgardie.[8] Hence, George and Polly Dodson formed the genesis of a dynasty that ranged across two colonies.

On his 63rd day at sea, on 17 December 1875, George Dodson wrote to his 'Mother, sisters and friends',

> I am pleased to say that we are all well and happy and as comfortable as possible with the exception of our dear Beatrice. She is rather funny, not altogether sick, but she seems as if she has St Vitus Dance coming on. The Doctor will not give her anything. He says that she will be alright when we get on shore. The rest of the children are all looking very well. The boys are very brown.

The symptoms of St Vitus Dance, now known as Sydenham's Chorea, include asymmetrical random writhing movements, usually temporary, which often disappear after a short time.[9] Beatrice may, however, have been merely suffering the restlessness that affected so many children at sea. In spite of Beatrice's temporary affliction, George and Polly Dodson's six children, the oldest celebrating his 11th birthday at sea, blossomed in the sun and fresh air on this large 254-foot long ship, where children had ample room for games, and the adults for promenading. And the food suited them admirably: 'Today we had whole boiled potatoes, Australian Beef (hot) and baked Plum Pudding'. With the advent of refrigeration, and far more room for livestock, food tended to be fresher. The ship had arrived at Latitude 43 degrees South, a distance of 12 800 miles, in just 63 days, and, with about 1502 miles to go, George observed, they were likely to reach Port Adelaide in five days. Regularly running over 300 miles a day before a following sea and a stiff breeze, he told his father that, typically for the Great Australian Bight, 'We are rolling about a bit today, and the waves are rather wild and large, and not very particular when they come aboard, who they wet'.

George was very pleased that they had passed a vessel that departed Plymouth 30 days ahead of the *Lady Jocelyn* because it meant a 'better chance to get work, as we will be the first on the market'. He assured his father that he had nothing to complain about,

> and have had but little at any time, but you know some folks will grumble, let everything be ever so well conducted. I think it might have been prevented if the Doctor had held the reins at the first, with a firm hand.

With telegraphic communication in place, he assured his father that since Lloyds of London would know of the vessel's arrival in Port Adelaide within two days of its (expected) arrival on Christmas Eve, his father would soon know of their safe disembarkation. George regretted not sending stamps to the Emigration Office in London with a request that a telegram be sent immediately to his parents upon its hearing of the ship's safe arrival. He knew that his father would have heard of their disembarkation long before his letter/diary reached him but, as with all of the diarists, he conversed, as it were, with his father in real time. Not only were ships larger and faster, but technological advances in communication meant far less worry for folk at home.

The Dodson family's experience of the emigrant depot had been an unhappy one, and he had evidently shared his fury in earlier letters, now lost:

> There are a great many couples with us who had hardly been married five minutes before they came to the Depot.
> Hang the Depot, I cannot bear to think of the place. We were all treated like convicts.

Like numerous blue-collar workers, George Dodson reacted far more strongly than poorer emigrants. He was, however, consoled by the treats he had brought on board, including a 'good, strong' cheese sent by his father, which had lasted a month.

With just a few days left to go, he made the promise that a tragedy prevented him from keeping: 'Ten weeks has gone', and 10 years soon will roll round, and if you do not come out, I may then I hope, (if all is well, and all things else is well) run home and see your dear face. May the Good Lord spare us for that distant but happy meeting, is my dearest wish.

As the vessel began its run up the coast towards Adelaide, like so many of his peers before and after, George's anxiety about their future increased. Still, he told his father,

> provided Polly, children and boxes are allowed to remain on board, I will go on shore and go right away to Kapunda to Mr Days home with his parcel, and then go to see the two gentlemen that Mr Day has given me a letter for, and who are M.P.'s and Good Templars. I will show them my testimonials and ask their advice. I and Polly think that this will be the best course to follow, unless I am engaged for the Railways at once. I believe there are some miles of the new Railways opening up, and they very badly want men.

George Dodson had done his homework. Moreover, like so many emigrants, he already knew people in the colony from whom he expected help. Not only did he intend networking friends, for whom he had done a favour by bringing a parcel from home, but his membership of the Knights Templars, like Freemasonry, was expected to pay dividends.

Their usual speed was, however, impeded by contrary winds as the *Lady Jocelyn* coasted towards Adelaide. Frustrated and vexed by the infidelity of the winds and currents, he was also worried about his daughter again:

> I am anxious on Beatrice account as I am afraid she has a slight attack of St Vitus Dance. I have seen our young Doctor, and he says that the symptoms are not well defined. He has given me a powder and a bottle of stuff for her, which we hope will do her good, but I am afraid that she will not improve much till we get her on shore, so that she can run around and get her proper diet.

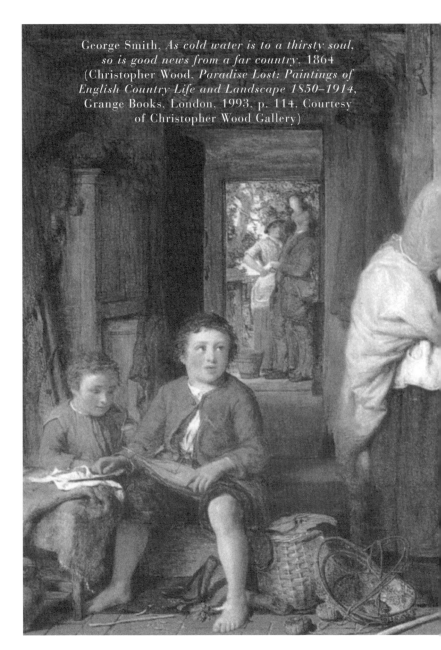

George Smith, *As cold water is to a thirsty soul, so is good news from a far country*, 1864 (Christopher Wood, *Paradise Lost: Paintings of English Country Life and Landscape 1850–1914*, Grange Books, London, 1993, p. 114. Courtesy of Christopher Wood Gallery)

The symptoms of St Vitus Dance were well understood, and the classical nomenclature remained an accepted cause of death in late 19th-century nosological indexes. However, parents often used the term to describe over-energetic children, and given that Beatrice thrived, producing four children of her own, the doctor was undoubtedly right. She was either suffering a temporary attack of a well-known condition or she was merely suffering acute restlessness. Perhaps her behaviour reflected an anxiety she had absorbed from her parents whose own restless apprehension was palpable as they drew closer to their destination.

Typically, as the ship neared shore, the family's health — perhaps exacerbated by shared excitement, fears and trepidation — began to deteriorate. In spite of a splendid thunderstorm as they approached Adelaide, which 'lighted up the heavens all around', the ship had been forced to tack, causing more lost time, and 'we are 9 minutes further away than we were yesterday at 12 noon'. With his frustration mounting and the coast receding rather than drawing closer, he observed that

> Beatrice I am sorry to say is no better, Polly is still poorly, if any difference, worse. I hope they will soon be better. George is not very bright, and it is his eleventh birthday. He is a good boy, and I cannot complain of any of our children. They are not near the trouble that most of the children are on board.

One might speculate that, given the frequency with which parents reported the declining health of children as they neared shore, and confessed their own fears and trepidations as the passage drew to a close, that children absorbed their parents' anxieties with such intensity that their health suffered. The journey was gruelling for children, but the extent to which their health broke down towards the end of the passage as their parents' apprehensions heightened is suggestive of a psychological, as well as a physical, dimension.

Typically, a child was born in sight of port: 'We now have our full complement of passengers. A boy and a girl have died, and a boy and a girl have been born. If we had to be on board for another month, there would have been 5 or 6 more births.' With his wife and children cheering up and excited at the prospect of landfall, George wrote movingly to his father. Echoing his own determination to maintain good spirits in the face of an unknown future, George exhorted his father to 'Keep up a good heart', concluding by emphasising his family's good fortune on the passage:

> What a splendid passage we had. A small boat could have followed us with the exception of the storm from Thursday to Tuesday. It is only 67 days from losing sight of land. You will, I know, not be afraid to take the trip if needful to do so.

The *Lady Jocelyn* was the largest ship ever to sail into Port Adelaide, and could not be towed into dock until space was available. On the following day, while the vessel remained anchored in the harbour, George Dodson was ferried ashore with other job-seekers, reporting that Adelaide's dreary port looked — as it did to vast numbers of his peers before and after — 'very rough and very wild. Not many houses, and what there is are scattered'. Arriving in December after an extensive heatwave, he found the country brown and 'burned', but was revived by a meal of ham and eggs, coffee and bread, 'Quite a treat you may depend, and this is Christmas Eve away from home and friends, and away from my own family, in a strange land, and among strangers'.

Adelaide City in 1875, George reported, was 'a pretty fair town, nothing like as large as Oxford'. Finding that it would be easy to get work, he bought a box of fruit for the children and some Christmas gifts and returned to the ship, before setting off the next day by train for Kapunda, a rural town 50 miles to the north of Adelaide, to deliver the box entrusted to him by a family friend. On his return that evening, he found he could not board the ship, still anchored in the harbour, until the following day. Taking lodgings overnight, he enjoyed more fresh meat, vegetables and fruit: 'It was very nice to sit in a chair to a table and have a cup & saucer, and get alongside a fire … We are in capital spirits and do not regret coming out'.

The *Lady Jocelyn* was bombarded by employers seeking female ser-vants and tradesmen: 'It is very nice to see friends come for their friends, and seem so glad to see them, and hurry them off and away and so sure there is plenty of work at good wages. Men with trades will do best'. On his travels, he had been asked whether there were stonemasons, car-penters and bricklayers on board his ship, 'as there was so much build-ing going on, and no men to do it'. Wages were high for men and for young female servants. The family remained on the ship still anchored in the harbour, while George formulated his plans for approaching the railways, which were not privately owned as at home. He told his father that, while they remained on board

> We now get fresh bread and mutton, also fresh potatoes, and of course we are all picking up fast. Only going up to Kapunda, I got as brown as the Colonials, I think that I can soon adapt myself to their ways, and also agree with them. They are very kind, if you know how to treat them.
>
> We are all well. Beatrice is better, and we hope will soon be as well as usual.

Perturbed by his inability to seek work owing to the Christmas hol-iday followed by a holiday on 26 December, 'the anniversary of the Colony', he wished they had arrived 'a week earlier or a fortnight later'.

Still, in spite of the annoyance of the vacation, he was delighted with the fresh food and the cool, changeable weather that had followed the heat: 'We are all in good spirits and well … The little ones are all looking well and hearty, fat and well'. He had noticed that the cottages supplied to railway workers all had a very good sized plot of land, and he supposed that the reason that no vegetables were grown was because of an infestation of locusts, 'every bit of green stuff is eaten up'.

Five days after arrival, the family were still living on the ship owing to the inability of the tugs to manoeuvre the giant vessel in the rough conditions. Meanwhile, George trekked again to Kapunda, where he was able to consult a 'gentlemen of influence' who endorsed his testi-monials and gave him letters for the head of railways in Adelaide. His strategy was successful and, within days, he was a paid employee of the South Australian Railways.

In the 1870s, little in the way of hygienic practice or ventilation had changed en route since the mid-1850s. Comfort had increased, owing to the greater capacity of these high-tonnage ships, enabling an ample fresh water supply, a wider variety of stores and livestock for consumption during the passage, and far greater allowance for space for emigrants, both below decks and on the main deck with its long promenade. Compared with the 350–800 ton vessels of the 1830s to 1850s, the facilities on these ships were vastly superior. On the few high-tonnage double-deckers of 1852–53, high mortality had resulted from allowing far larger numbers to embark, including a high proportion of children, and from the presence of epidemic disease at Liverpool. Water distillation, and ventilating procedures (including massive ventilation shafts) had also improved by the 1870s, after decades of testing a range of equipment.

When Dr John Sprod arrived at Port Adelaide on the 1238-ton *Forfarshire* in November 1874, he was eulogised by the local press for his supervision of regulations that had 'been so well observed on the voyage that the mortality has been very low'. Four deaths (one an adult and one an infant born on board) and seven births at sea was then considered an excellent record for a ship arriving with 511 souls, including 166 children. On this ship, Dr Sprod found that Gravely's distilling apparatus had produced good, wholesome water, averaging 280 gallons daily, and using ten hundredweight of coal during the 76-day voyage.

Nevertheless, in spite of technical improvements, the tropics remained problematic, especially for children. Dr Sprod reported that, for a period of three weeks from 7 December (14 days after departure from Plymouth),

> the thermometer stood very high — averaging 80° in the shade. During this period there was a great deal of sickness. Two patients were admitted into the Hospital suffering from Cerebral Congestion, one child from

convulsions, and <u>one woman</u> Ellen Nolan <u>from mania</u>.
<u>Two patients</u> were admitted into the Hospital suffering from <u>simple continued fever</u>. And at the same time a <u>great many people suffered from excessive debility</u>.
The <u>principal disease</u> during the voyage has been <u>diarrhoea</u>. <u>People of all ages</u> were attacked — but a large number of the children suffered severely from this complaint.
There were <u>several cases of jaundice among the children</u>.[10]

With diarrhoea prevalent, Dr Sprod had done well to contain the deaths to four, including one from 'Angina Pectoris' and a premature birth. The response to Dr Sprod's disciplinary procedures on board was primarily responsible for the health of his charges on arrival:

> The regulations were well observed on board and the instructions for the order and cleanliness of the ship were well carried out. At the musters the people always presented a clean and tidy appearance. The school on board was well attended, and the children made good progress. About 20 young men made great improvement under the Schoolmasters instructions. Divine Service was regularly conducted.

In spite of his youth and inexperience (he was a young graduate returning home to South Australia, having completed his medical education in Britain), Dr Sprod was one of a legion of surgeons whose strict supervisory routines were responsible for the safe delivery of hundreds of thousands of emigrants.

Storms and sickness, 1877

George Fletcher, bound for Queensland in October 1877, dwelt — as had so many correspondents over the past four decades — on the Dickensian fog of the wet and inhospitable Thames marshes as his ship, the *Essex*, was towed from London's West India Docks to Gravesend through a dripping, grey and eerie landscape. George

Fletcher's unpleasant three-hour experience was ameliorated by his first meal on board of roast and boiled beef and potatoes.[11] Two of his six messmates were travelling to Australia for the sake of their health, as consumptives were encouraged to do during a period when Australia was promoted as a health resort for tubercular patients. Several of the other emigrants in third class had been to Australia before, one a Canadian traveller in dry goods. After an unpleasantly foggy journey to Plymouth, they were permitted to go ashore to visit the stalls on the quay, which sold sweetmeats, vinegar, fish, chocolates, fishing lines and hooks to emigrants.

The *Essex*, carrying 29 saloon and 28 second- and third-class passengers, along with a cargo of liquor, hardware and soft goods, put to sea in 1877, just as the worst storm for 15 years hit the channel, forcing the captain to take shelter in Portland Harbour, where another emigrant ship struggled in with its mast and rigging wrecked. Upon leaving Portland Harbour, the *Essex* was followed by the worst storms, according to George Fletcher, that the crew had ever seen. As on so many other vessels that had left in autumn or winter, the hellish experience of tempestuous weather at the commencement of the voyage set the scene for horrendous seasickness. Nevertheless, George baked some excellent pies for his messmates. With the storms abating, 'after breakfast we had to turn out while the sailors cleaned and fumigated our saloon'. Ships carrying so few emigrants were often referred to as 'short ships'; if fewer than 50 passengers embarked, they were not required to carry a surgeon. It is possible that, on this ship, the emigrants were not required to contribute to the cleaning routines as on a vessel carrying a full complement of emigrants.

Christmas Day saw the third-class passengers consuming one pound each of hot roast pork, potatoes, beans and Christmas pudding with a pint of stout. This was followed by energetic sports on board. Grand dinners, too, were regularly given, with lobster, sardines, baked jam rolls, jam tarts and apple pie. Sharks were caught and eaten on this vessel before the ship sailed into southern waters, where wet, foggy and rough weather brought gales with waves 20 to 30 feet high. One male adult had been 'committed to the deep' about six weeks after departure. About three weeks before arriving in Melbourne, during a period of heavy and terrifying storms, a passenger — perhaps understandably — succumbed to acute paranoia and was kept under lock and key at night.

Ten days before landing, a 'fine boy' was born, but, with the vessel running short of provisions, the sailors were put on half-rations. The banquets early in the voyage had been consumed at the expense of the diet during the last fortnight. With the vessel nearing shore and food running low, the third-class emigrants, with a Swiftian flourish, subversively entertained the saloon passengers when the four-day-old baby was 'sent to the Saloon under a cover on a dish at dinner time of course the Captain had no idea what was under the cover so it caused a great deal of fun'. Arriving at Williamstown, like so many before him, George Fletcher was met by a friend, and 'thus ended the voyage'.

Although George Fletcher failed to remark upon the noisome consequences below decks of a boisterous passage, one young surgeon, who endured a horrendously stormy passage to Rockhampton, Queensland, in 1878 on the 816-ton *Scottish Bard*, and who was not yet 'stink-seasoned' as were his more experienced colleagues, was not so hesitant to record his reactions, though his own responses to the olfactory mayhem in steerage are exceptional. Encountering rough seas off the Devonshire coast, he wrote, 'the amount of "sicking" is prodigious, and I am running and scrambling all over the blessed ship looking after the "sickers"'. Three days later, under a fair wind, he described the single men and women as the most troublesome, and, although the married quarters were 'quiet enough', 'there is an awful smell of babies, which I find almost impossible to do away with'. Not only was Dr Lightoller's nose assaulted at every turn, but, three days into the voyage, with heavy seas crashing and the wind howling through the rigging, he had delivered three infants, and he was soon to be troubled by cockroaches in his cabin. His greatest horror, though, was to discover a case of measles on board two days after departure, 'Had him separated from the rest of the passengers, and am taking all precautions to prevent infection'. This strategy, however, failed to curb the infection, which saw him burying several children at sea. Meanwhile, with the vessel riding badly in the incessant gales, creating pandemonium on board, Dr Lightoller reported that he had

> just been to see one of the girls who is very bad. She had just given me the benefit of part of the contents of her gastric organ, so I have just had a rattling good vomit myself. It is enough to make anyone laugh.[12]

To a modern sensibility, this would be no laughing matter, but Dr Lightoller's sense of humour carried him through a nightmare voyage where massive waves in the Southern Ocean swept away the steering wheel and the women's bathroom on the poop deck and caused numerous other life-threatening accidents. Although this 27-year-old novice surgeon superintendent, who set up practice in Ipswich after arriving in Queensland, cannot have previously experienced anything like life in steerage during frightful storms, when the air below was damp, sour and fetid, as a 19th-century medical practitioner he had seen and smelt much that would turn the stomachs of modern observers.

It is difficult to know what proportion of voyages suffered such frightful storms, but numerous emigrants and surgeons reported fine passages with fair winds, and only a handful of ships carrying assisted emigrants were lost at sea during the entire century. That ships like the *Scottish Bard* did not founder while hove-to into the wind for 24 hours during a frightful storm in the Southern Ocean, as repairs were made to the steering gear while the smashed superstructure was rebuilt, is a great testament to the shipbuilders and crew of these transoceanic vessels. Ships like Dr Lightoller's encountered weather almost beyond endurance in the freezing southern latitudes, where emigrants battened below prayed and sang hymns while huge seas washed over the decks and down every available opening, drenching the passengers, beds and lower decks already awash with the contents of larders, stomachs and water closets.

Yet, rarely do we find an emigrant, or a surgeon, mentioning the sheer noisome horror of it all. Theirs were senses dulled by streets awash with horse and cattle manure, open drains and cesspits, ash or earth privies, and the stink of industrial or domestic waste. Their own bodies remained undeodorised; even an occasional strip wash was a luxury. Even for the respectable poor, conditions below decks may have been little different from the malodorous environment they had recently vacated.

A surgeon's wife
observes the voyage,
1882

In 1882, Dr James Thomson, a young surgeon barely out of Durham University's medical school, was accompanied by his new bride on his first commission as a surgeon superintendent. His ship, the 1237-ton *Selkirkshire*, was bound from Glasgow for Queensland with 400 Scottish emigrants. Dr Thomson and his wife Frances had been engaged to be married for several years while he studied for his medical degree and completed his internship at the Newcastle-on-Tyne infirmary. When he was given the opportunity to sail in charge of emigrants to Queensland, and to take his wife as a paying passenger, they married at short notice under special licence on the same day they left from Darlington, in North Yorkshire, for Glasgow to embark.[13] Frances Thomson recorded their experience as novice sea travellers. Given only two days' notice to take charge of the vessel, they arrived in time to find it 'all in confusion'. Dr Thomson's duties were no different from those of his predecessors four decades earlier: he checked the stores, the accommodation, and examined the emigrants. For his 28-year-old wife, 'it was the first time, I had ever been on a ship in my life. I had no idea they were such a size. They had prepared a nice cabin and another little room next to it for us'.

On the following day, Frances Thomson observed the emigrants as they boarded the steamer that was to take them via the Clyde to the 'tail of the bank where the *Selkirkshire* was lying':

> They are a fine respectable looking lot of people, mostly Scotch, and all appeared remarkably cheerful, I only noticed two crying. In about an hour and a half we got nicely off cheered by thousands of people who were watching at the Quay side.

The owner of the ship visited as the emigrants boarded and instructed the captain that Frances Thomson was 'to have everything done that I wished in any way'. Officials from the Board of Trade arrived to test the firing of the cannon, 'if it had not gone off properly, we should had to have waited until a new one was got'. The lifeboat was activated in three minutes to the satisfaction of the officials, who left the ship while the sailors prepared to weigh anchor. During the midsummer evening, the sailors sang traditional songs while they hauled the anchor, and numerous small boats, 'with young men, and girls, in them, stayed near the ship all the evening, they sang Scotch songs, which sounded very sweet as their voices floated up to us every now and again'.

As usual, the emigrants and passengers, including Frances Thomson, were beset with seasickness as the ship began its journey, 'I could not eat any of the good things provided for me, by our cabin steward, a pleasant looking black man' whose English wife remained behind in Glasgow. For a cabin passenger with the added benefit of being wedded to the surgeon, treats were laid on. In contrast to the diet of the emigrants, Frances described the menagerie sent on board for her own personal consumption: 'One additional sheep, one pig, 2 dozen fowls, 1 dozen ducks, fruit, biscuits, and many things to numerous to mention'.

Although Frances was well within days, many of the emigrants were so ill that she barely saw her husband. In his absence, she turned to versifying, echoing the sentiments of hundreds of thousands of seafaring travellers:

> *A life on the ocean wave,*
> *The man who wrote it was green,*
> *He never had been to sea,*
> *And a storm he never had seen*
>
> *He never had been aroused*
> *From the mornings gentle dose,*
> *By the sound of the splashing water,*
> *As it fell from the horrid hose.*
>
> *And Oh he had never been sea sick,*
> *And crept into bed in his clothes,*
> *While every motion aroused his throes,*
> *And his feelings were all in his throat.*

Four days into the voyage, having enshrined her misery in verse, Frances took her place at the table while her husband, already steady on his sea legs, took great delight — as did so many gun-toting cabin passengers — in shooting dolphins and sharks with his rifle. Dining with the captain every day, the couple consumed

> three or four courses to dinner every day and everything of first class quality. Today we had two kinds of soup, roast fowl, boiled fowl and sailors corned beef, mashed potatoes, carrots and turnips, cauliflower, then tarts and pudding, for desert almond's, raisin's, nut's, fig's, and other things. Breakfast is a substantial meal to — potatoes beefsteak, curried lobster, whitting [whiting], and other things to numerous to mention, I don't think any of us will starve, about 4 in the afternoon the steward brings us a cup of tea, and a biscuit, then about eight o'clock we have a kind of tea supper.

Encountering storms, Frances assured her readers that

> I could not sleep at all <u>rocked in the cradle of the deep</u> sounds very charming in a song, when we are safe on land, but I can assure any-one of an enquiring turn of mind that it is not half so pleasant in reality as we are led by the song to suppose.

On the *Selkirkshire*, Frances Thomson helped her husband to muster the children for his regular observation of their health. As we have seen, sweets and nuts were distributed to gain the confidence of parents. On the first occasion, she wrote,

> I amused myself by giving out sweets to the little children from the store of Medical Comforts. Children appeared as if by magic. I don't know where they all came from. I never noticed so many before, women brought little babies, without a single tooth in their head for a share, and

assured me they were very fond of them. Fancy a government giving the best London mixtures [of boiled sweets]
to children. It makes me think of the Lion, and the lamb,
lying down together, and things of that sort.

The children, Frances Thomson maintained, 'are very good, and run
about as happy as the day is long', and the people were all very well
conducted. Her husband was occupied from his first round at 8 am,
attending people 'all day long … who are always wanting something'.

As had been the case since the 1830s, for many people their
encounter with a doctor at sea was the first in their lives. What is more,
his service was free, and they were determined to make the most of it.
On this voyage in 1882, the usual rounds of daily prayers, Divine Service
on Sundays, inspections, music, dancing and exercise on deck continued
as it had done for decades. The winds were unfavourable and the vessel
progressed slowly. As usual, there was great excitement on the days that
boxes were brought on deck for a change of clothing and to retrieve
stored treats. The sailors, too, looked forward to Sunday afternoons:
when 'they have no work to do they amuse themselves by turning over
their things, very trivial things please people at sea'. On the *Selkirkshire*,
'one of the single women got into trouble, and James ordered her to be
confined between decks for 24 hours for punishment': basic procedures
had not changed for half a century. As usual, when another ship drew
near, the captain and his cabin passengers — in this case, the surgeon
superintendent and his wife — were invited to row over to dine with
the captain of the other ship, their departure creating amusement for the
emigrant onlookers. Later that evening, as the ships parted company,
rockets flared from both vessels, and the emigrants sang parting songs.

During the blazing heat of the tropics, the first of four deaths
occurred: 'During the night a poor little child died, it was buried at 8
o'clock the same morning. James read the service over it'. With tropical
thundery downfalls in the Doldrums cooling both the ship and the emigrants, Frances Thomson — like so many women diarists before her —
was terrified when the fire alarm was raised:

> Tonight a dreadful scene took place, such as I hope I may
> never see again. The people were having a concert and all
> was going on very nicely when a man rushed into the
> midst of the people, crying, Ship on Fire. At once a dread-
> ful <u>panic</u> took place, men, women, and children rushed
> madly about, shrieking and crying. The noise was deafen-
> ing, women fainting on all sides, little children neglected
> by their mothers, went about with their little hands
> clasped, begging some one to save them. About fifty of the
> single men at once tore the covers of the boats and got
> into them ready to save themselves. Happily it turned out
> after all to be a false alarm, one of the sails had fallen
> down that was all, they found the man who gave the
> alarm and put him in irons.

Following an enquiry, the culprit 'was ordered to be kept in irons
for a week', a punishment undoubtedly endorsed by the emigrants
whose panic was probably no less extreme than that of the surgeon's
wife. So traumatised was Frances Thomson by the incident that for the
remainder of her life she was unable to visit theatres or places of enter-
tainment where she might encounter clapping or shouting.

A few days later, as the ship picked up the trade winds, another
16-month-old child died during the night and was buried the following morning, an event followed a day later by the birth of the first child
on board, a boy named for the surgeon. As the ship began its south-
easterly run around the Cape of Good Hope, Frances Thomson's diary
ended. She may have begun to ail in the rough southern latitudes or
merely become bored with her observations. By the time the voyage
was over, though, Frances Thomson was about two months pregnant.
Morning sickness, compounded by the heavy weather in the Great
Australian Bight, may have put an end to her diary. After touring
Australia, she and her husband returned to England via the Suez Canal,
just six weeks before her first and only child was born in May of
1883. Dr Thomson practised as a doctor in Southport until 1902. His
commission as a surgeon superintendent had not only given a novice

practitioner experience, presiding over the health of 400 emigrants, the deaths of four children and the delivery of four others, but he had experienced a grand tour at minimal expense.

The Suez route:
steam versus sail

On 3 December 1884, a young single man embarked on the 3123-ton SS *Duke of Buckingham* bound for Queensland via the Suez and Torres Strait to Queensland.[14] At the beginning of the voyage, Reuben Percival described the routines and entertainments on his steamer, which exactly replicated those on sailing vessels over the past five decades:

> Our Captain and also the Dr are very particular about our places being kept clean and orderly you would have been pleased to have seen a lot of us [single men] using the holy stone its like that stone what you scour the house with only about the size of a brig we have to sprinkle some sand about and then scour the floor with these stones which makes the boards look nice and white we shall have a jolly time of it I believe when we get properly use to it.

The young men were permitted to swim in the Suez canal during overnight stops but, after clearing the canal, the ship was whitewashed as a precaution against infection. Although on many voyages emigrants were not permitted to go ashore at ports of call for fear of disease, the emigrants on the SS *Duke of Buckingham*, who included English, Irish, Scots, French and Italians, were allowed to visit the ports of Malta, Aden and Colombo when the ship called in for coal. Steaming through the Suez cut the time considerably, but for the first time since ships called at the Cape of Good Hope en route to take on water or supplies (before the mid-1840s), emigrants were at great risk of picking up either airborne or water-borne disease. The single men were exhorted to take pains with their personal hygiene: 'I suppose you would think it rather strange to see 20 or 30 men washing their clothes but we are obliged to keep very clean.' After Colombo, though, the captain refused to allow the emigrants to disembark at ports where the vessel refuelled, or to buy fruit from traders who approached in small craft 'in case of fevers for it is very unhealthy here'. The captain, mindful of the risk to the emigrants, kept abreast of the health status of each port, but bad water taken on during stopovers occasionally caused great distress to the emigrants over the next 80 or more years.

During the voyage, the SS *Duke of Buckingham* met a vessel travelling from Calcutta to Jamaica, possibly with indentured labourers on board. Responding to its distress signal, the captain discovered that it had only a few bags of rice left. He sent over 40 bags of rice and biscuits. The distressed vessel may have met with unfavourable weather that had stretched its time at sea far beyond its capacity to feed its human cargo.

Carrie Soper, a second-class passenger on board the 1051-ton fully rigged sailing ship *Ann Duthie*, en route to Sydney in 1882 with her husband the Revd JA Soper and their baby Florence Louisa, suffered the usual distress in the English Channel and Bay of Biscay. Like numerous husbands, Mr Soper was a great help with the baby while his wife was ill, and took care of the washing. The usual class distinctions meant that the clergyman and his wife, as mere second-class travellers, did not mix with the first-class passengers. However, while her husband bathed on deck using the shower baths set up for men, Carrie Soper was able to bathe privately in her cabin, a luxury by maritime standards. Striking up an acquaintance with the captain's wife, a marine veteran, Carrie learnt that she ought not bath the baby in seawater if she wished to avoid prickly heat, the scourge then, as now, of children in the tropics. In spite of the warning, Florence was miserable with prickly heat.

On this vessel, too, a sailor was lost overboard, and Carrie Soper described a near-death experience when the captain, 40 miles awry in his calculations, bore down towards an island in the half-light. Only by the super-human efforts of the sailors was the ship put about with just two minutes to spare. More mundane problems also created discomfort: the condensed water became unpalatable as the journey wore on, even in porridge. It was only after the intervention of another passenger, who mended the apparatus and cleaned its filters, that the water became drinkable again. On this private vessel, it would seem, no person had been employed to maintain the condenser. As was the custom half a century earlier, Carrie Soper swapped ingredients and exchanged cooked food, including pies and puddings and cakes, with other passengers. After a last big washing day on board, she ironed their clothing in readiness for shore. For Carrie Soper, her husband and infant daughter, the voyage was a pleasant one. Like numerous emigrants in the past half-century, they arrived fitter than they embarked: 'We are all very much better than when we left England, indeed our friends would scarcely know us'.

Carrie Soper's daily entries expressed a great deal of satisfaction with the voyage and the conditions on board, but she advised friends not to sail via the company with whom they had travelled, nor on the *Ann Duthie*. Her family, she stressed — contradicting her own commentary — would not have chosen the vessel had they known how uncomfortable it would be. They had been taken in by the owner's advertising, which assured them that a cook would provide meals, whereas she had no choice but to prepare their food. Although they had chosen a sailing vessel (reputedly much cleaner than a gritty, sooty, noisy steamship), she believed that a steamer would have provided them with fresh meat daily. Following the long tradition of emigrant letters, she packed her commentary with useful hints and information for friends and relatives preparing to follow, guiding them through the process and suggesting ways in which they might increase their own comfort.

Another well-to-do woman, writing to her brother after arriving in Queensland in 1884, offered an amusing account of her alleged encounters with 'alligators', fleas, snakes and other venomous or dangerous creatures. 'If you go to New South Wales', J Dixon wrote to her brother Walter, 'you will find everything as tame as at home, but Queensland is the place for adventures'. On a sailing ship, she advised, he would consume pea soup and 'plenty of boiled rice and Australian tinned meat and then when you land it will be Beef, Beef, Beef, for breakfast, dinner & tea, nothing but beef'.[15]

In 1889, a working-class man bound for Maryborough in Queensland with his wife and two daughters, boarded the SS *Dundee* in Dundee and made his way to the London Emigrants' Home before boarding the SS *Chyebassa*, 'a fine looking craft of 1,800 tons built in Port Glasgow in 1874', and belonging to Glasgow owners. Alan Aitken, a patriotic Scot, described the Emigrants' Home as having 'a splendid view' over the Thames from London's East End. Formerly the Brunswick Hotel, it had been purchased by 'a wealthy gentleman' for 'a Emigrants Home and it is a home in the full sence of the word'.[16] Emulating the emigrant depots of the 1840s to 1860s, it was 'all got up as aboard ship', with bunks, messes and bathrooms. The conditions, he reported, were excellent. Coffee, bread and butter were provided for breakfast, free of charge, and dainties could be purchased very cheaply. Plates of ham piled high could be bought for threepence. He was more than satisfied with his dinner of lentil soup with bread, beef and potatoes in large quantities, while supper brought bread, butter and tea in unlimited quantities. He had only to suffer the hard beds for two nights before embarkation.

Typically, the emigrants were given canvas bags by the storekeeper to store enough clothes for the first fortnight, until boxes were brought on deck for the usual change into light clothing for the tropics. The examining officer examined both the canvas bags and the boxes, taking a long time as he thoroughly scrutinised their contents:

> there was a great excitement going on amongst the passengers every one running hither and thither all full of bussell the boxes that was wanted on the voydge had to be empted to let him see that we had the required amount of articals mentioned in the Government regulation list the inspecting officer was one of those surly dogs that liked to show his authority and get the passengers excited a bit. I got passed very well. I had everything that was required. I had no firearms gunpowder spirits or offensive weppons so I started and closed up the boxes again.

As had happened in earlier decades, people with insufficient clothing were obliged to purchase appropriate apparel from the depot's store. On the day of embarkation, the surgeon handed out embarkation orders that had been surrendered on entry to the home.

Once the surgeon had notified the emigrants that he wished to choose constables, Aitken put himself forward and was immediately chosen to assist the surgeon and examining officer to inspect the emigrants, a procedure that took all day. It is impossible to tell whether these thorough procedures were typical of the Queensland Immigration Service, but it would seem from Alan Aitken's commentary that the routine was well entrenched. During the inspection, about six men were rejected: 'I was very sorry for them but there was no other help for it, the word was said and that was enough'.

Characteristically, Alan Aitken left the depot to purchase 'articals to help us on our journey we got orders to have everything in readiness for getting embarked at eleven o clock on Wednesday morning'. At the appointed time, the SS *Chyebassa*'s emigrants were marshalled again 'in riddieness to pass a second Dr before we went aboard of the tender which was to take us down to Gravesend where our nobel vessel was waiting on us'. During this trip down the Thames, the surgeon swore in ten constables. Each was allocated special duties. Alan Aitken and two others were appointed 'to look after the young weamon of which there are nearly 100 on board'. Nothing much had changed since the 1830s. In 1889, the women were securely enclosed so that no intercourse was possible with the other passengers below decks, although they mingled on the main deck during the day. Four-hour watches, as usual, were instituted, with four on and eight off in rotation until 10 pm. All three constables were, typically, expected to carry the food from the galley to the women's messes, and to see to their comfort: 'The Dr told us that our job was the most responciable bit of it all'. At the end of the journey, if they performed their duties satisfactorily, they were each to receive £5, an increase since the 1850s, when £2 was the going rate for a constable. On this ship, the constables were paid according to the responsibilities entrusted to them. The single women's constables and the sanitary constable were the highest paid, with the others receiving £3 each. They included one lamp trimmer, one 'surgent's assistant', two 'young men's constables', and two to assist the married people and children.

Alan Aitken's first dinner on board he thought was splendid: 'Scotch broath, potatoes & fresh beef. Everyone washes their own things.' The black crew, he reported, were very small in stature, and ate their meals sitting on their haunches 'in a ring and a big bason of rice [and curry] in the centre', which they shared. Having crossed the bar into the Channel, the ubiquitous seasickness began after the smooth ride down the Thames but fortitude was all: 'it would not do for one of the Queensland Government Constabels to be seen sea sick'. The SS *Chyebassa* was awash with musicians. Among the 'merrie company', he reported were three or four sets of bagpipes, two fiddles, any amount of melodians and flutes 'so we are prittie well set on for Music on our part of the deack there is dancing going on in great Spirit to the Irish bag-pipes in other parts we have concerts English Scotch & Irish'.

Although mattresses in mid-century were stuffed with straw, by the 1880s Allan Aitken was equipped with 'comfortable flock mattresses, 2 sheets, pillows, 2 heavy blankets'. Privacy, too, had improved. Each berth was partitioned, much to his satisfaction, with a sliding door and curtain enclosing the bunk he shared with his wife, and another shared by his two daughters. A central table was lowered from the roof whenever required for meals, and raised to provide more room when not in use. After a smooth run down the English Channel, they entered the Bay of Biscay, 'the much dreaded Bay — off they went sick again in all direc-tions, men, Wimming and children', even though the ocean was quite calm. Alan Aitken maintained that 'If they had not been told that it was the bay of Biskie there would have been no word about Sickness.' As a constable, it was his duty to assist the sick to their cabins and all consta-bles and married men who were not recumbent were enjoined to keep their eye on the married compartments by checking every ten minutes to see that no one was in distress. Every four hours, a bell was rung and the watchmen reported on deck to the Commanding Officer, 'All's well, Sir, in the Married Compartment', or whatever section they represented.

Alan Aitken was so proud of his status as a 'Queensland Government Constable' that he drew a picture of the red insignia embroidered on the blue jacket he wore as a symbol of his station. The Queensland

Immigration Service, by supplying uniforms and developing an officially recognised status for its constables, had imbued them with a sense of importance that augured well for the fulfilment of their duties. It was a canny move that impressed both the constables and the people under their charge who had already seen, at the depot, that officialdom could be heavy-handed. Besides their uniformed jackets and gratuities, constables who fulfilled their duties to the satisfaction of the surgeon superintendent received certificates commending their good conduct. They were also given preference for any available government jobs: the surgeon on the SS *Chyebassa* claimed to have found work for every constable he had taken out.

Alan Aitken was impressed with the facilities on board. There were baths in specially designated bathrooms and the seawater, which he found refreshing, did not put him off at all. Four Scots engineers who were eager to show him around ran the engine room, and 'Everything that can be done for the comfort of us Emegrants is done — we are treated more like Second class Passengers than anything elce'. Alan's daily routine included bathing before fetching the water and bread produced by two bakers on board at 6 am every morning, for the single women. For his own mess of about a dozen people, at about 7.30 am, he fetched the bread, coffee and porridge, which was available in unlimited quantities, for an 8 am breakfast. At 10 am, milk was served to the children, and at midday, beef-tea was served to the women and children, who were allowed two eggs weekly in lieu of beef-tea. At 12.30 pm, a dinner of Scotch broth, potatoes and fresh beef was served on five days, and duff, green peas and salt meat twice weekly: 'We are all getting fat with the feeding', he observed, as had many of his peers before him. Tea was served at 4.30 pm. Among the twice-weekly distribution of rations, he received brown sugar, molasses, jams, pickles, cheese, a large can of mustard, pepper and salt. People helped themselves to ships' biscuit from large barrels whenever they liked.

Occasionally, grand concerts were held. A stage was decorated with British flags and lit by 40 bright lamps, emulating a concert hall at home where Scots, English and Irish songs and recitations entertained over

400 emigrants, crew and officers. In spite of the grand concerts, Alan Aitken found 'not the least sign of drunkness amongst us for a very good reason it is a TT boat'. This teetotal boat, or 'tea-total' as Alan Aitken put it, was one of many Australia-bound vessels to forbid the consumption of alcohol. However, the emigrants did not go thirsty. Although Alan stuck to water, tea and coffee, 'Gingerbear and leamonade is sold at fivepence per common bottle I can live fine without any of them'. Stout was available as usual for pregnant and nursing women and it seems that if one had a full pocket even on this teetotal vessel, stout could be purchased for recreational drinking, but 'If we are not good templiars one would have to be very flush of money', with stout costing two shillings for three pints. The Knights Templar was an American temperance society organised on Masonic lines, and Alan Aitken appears — like many of his companions — to have been a member. It is possible that the ship's owners, too, imposed a regime recommended by the Templars, in consequence of which emigrants like Alan Aitken believed themselves to be temporary members under the ship's regulations.

The attendance of a pharmacist on board was another innovation of the 1880s, and was an index of the extent to which the Queensland government insisted that its contract carrier provide an environment and personnel guaranteed to ensure the safe transit of its recruits. As the ship drew into Malta for recoaling, the captain was advised that cholera was prevalent, so 'we gave it a wide birth'. Able only to observe Malta from the ship as they sailed on to the next coaling station, Alan described towns of great beauty, 'but it is better to pass than run any risk for to have distress aboard ship is something awfull.' A child, who had been 'weakly since coming on board … [died and was] consigned to the deep' two hours later. As usual, the doctor read the burial service. Alan was perplexed by the sickness on board in spite of the calm, docile weather: 'There has been a great many sick amongst the weamon & childern there was 150 that was not able to take their dinner. Arraugh root & beef tea had to be made specially for them'. So many children were ill that the school was closed.

On Sunday afternoons, the children were all lined up and the doctor, flanked by two constables, examined their eyes and tongues while the constables distributed sweets by the handful. The doctor, observed Alan Aitken, 'did everything to keep them in good spirits'. As the ship approached Port Said, the first port of call for this vessel owing to cholera in Malta, the surgeon gathered everyone together to lecture them on the iniquities of the town in a fire-and-brimstone speech. It was:

> the dirtiest wickest place in the world it is just a gambling hell and full of all other vice and cryme known. And no-one was allowed to go ashore. And no-one was allowed to come on board without permission from the Dr.

The surgeon told the emigrants that swarms of people in boats would come alongside and attempt to board. They were to have nothing to do with this invasion, although it seems that emigrants purchased grapes, watermelons and lemons for one to threepence per pound each. In spite of the risk of cholera or typhoid, the fresh fruit would have been conducive to a healthier voyage than that of vessels that sailed directly to Australia via the Great Circle route.

At this refuelling stop, 360 tons of coal were taken on board, shovelled in baskets from barges that came alongside by men who ran up and down planks. Within a few hours, the ship headed for the 'Sewis Canal' where the going was very slow, up to 50 hours at five miles per hour. Immediately after the call at Port Said, Alan developed an acute sore throat and was taken off duty by the surgeon, who ordered him to hospital, where a constable was appointed to care for him. Served beef tea, arrowroot, 'saggo' [sago] and 'shiree wine', as well as 'three different medicines and stout', he made good progress.

Released from hospital, Alan Aitken continued his duties. As usual, the emigrants slept on deck during the scorching heat, and received liberal quantities of lime juice every day when everyone was 'half-roasted and fairly forfoughten with the heate'.[17] Another nine-month-old baby surrendered its life just before the ship negotiated the 'Hellgates' separating the Red Sea from the Indian Ocean. Here, a British signalling station kept ships abreast of news, including the health status of refuelling ports. It was also a convalescent station for soldiers sent from Malta to regain their health and vigour. Although it was hot, the climate at this confluence of the two seas was considered to be healthy.

At Aden, small boys dived for coins while the doctor visited shore briefly after ordering his constable to keep strict watch on the single women. He had no intention of delivering a single girl to Queensland whose reputation was tainted by an unchaperoned shore visit. Alan bartered for 24 'Ostridge feathers', purchased for one shilling, a 30th of the original price, with which he was well pleased. After loading 200 tons of coal, the ship left Aden a few hours later, immediately encountering heavy weather. The young women were all in their bunks with 'a basin at their heads it blew something terriable'. The following day, few emigrants sought fresh air on decks, 'this is what is call a typhune'. Once the hurricane dispersed, the concerts and dancing began again and all seasickness was forgotten.

A great deal of food was thrown overboard every day on this well-provisioned vessel, even though everyone was eating well. In spite of the temperance status of the SS *Chyebassa*, the surgeon, as his predecessors had done for 50 years, gave each constable a glass of rum every Saturday and a pint of porter on Wednesday. A month after leaving Dundee, the Aitkens experienced the first shower of rain since leaving Scotland. On reaching Colombo, the emigrants were again refused permission to go ashore while the ship took on 300 tons of Welsh coal, although the cabin passengers were permitted to go sightseeing. For the first time in his life, Allan Aitken saw, and tasted, a banana. His new-found discovery intrigued him as much as he knew it would fascinate his readers in Scotland. Having purchased some, he searched for words to describe this unusual and captivating fruit. It was, he wrote, 'about 5 [inches] in circumferance you open the pod the same as a garden bean after the husk is off ... it is a solid piece of deleasious froot'.

As the ship sailed past the Indonesian island of Krakatoa (Krakatau), the surgeon told Alan that, four years earlier, he sailed past just six hours before it erupted. At the time, it was burning fiercely but, he told Alan, when it blew it took with it 75 000 souls, creating a tidal wave 60 feet high (in fact 36 000 people inhabiting coastal regions in the Sunda Strait were killed and the tsunami waves were as high as 120 feet, or 40 metres, in some areas). His ship was 84 miles away by the time it erupted, but, even so, the surgeon alleged, it was covered with cinders. The famous eruption of Krakatoa, located 40 kilometres from Java (latitude 16.7°S, longitude 105.4°E), occurred on 26 August 1883; if the surgeon's memory is correct, this places Allan Aitken's undated journey on the SS *Chyebassa* in the year 1887, rather than 1889, as recorded on the notes to his archived file. The surgeon, though, may have miscalculated the years since the eruption, or perhaps even fancifully placed himself in a time and place about which he had heard so much — although this is unlikely, given that his story could be falsified by other crew members. At a distance of just 84 miles, and given the magnitude of the tidal wave, his vessel, however, might have been expected to suffer a more dramatic experience than a rain of cinders. After all, during this multiple eruption, which exploded with devastating fury, energy was released equivalent to 200 megatons of TNT (compared with the 20 kilotons of energy released by the bombing of Hiroshima).

Apart from the tidal waves, the explosions were heard as far as away as Australia. Fine ash rained on New York, the effects of the tidal wave were felt in the English Channel, the blocking of the sun plunged the immediate area into darkness for three days and varying degrees of sunless gloom were experienced for up to 257 miles. Volcanic dust in the upper atmosphere affected the earth's weather for several years, and global temperatures were reduced by about 1 degree centigrade. This eruption 'was one of the most catastrophic natural disasters in recorded history'. Hence, if the surgeon superintendent on Alan Aitken's vessel witnessed this eruption at a distance of 84 miles, he was exceptionally fortunate. Substantial deposits of ash reportedly covered vessels up to 120 miles away from where thick black smoke could be seen billowing from the explosion. It is probable that the surgeon witnessed the first explosion far enough away to be free of danger by the time of the second, massive, triple explosion, a day later, which caused 'the most severe violent volcanic explosion on Earth in modern times'.[18] Given that most Queensland-bound vessels sailed close to the Indonesian coast, it is fortunate that this, and other vessels, were not near enough to be obliterated at the time of the explosion.

At Batavia (Jakarta), Alan Aitken's vessel took on another 300 tons of Australian coal: 'dirty looking stuff they are nothing like English or Scotch stuff'. Again, emigrants were not allowed to disembark, nor were Batavian locals allowed on board:

> Batavia is a very unhealthy place if we had allowed any of the natives on board we would have been compelled to have ridden ten days Quarantine at Thursday Island before we were allowed to enter the Harbour there.

Queensland government officials on Thursday Island, at the tip of Cape York — the first port of call in Northern Australia — were taking no chances, in the late 1880s, of importing disease into the colony. However, the shipping company had no compunction about allowing the emigrants to act as stevedores at Batavia, paying each volunteer an hourly rate of one shilling for nine hours to unload cargo on the wharf.

The emigrants were delighted to see a 'splendid Java bull' brought on board to be slaughtered the next day for fresh meat and, in spite of the heat, they enjoyed Highland Games on board, including tugs of war, jumping, sack-racing and dancing. As the emigrants began to weary of deck games, Alan Aitken reported that they discovered 'a fine liberary on board'. Like many surgeons before him, the medical officer on this ship posted notices whenever he wished to communicate orders to the emigrants. On one occasion, a notice ordered all emigrants who had put their flannels away to put them on again as it was too chilly in the mornings and evenings 'or they will catch cold'. Alan himself was disappointed that it was not as hot as he had expected. That emigrants obeyed instructions concerning their mode of dress is an indication of the extent to which the majority — as they had done for a half a century — remained willing to subsume their individual rights for the sake of the collective good. Moreover, it is another indication of the authority wielded by surgeons, whose maintenance of discipline remained crucial to the success of the voyage.

On this vessel, as on its predecessors, the surgeon's word was law. As they steamed towards northern Australia, Alan Aitken reported that

> This has been what I would call a read letter day for us three younge women Constables [A red-letter day for the three constables charged with the wellbeing of the young women. We] were called to the bridge this afternoon and had to stand Coartmarchal before the Dr Capton and first Officer for some complaints that the Matron had lodged against us but we came out clear without a stain on our character it was proved that we had don nothing but what we were ordered by the Dr as the Dr is Supreame over all on board bar the Capton and officers we had done nothing but our deuty.

Children's tea parties were an institution on vessels carrying 'ten pound poms' after the Second World War; but they were already a feature of voyages in the 1880s, after which procedures on board changed very little, as we shall see, if we compare the experience of the Aitken family with that of families in the 20th century, discussed below. Attended by six single girls acting as stewardesses, children aged two to 12 were given a 'grand tea party' with food treats beyond their dreams. Afterwards, the ship's stewards, exhibiting 'great taste' and refinement, served the voluntary constables and stewardesses fresh 'salmond', sardines and puddings. After the celebratory dining during the last fortnight of the voyage, including superb teas for the women and children, the SS *Chyebassa* was prepared for its first Australian examination on Thursday Island by whitewashing and cleaning: 'everything must look fresh'.

Following the usual procedures, four passengers and 200 tons of cargo disembarked on Thursday Island. Volunteer emigrants, as in earlier ports of call, were hired to discharge the cargo onto a large hulk in the harbour. Alan Aitken had been warned that employers would come on board to recruit labourers. As expected, he was offered a job as a water policeman by a police sergeant who boarded in search of volunteers, but declined it. At the next port of call, Cooktown, six single women and two single men landed, and 200 tons of cargo was discharged, principally iron. Another inspector boarded and thoroughly examined the emigrants, passengers, crew and ship. The servant girls were hired at 12 shillings weekly, including board and lodging.

At Townsville, the same routine saw 80 emigrants disembarking, while 300 tons of cargo was off-loaded, mainly liquor including brandy, whisky, rum and stout. This teetotal ship was not averse to carrying alcohol as a cargo. Presumably, by naming the ship a teetotaller, contractors were able to impose an even greater discipline among emigrants for whom the boredom at sea often led to a fondness for drink that could have unpleasant results for the more sober travellers, or for wives. Alan Aitken's descriptions of the beautiful scenery as the ship coasted down the east coast of Australia completed his observations, and it is to be hoped that his certificate of good conduct, signed by the medical officer, saw him in good stead when he reached Brisbane.

'We put 14,000 miles between us and home and friends'

1900–1950

Steamers, tourism and a new era

I n July 1912, another father embarked for Australia with his wife and children. After joining friends for a last supper at the Post Office Buffet, 40-year-old Isaac Tarbitt and his family left Newburn, near Newcastle, by train for King's Cross. Like many emigrants, he saw the first leg of his journey from home as a grand opportunity for sightseeing in London before leaving England, perhaps forever. Having breakfasted at King's Cross, he took his children to the Regent Park Zoo, a 'wonderful place'. He took them riding on the underground rail to visit the Houses of Parliament, where he spoke to a number of Labour politicians, including his hero Ramsay McDonald.[1]

The next day, the family — the first in this book to emigrate under the auspices of the Commonwealth of Australia after the federation of the colonies in 1901 — rose at 6 am to join the commotion at St Pancras Station, where two special trains had been engaged to take third-class passengers, and another to take first- and second-class passengers, to the Orient Line's 12 927-ton SS *Orama*, which was waiting at Tilbury Docks in Essex, the quayside from which many thousands of post-war migrants were to depart in the 1940s and 1950s.[2] By the turn of the 20th century, great technological advances in engineering had produced far more efficienct triple- and quadruple-expansion engines driving twin or triple screws, allowing ships to sail at a steady

15 to 18 knots. And advances in the space and comfort available to assisted emigrants continued.

Typically, separation of the classes began at the station rather than the dock. After a three-hour train journey, the third-class passengers 'formed a Procession to show passes'. The doctor particularly examined the children's heads for lice. Once the bell had rung for all friends to leave the ship, Isaac Tarbitt noted many 'sorrowful partings probably never to see each other again'. He went on: 'the feelings expressed and suffered at these times are such as make themselves physically felt and wear out the body in passing'. Even in an age when return to the United Kingdom was so much easier, partings were no less distressing. Upon arrival at Plymouth Sound, the SS *Orama* was coaled at sea owing to a dockers' strike.

Seasickness was as troublesome in 1912 as ever, and on this ship passengers were permitted to go ashore at Gibraltar, where they purchased fruit, tobacco and fancy goods from boats, and amused themselves by throwing coins for the diving youths. On shore, Isaac Tarbitt took his family to visit the university and other fine buildings, vividly describing their experiences during 'six hours of life never to be forgotten'. At Taranto, in southern Italy, they were also permitted to go ashore, but he preferred to stay on board. Again, there was no limit to the amount of food available at each meal. Breakfast included porridge, hot and cold meats, a choice of potatoes, brawn, sausage, bloaters (herrings), liver and bacon, and fish on Fridays. Bread, butter, jam and marmalade were bounteously provided. Lunch included soup, potatoes, hot and cold meat, rabbits, haricot beans, cabbage, pumpkin, turnips and various puddings. At tea, he could choose from hot or cold meat, hotpot, bubble and squeak, bread, butter, jam and marmalade.

At Port Said, the Tarbitt family went ashore, where they dined on ham and eggs and where Isaac noticed local barterers with ostrich feathers and other fancy goods. It was, he wrote from Port Said, in a tone and sentiment characteristic of his era, a 'pleasant change to be in an English town'. Like his peers for over three decades, he found the slow journey down the Suez hot, exhausting and trying, especially as an adult male was buried as they negotiated the narrow channel.

At Colombo, they were permitted to go ashore on tenders at a cost of two shillings each. While the passengers were sightseeing, local men, women and children ran up and down the planks with baskets, loading 2000 tons of coal. On this voyage, the vessel did not sail through the Torres Straits to Brisbane, as Alan Aitken's had done in 1889, but headed straight for Fremantle, where it docked nine days after leaving Colombo. As was now traditional, children's teas, adult parties and dinners were given as the ship approached Australia, in what appears to have been a public relations exercise introduced by Australian authorities anxious to convey the impression of a bounteous country. As the vessel approached Fremantle, the passengers were obliged to seek tickets from the doctor 'for medical inspection at 6am tomorrow'. The ticketing system undoubtedly streamlined the official inspection procedures. At 6 am, an official medical inspector boarded and the emigrants, who had been up since 5 am, were individually inspected in the dining hall. Isaac believed that, since this was the first port of entry into Australia, no more inspections would be necessary. However, three days after leaving Fremantle, he discovered that they were to be examined again before arriving in Adelaide: 'This is done 14 days after leaving an Indian Port, ie Colombo 2 or 3 cases of measles reported this morning among the men'.

In spite of the measles on board, tourist activity was encouraged and sightseeing was on the agenda again in Adelaide. The Tarbitt family took a train from the wharf to the city, paying one shilling for a return fare. The city was, he wrote, 'A very nice town, the best we have seen so far'. After a day's sightseeing, they were back on the boat at 4 pm, ready to sail an hour later. In Melbourne, too, they visited the zoo, while 300 passengers disembarked. In Sydney, they visited the Botanic Gardens and an Aboriginal camp, as well as other venues to which tourists were directed. In Brisbane, Isaac Tarbitt endured a deal of trouble getting his boxes through customs. Once they had left the red tape behind, the family was met by friends who escorted them to Bulimba by train 'to an old country welcome ... We put 14,000 miles between us and home and friends'.

As with many of Isaac Tarbitt's predecessors, the ordeal of negotiating entry into the social and economic life of Australia was softened by friends, who offered him hospitality, helped find a house and introduced him to colonial habits. Entrepreneurial like so many others, Isaac visited the Premier, who promised to try to secure him a rebate on the family's passage money. He selected a site for a house — the land was part of his immigration package — organised tools and seed, and transported his family by train and wagon to Widgee, where he built their dwelling. By the following year, after quarrelling with his friends and finding his feet, he in turn attempted to nominate a friend (or relation): 'Over to migration office this morning but nominations have stopped so couldn't get Ned's people nominated'.[3] As usual, funding for assisted emigrants depended on the rhythms of the economy, and Isaac Tarbitt had chosen an inauspicious moment to attempt to nominate people for whom he wished to pay a deposit as his friends had undoubtedly done for him.

Another Scot headed for Sydney a decade later. Travelling on one of the Commonwealth Government's famous 'Bay boats' (which included the SS *Hobson's Bay*, SS *Largs Bay* and SS *Esperance Bay*), James Cameron travelled as an assisted immigrant on the SS *Moreton Bay* in 1922.[4] As with all of the 15-knot 'Bay' liners, there was accommodation on this new 14 376-ton oil-fuelled vessel for 720 third-class emigrants and 12 cabin passengers. Further steps in maritime technology meant that not only was this liner, like its sister ships, oil-fuelled, but it sported a double-reduction geared turbine driving twin screws, increasing its power and stability, and enhancing the comfort of passengers. These liners 'soon made a name for themselves as comfortable roomy ships' providing voluminous refrigerators for taking Australian frozen meat to Britain on the return journey.[5]

In spite of space, comfort and advancing technology, James Cameron on the SS *Moreton Bay*, found the Suez hot. The promenade deck on his ship was enclosed in canvas to provide shelter for the passengers. Even so, three of his companions suffered fatal heat exhaustion and were buried in the Suez Canal. Advanced technology and a smoother passage far from the buffeting of the great Southern Ocean, were unable to save emigrants on the more stable steamers from the punishment dealt out by tropical heat.

Arriving in Fremantle direct from Colombo, James Cameron claimed that Western Australia was known as 'the mendicant State'; when he reached Sydney, an employer came on board and chose him as 'a likely lad'. He was occupied lumping wheat sacks for six days a week until he sought his fortune further afield, following work around New South Wales. Eventually, he made his way to South Australia where, he claimed, marriage was a boon in the Depression of the 1930s, because single men could not get government relief.

Twenty-five years later, in July 1947, the family of 35-year-old Mildred Howell were among the first 22 assisted immigrants to arrive in Brisbane after the Second World War on another of the Commonwealth Government's 'Bay boats', the 26-year-old 14 362-ton twin-screw, double-reduction, geared-turbine SS *Largs Bay*. This was a vessel similar in every respect to the SS *Moreton Bay* on which James Cameron travelled in 1922.[6] Commissioned in 1921, built in Glasgow for the Australian Commonwealth Line, and used as a troop ship during the Second World War, it resumed its assisted passenger run to Australia between 1947 and 1957, the year in which it was decommissioned and broken up.[7]

Travelling in 'tourist', or third, class with Mildred Howell were her husband Frederick Leslie (known as Les) and her children Henry and Yvonne, aged ten and nine. Again, the Howell family's experiences of official procedure barely differed from those of their predecessors a century earlier. The greatest differences included the abundance of luxuries offered on board, and a quite dramatic change in the accommodation and service. Meals were taken in dining halls, prepared by cooks and served by stewards, and third, or tourist, class cabins replaced steerage class in which each family's berth was barely separated from their neighbour's. Children, however, still suffered from epidemics of measles and scarlet fever, and adults still succumbed to tropical heat. The Great Australian Bight, too, claimed its victims. Medical examinations, and fitness for the voyage, remained important criteria for acceptance as an assisted immigrant, and character testimonials and certificates of medical fitness were mandatory, as were examinations upon arrival. Most changes to accommodation, cleaning routines (by the crew instead of the emigrants) and diet had occurred by the 1920s; hence, by the time of the great post-war immigration of the late 1940s to the 1960s, further differences were minor.

As in 1922, post-war migrants dined, at separate sittings (as, for example, a first, second or third sitting), in vast dining halls where concerts were also held. The sugar-starved Howells, who had left a country still in the grip of severe rationing in 1947, were astonished to find one-pound boxes of chocolates for sale very cheaply on board; the food was beyond their dreams, both in quality and quantity. One major difference was that, instead of housing the married couples and their children together, as had been the case throughout the 19th century, by the mid-20th century, wives shared cabins with other women, both single and married, their daughters and younger sons, while husbands shared with other men and their sons over the age of ten. For many couples who had spent years apart during the war and during demobilisation, this loss of privacy and intimacy was a severe blow, but they found ways and means of organising the odd romantic moment.[8]

Mildred Howell and her daughter shared a cabin with other women, while her husband and son shared with other men and boys. In the following year, another 30-year-old emigrant travelling to Adelaide with her husband and three daughters, aged nine, eight and 20 months, left Tilbury. Embarking in October 1948 on the P&O's SS *Ranchi*, a 16 738-ton vessel that carried 'ten pound poms' to Adelaide and Melbourne also in tourist class, Elizabeth Britton, too, was surprised to find herself separated from her husband:

> We were allocated cabins, but not as a family — myself and the girls shared a cabin with six other women, the men shared cabins. We were lucky in our cabin — we all got on very well, not a cross word the whole voyage. But there was a lot of discord in some other cabins.[9]

For this family, too,

> One of the great joys of the journey was the food after
> being on rations, and the children's meals were great. Most
> of them would have second helpings, especially dessert.
> There was always entertainment for the children, in some
> form or other, like films, and shows, then sometimes they,
> the children, gave their own concert.[10]

Upon arriving at Port Said, the captain on Mildred Howell's ship
broadcast the rules over the public address system. Passengers were not
to purchase anything to eat under any circumstances. At Aden, the SS
Largs Bay's water supply collapsed. In spite of technological advances,
breakdowns still occurred, putting the passengers at great risk: 'We have
had to buy Adenese water which is putrid, and filled two hospitals with
dysentery'. In spite of the rancid water, the Howell family went ashore
in Aden, which Mildred found cleaner than Port Said. There, where it
was 100 degrees in the shade, they purchased films, soap and jars of
boiled sweets during the few hours the ship spent refuelling. Three days
later, Mildred Howell collapsed from heat exhaustion and was bed-
bound for some time. In Colombo, the family was ferried ashore in a
motor launch, encountering the usual hassle with passports. Mildred
Howell is the first diarist in the series examined in this book to discuss
passports. If they were required of earlier emigrants after Federation,
diarists did not mention them. In Colombo, the family purchased
coconuts and oranges during the half-day allowed on shore.

Mildred Howell found the ten days between Colombo and
Fremantle tedious in the extreme — it was dull, she wrote, only miles
of water, with no land or lighthouses. Nineteenth-century emigrants on
sailing ships would undoubtedly have smiled, having endured three
months of water, sky and their own company, with no landfall at all. As
the SS *Largs Bay* approached Fremantle, the usual fancy-dress children's
party was held, just prior to another sea rescue where, again, the medical officer was ferried to a ship in mid-ocean to attend a badly burnt
engineer who was brought back to the SS *Largs Bay* to be taken on to

Fremantle. Photographing the scene, Mildred Howell, observed 'A nice bit of work by the boat crew'.

Yet another children's party brought the family more good fortune when the Howell children won a box of chocolates for a recital. These routines and special menus for children were adopted on all post-war ships where, on the SS *Ranchi* in 1948, for example, the 'Children's Breakfast', for which special menus were printed daily under the ship's own coat of arms, included oatmeal porridge, cornflakes, poached eggs on toast, puree tomatoes, white and brown bread, jam, marmalade, tea, milk and cocoa. The 'Children's Tea', which also changed daily, included, on 7 October 1948, Mongole soup, minced chicken and spaghetti, creamed potatoes, jelly Napolitaine, currant buns, tea, jam and milk. The food on these vessels was almost beyond the comprehension of children raised during five years of austerity and for whom rationing had remained a daily burden during the previous two years.[11]

As usual, the emigrants on the SS *Largs Bay* were instructed to rise at 5.30 am to be examined by Australian medical officers on arrival in Fremantle, just as Isaac Tarbitt had experienced 25 years earlier. Once on the dock, the family formed a small circle. Henry Howell recalls that his father 'then informed us that, now our feet were on Australian soil for the first time, we would henceforth regard ourselves as Australian, which we did'.[12] Mildred Howell was delighted with Fremantle's and Perth's 'marvellous houses, lovely trees, all smothered in blossoms all beautiful colours. There are verandahs running all around the houses'. For English arrivals, the unfamiliar terrain, flora and fauna were ceaselessly amazing. Mildred admired tall, clean, Perth; she thought that the babies' prams were wondrous, just as she had seen in Hollywood films. Perth's shops also gave up their bounties, including coloured wools of such quality and vividness never before seen by this avid knitter. Biscuits in cellophane were a novelty that the family could not resist, along with huge quantities of fruit. Mildred was overwhelmed by the availability of inexpensive clothes, shoes and other goods. She purchased shoes for her children and two pairs of fully-fashioned stockings — box and all — for one and sixpence a pair, and before you buy them, they put them over a glass leg and revolve it slowly so that you can see that there isn't a flaw in them. No coupons either … Isn't it grand.

A café lunch in Fremantle was unbelievably sumptuous, and cheap to boot:

> We had a wonderful lunch in a café called Lucas; we had ham and two eggs, lettuce, beetroot, tomato and chips all on one plate; then bread and butter and tea for four of us, and the bill was only nine-and-sixpence, and they don't allow tips.

Negotiating Australian customs, mores and terminology was always tricky for new arrivals, in spite of shared language; the no-tipping rule was a great bonus on top of the cheapness of the meal. As emigrants in the mid-19th century had found, that first meal on land was always memorable. After a day's sightseeing, the family re-embarked, and, although they endured the characteristically terrible storms in the Great Australian Bight, Mildred claimed that she had known worse. The port-holes were screwed down and watertight doors battened. During the storm, Mildred wrote, 'another incident on the ship. A newly-embarked passenger died during the night, and had to be buried at sea'. Typically, the assembled emigrants attended a solemn burial service.

The round of tea parties continued while the emigrants packed, washed, ironed, and entertained themselves in the evening with sing-songs. Mildred Howell, too, enjoyed the company on board her ship. As they approached Sydney Harbour, the crew busily hooked sharks. The Howells were delighted by the harbour lights and thrilled by the sight of people crowding the quays, waving handkerchiefs and Union Jacks: 'Then our people from the Immigration Offices of Brisbane came aboard to welcome us, namely Miss Connie Clayton, who looked after our affairs for us, and her boss, Mr Longland'.[13] Mildred continued,

We had an agonising hour in the Customs Sheds but afterwards we were taken to a large hotel called the Wynyard and they gave us a wonderful lunch, and afterwards we went to the Botanical Gardens where the kiddies had a good romp on the grass, and we all had a good chat. Then we all had tea in some gardens and it was all free. Then we got together, twenty-two of us, and had an orgy of shopping. I bought some lovely yellow wool, all coupon-free for a woollie. You don't know which colour to buy and we bought some cream slices, biscuits, and chocolate (milk ones, I mean) and then came back to Wynyard for a wash and brush up, and then we had dinner, and they had to tell us that we weren't eating enough, but you ought to see the food here!

Typically, freedom from coupons, and the luxury of unlimited food, nylon stockings, and clothing, remained an extraordinary novelty for a war-weary family.

After a 'nightmare' 19-hour train journey to Brisbane, sitting up all night nursing her daughter, escorted by 'the redoubtable and greatly loved Connie Clayton' of the Queensland Immigration Department, the Howells were given a grand welcome party by relatives who were waiting at the station for them. As had so many of her predecessors for over 100 years, Mildred Howell ended her diary with, 'Well, that is the end of our trip across fourteen thousand miles of sea and land'.

Quarantine remained an issue in 1948 when Elizabeth Britton's youngest daughter arrived in Adelaide with measles on the SS *Ranchi*. Having been told earlier by the medical officer on board, that the 20-month-old child was unlikely to survive such a severe attack with complications including an ear abscess, the determined mother had nursed her daughter through the crisis. She was not about to surrender her to alien officials. Reporting 'a confrontation with the authorities' who wanted to place her daughter in 'the isolation hospital', she declared that 'I wouldn't let her go and as we were going where there weren't any children they gave way'.

For emigrant parents arriving at any time between the 1830s and 1950, the health of their children was a major anxiety during their voyage, arrival and settlement. Apart from medical advances including aspirin and inoculation for a range of other diseases besides smallpox — antibiotics were not available for general use before the mid-1950s — major differences in the experience of emigrants from the 1870s were primarily due to advances in steam technology and to the massively increased space created by advances in shipbuilding, which ushered in the new transoceanic liners. Supplementary benefits of stream-driven engines from the late 19th century included high-volume water condensers, more powerful refrigeration, and fan-driven ventilation. Auxiliary steam engines driving screws on sailing vessels such as the SS *Great Britain*, had considerably reduced the passage, disarming the tyranny of distance. The dirty, noisy and polluting coal-fired engines that propelled the migrant ships of the 1880s to 1920s were gradually replaced by cleaner, more efficient and easily refuelled, oil-fired engines typical of many of the migrant ships of the mid-20th century. So appalling was the reputation of steamers in the late 19th century that, from the 1880s, numerous emigrants preferred to book passages on sailing ships, believing the voyage to be far more pleasant than the sooty, vibrating, coal-fired steamers of their day.

In spite of the mode of travel, bureaucratic procedures and on-board regulations aimed at increasing comfort and saving life changed remarkably little for a century after 1850. From the 1880s, with high tonnage and spacious ships the norm, food, exercise and accommodation were far superior to that of earlier decades. Nevertheless, the emigrants were linked together over time by their hopes, aspirations, fears and trepidation as they sought a new life in a country to which they had been drawn by its climate, its imperial ties, and its offer of plentiful work, land and housing. 'The Australian Dream' of a house on a quarter-acre plot of land was, essentially, shared by 1.5 million migrants from the United Kingdom in the 19th century, and hundreds of thousands thereafter. And they were prepared to cover a great distance to fulfil an aspiration when beckoned by letters from friends and relatives in Australia, or by an expanding range of promotional material touting an Australian paradise. This book, however, is peopled with successful settlers; many others were scooped up by, or fell through, the web of philanthropic and government welfare agencies, enduring mean and meagre lives in and out of institutional care. These, and their fellow immigrants for whom rural life in a cruel and unforgiving environment left enduring scars, bequeathed little personal testimony of the purgatory to which they had been propelled by wind or steam.

Most passages to Australia were relatively uneventful, even tedious to the point of distraction. This book has, unavoidably, focused on some of the more dramatic voyages — the horrific episodes where high mortality attracted the attention of authorities and the press — over which a great deal of ink was expended. From these exceptional voyages, however, and the official reactions to the death toll and the conditions on the ships, we can see far more clearly why all but 1 to 2 per cent of immigrants arrived safe and well after a 15 000-mile voyage through all seasons and weathers. The selection of personal testimony, too, has introduced a bias. Inevitably, the more mundane narratives from fair-weather ships, written by immigrants with little interest in procedures on board have been excluded in favour of those that dwelt on the health of children and the monitoring of cleanliness routines on board. And it is these eyewitness accounts, with their emphasis on illness and bereavement, that project the most vivid images of life and death on board.

From the experiences on a few ships in the late 1830s, when distraught mothers faced the unspeakable consequences of epidemic disease, emigration officials counted the human costs of the passage. A flurry of official excitement was prompted by sporadic tragedies in each decade until the 1880s, by which time faster steamships had considerably reduced the risk of death, even to infants. From the early 1840s, an authoritarian Colonial Office agency in London mobilised emigrants in co-operation with a modernised and muscular inspectorate of colonial civil servants led by Immigration Agents in Sydney, Melbourne and Adelaide. Under the new regimen — operating at both ends of the voyage — regulatory improvements to personnel, accommodation and diet on these well-scrutinised voyages were introduced and maintained by civil servants whose authority went far beyond that wielded by most inspectorates in an age of laissez-faire when the civil service, as we know it today, was in its infancy. By the mid-1850s, their success was evident. Adults were delivered to Australia at no more risk to their lives than had they stayed at home.

One question often asked in relation to the gradual improvement in British civic life from the mid-19th century, and central to the themes explored here, is this: 'Did government intervention in the lives of ordinary citizens really matter'? This book has shown that official initiatives introduced to monitor and deliver health and well-being on government-operated ships significantly reduced maritime mortality. The number of well-off private fare-payers who chose to travel as cabin passengers on government ships, rather than on private vessels with companions of their own class, confirms the high public regard for government ships in the mid-19th century. Confidence in the government service was shared by all sectors of contemporary society. This confidence was intermittently undermined by sensationalised reports in years when cholera or other epidemic diseases were prevalent, or on the relatively rare occasion when a ship was supervised by an inhumane or incompetent surgeon. But public exposure of 'fever ships' led to further initiatives that improved the lot of prospective emigrants.

Precisely how far the methods used to reduce mortality on these ships spilled over into the realm of local or central public health on land is uncertain. Undoubtedly, the Emigration Commission treated government ships as laboratories for the successful implementation of measures to promote health and hygiene, leading the way by rapidly and substantially reducing civilian mortality at sea. Given the frenetic correspondence between the Emigration Commission, the Home Office, the Admiralty, the Poor Law Board and the Board of Health — and the close personal and kinship ties between many senior personnel in these departments — information was circulated constantly. The implementation of pioneering legislation via the Passenger Acts, and the successful enforcement of regulations controlling the conveyance of government emigrants, demonstrate that, in so far as the maritime sphere is concerned, government intervention really mattered.

Children aged three and under represented about two-thirds of all deaths on government-assisted ships in the 19th century. In the early 1850s, the Emigration Commissioners sought expert opinion on ways to reduce deaths among the youngest emigrants. It was already clear that improvements in sanitation, which worked for their parents and older siblings, were not enough to prevent excess infant mortality; hence the Commissioners introduced a new dietary regime for babies. Unfortunately, this strategy appears to have worked for toddlers and young children, but not for their younger siblings. Without specialised knowledge on infant nutrition, even the introduction of alternative supplementary fine cereals and milk substitutes was unable to make much difference, at that point, on land or at sea: another half-century was to pass before the infant death rate would fall dramatically on shore.

However equivocal the success of measures introduced to save infant life at sea, they ensured that women were given the best possible care during and after their confinement, including rest, food treats and comforts such as fresh meat, porter and wine to assist with breastfeeding. The focus on mothers and babies ensured better quality food for nursing mothers and the supervision of meals for young children. Perhaps the infant food introduced for babies after 1854 may ultimately have encouraged mothers to wean their babies at sea too early with tragic results, due to a general lack of understanding of measurements, volumes and special hygiene required for successful artificial infant feeding.

Yet it ought not be thought that emigration officials promoted artificial feeding at the expense of breastfeeding, as was to happen on land in the second half of the 19th century, with the support of both the medical profession and commerce. Rather, it was well understood that nursing mothers were likely to lose their breast milk during or following seasickness; artificial feeding was considered a necessary evil in the maritime environment. And many surgeon superintendents were critical of mothers who weaned their infants too soon.

Ironically, the greater value placed on the specific needs of infants at sea was the key to reducing the mortality of all but the target group, those who were at greatest risk. Acting as Medical Officers of Health, but with greater authority, surgeon superintendents may be seen as precursors of the welfare and mothercraft movements that contributed to the saving of infant life on land at the turn of the 20th century. Without them, and the authority invested in them to oversee the welfare of emigrants on the longest transoceanic route, the death toll on Australia-bound ships would undoubtedly have been far higher. We should bear in mind, though, that it was not their expertise as doctors, or the content of their medical bags, that saw a remarkable decline in maritime mortality. Rather, it was their supervision of the housekeeping routines and the diet on board that was responsible for such an outstanding outcome. As representatives of the State, they supervised strategies that, over time, saved the bitter tears of numerous parents travelling in steerage to Australia.

Some strategies and innovations were beyond the control of surgeons. The adoption by colonial governments of long-distance, capacious passenger steamships via the Suez Canal route in the 1880s provided faster voyages, shortening the time infants and their siblings and parents were at risk. More spacious accommodation was also conducive to a far healthier passage, compared with the crowding of earlier decades. It was in this age of maritime innovation, coinciding with an era when the focus on land was swivelling towards mothers and babies, and when emigration was winding down to all colonies but Queensland, that the health of infants at sea truly benefited.

Although our attention has been drawn to the plight of young children at sea, we need to bear in mind that over 98 per cent of assisted emigrants bound for an Australian shore in the 19th century landed alive, and many claimed to be healthier than they had ever been in their lives. As we have seen, officials at both ends of the emigration process believed that the successful management of the ships was due to the diligent performance of surgeons, many of whom were repeatedly commended. Also worthy of mention are the assistants chosen by surgeons as their constables and matrons, whom they endowed with the authority to implement the procedures that contributed so successfully to the life-saving routines at sea. Surgeons, themselves, even in the late 19th century, when the risk of death at sea was far lower, knew the value of the volunteer men and women in whose hands they placed the routine welfare of their charges. As one constable wrote in 1889, 'The Dr told us that our job was the most responciable bit of all'.

A cleaner environment, a focus on private and public hygiene, and attention to diet, worked on the majority of ships. Yet, it is not surprising that the risks for young children remained high. First, it is uncertain how far cleaning up the environment minimised fatal airborne infections such as measles and scarlet fever. Even on the cleanest vessels, the importation of one case could result in several burials at sea. Second, infant health movements succeeded on land once a generation of women, born near the end of the 19th century, enjoyed the benefits of higher living standards, relative freedom from tuberculosis, and education in domestic and infant welfare. Better fed, educated and healthier, they bore heavier, stronger infants who benefited from their mothers' well-being. Surgeon superintendents on government-assisted voyages to Australasia in the 19th century had the authority to implement life-saving regimes, but not the specialist training in infant and maternal nurture, which remained undeveloped on land until social, political and scientific advances at the turn of the 20th century — including universal suffrage — propelled paediatrics towards a revolution in infant health.

If one were able to assemble in one place — say, on the deck of a modern luxury liner — all of the emigrants and surgeon superintendents who appear in this book, one can only imagine the wonder with which each would greet the stories of the others. Even within the same year, experience could be entirely different, especially before the advent of the modern steamers of the 20th century. In the age of aeronautical travel, the pioneers of modern airliners adopted not only the language of the nautical environment — [air]liner, bridge, cabin, crew, captain, pilot, steward, galley, gangway, and so forth — but its classes as well.

Hence, the economy class in which so many hapless passengers fly between the United Kingdom and Australia is, essentially, the modern steerage class. Many of these modern jetsetters — themselves subjected to a range of pathogens circulating in the recycled air in an enclosed system and at international airports, would doubtless welcome the opportunity of a four-to-five-week voyage on a liner of the 1940s and 1950s, in spite of the probability of seasickness. But few, I suspect, would volunteer for a three-month passage in a square-rigged vessel, with or without children, to test their reactions to life and death in the age of sail.

Endnotes

Preface

1 'Letter written on the Voyage to South Australia' by George and Sarah Brunskill to her parents in Ely, Cambridgeshire, 1838–39, 27 November 1838, MLSA, D 5203 (L), typed transcript.

Introduction

1 Robin Haines, *Emigration and the Labouring Poor: Australian recruitment in Britain and Ireland 1831–1860*, London, 1997; see also articles listed in the bibliography.

2 Helen Woolcock, *Rights of Passage: Emigration to Australia in the Nineteenth Century*, London, 1986; Don Charlwood, *The Long Farewell*, Ringwood, 1981.

3 Mark Staniforth, 'Dangerous voyages? Aspects of the emigrant experience on the voyage to Australia 1837–1839', unpublished MA thesis, University of Sydney, 1993; idem, 'Diet, disease and death at sea on the voyage to Australia, 1837–1839', *International Journal of Maritime History*, VIII:2, December 1996, pp. 119–56; idem, 'Deficiency disorder: Evidence of the occurrence of scurvy on convict and emigrant ships to Australia 1837–1839', *The Great Circle*, 13:2, pp. 119–32.

4 Haines, *Emigration and the Labouring Poor*, Appendix 2, pp. 264–67.

5 Robin Haines, *Children at Sea: epidemics, ships, and doctors in the age of sail* (in preparation).

6 *Historical Records of Australia*, Series 1, vol. viii, pp. 274–327; John McDonald and Ralph Shlomowitz, 'Mortality on convict voyages to Australia, 1788–1868', *Social Science History*, vol. 13, no. 3, pp. 285–313, especially Table 1, p. 288; p. 291. This and other articles on maritime mortality can be found in Ralph Shlomowitz, *Mortality and Migration in the Modern World*, Variorum, London, 1996.

7 McDonald and Shlomowitz, 'Mortality on immigrant voyages to Australia in the 19th century', *Explorations in Economic History*, 27, 1990, Table 6, p. 96.

8 Anonymous diary, Oxley Library, M1265.

9 Clark family memoirs, MLSA, PRG 389/9.

10 FK Crowley, 'British migration to Australia: 1860–1914: A descriptive, analytical and statistical account of the immigration from the United Kingdom', unpublished D. Phil. thesis, Oxford University, 1951; idem, 'The British contribution to the Australian population: 1860–1919, *University Studies in History and Economics*, July 1954, pp. 55–88.

11 SRSA, GRG 35.

12 The source for this analysis is the manuscript 'Register of deaths on emigrant ships', in

three volumes, 1847–54; 1854–60, and 1861–69', housed at the Public Record Office, Kew, CO 386/170–172, now available on microfilm (PRO Microfilms 6887–8). Another manuscript register (1854–64), PRO, CO 386/184, reports details of each ship and its emigrants by age-class and sex, and births and deaths on board, is the original of the published tables appended to the Colonial Land and Emigration Commission's annual reports. For an analysis of the quality of this and other sources, see Haines, '"Little Anne is very low"', Appendix 1.

13 Lower pay may have led to far less stringency on the part of surgeons on ships chartered by the new Queensland government after 1860, leading to a number of high-mortality ships. In addition to Woolcock, *Rights of Passage*, see Jennifer Harrison, 'A life on the ocean wave: Children on immigrant ships to colonial Queensland 1860–1900', *Journal of the Royal Historical Society of Queensland*, 16:6, May 1997, p. 264.

14 See the bibliography for a listing of emigrant tracts.

15 Charlotte Erickson, *Invisible Immigrants: the adaptation of English and Scottish immigrants in nineteenth-century America*, London, 1972.

16 Exceptions include Eric Richards, 'A voice from below: Benjamin Boyce in South Australia, 1839–1846', *Labour History*, November 1974, pp. 61–72.

17 David Fitzpatrick, *Oceans of Consolation: Personal Accounts of Irish Migration to Australia*, Cork, 1994.

18 Thirty-third General Report of the Colonial Land and Emigration Commission, Appendix 20, *BPP*, 1873 [c768], vol. XVIII, p. 81; Andrew Lemon and Marjorie Morgan, *Poor Souls They Perished: The Cataraqui — Australia's Worst Shipwreck*, Melbourne, 1986.

19 Frank Crowley, 'British migration to Australia', pp. 232–33; Don Charlwood, *Settlers Under Sail*, Melbourne, 1978, p. 4.

20 Simon Szreter, 'Rapid population growth and security: urbanisation and economic growth in Britain in the Nineteenth Century', *Common Security Forum: Centre for History and Economics*, unpublished paper, June 1995; idem, 'Economic growth, disruption, deprivation, disease, and death: On the importance of the politics of public health for development', *Population and Development Review*, 23:4, December 1997, pp. 693–728; Anthony Wohl, *Endangered Lives: Public Health in Victorian Britain*, London, 1983.

Sickness, Health and the Voyage in Context

1 Between 1831 and the early 1840s, emigrants were also introduced by private shipowners via various bounty schemes funded by colonial governments.

2 After 1860, each of the colonies appointed Agents General in London, who worked closely with the CLEC as they mobilised selected and nominated emigrants. Between 1872 and 1878, the Board of Trade (BT) gradually subsumed the CLEC's activities.

3 The average adult fare paid by the CLEC was £17 on its chartered vessels, but private steerage passengers paid far more in some years. John McDonald and Ralph Shlomowitz, 'Passenger fares on sailing vessels to Australia in the Nineteenth Century', *Explorations in Economic History*, 28, 1991, pp. 192–207.

4 Anne Hardy, *The Epidemic Streets: Infectious disease and the rise of preventive medicine, 1856–1900*, Oxford, 1993, pp. 268–69, 291.

5 Michael Sigsworth and Michael Worboys, 'The public's view of public health in mid-Victorian Britain, *Urban History*, 21:2 (October 1994), p. 248.

6 Sarah Brunskill to her parents, 7 December 1838, MLSA, D5203(L).

7 RI Woods, PA Watterson and JH Woodward, 'The causes of rapid infant mortality decline in England and Wales, 1861–1921. Part II, *Population Studies*, 43, 1989, p. 119.

8 P Atkins, 'Sophistication detected: or, the adulteration of the milk supply, 1850–1914',

Social History, 16, 1991, pp. 317–39; idem, 'White poison? The social consequences of milk consumption in London, 1850–1839', *Social History of Medicine*, 5, 1992, pp. 207–28; MW Beaver, 'Population, infant mortality and milk', *Population Studies*, 27, 1973, pp. 243–54.

9 Ian Buchanan, 'Infant feeding, sanitation and diarrhoea in colliery communities, 1880–1911', in DJ Oddy and DS Miller (eds), *Diet and Health in Modern Britain*, London, 1985, 148–77; D Dwork, *War is good for babies and other young children: a history of the infant and child welfare movement in England, 1898–1918*, London, 1987, pp. 44–51.

10 Graham Mooney, 'Did London pass the "sanitary test"? Seasonal infant mortality in London, 1870–1914', *Journal of Historical Geography*, 20:2, 1994, pp. 157–74.

11 Naomi Williams, 'Death in its season: class, environment and the mortality of infants in nineteenth-century Sheffield', *Social History of Medicine*, 5, 1992, pp. 85–94, especially pp. 87–90.

12 Anne Hardy, 'Rickets and Rest: Child-care, Diet and the Infectious Children's Diseases, 1850–1914', *Social History of Medicine*, 5:3, December 1992, pp. 389–412.

13 Hardy, 'Rickets and Rest', pp. 410–11.

14 Woods, Watterson and Woodward, 'The causes of rapid infant mortality'. Part II, pp. 121–32.

15 Bill Luckin and Graham Mooney, 'Urban history and historical epidemiology: the case of London, 1860–1920', *Urban History*, 24:2, 1997, p. 51. See also Smith, *The People's Health*, pp. 117–23.

16 Hardy, 'Rickets and Rest', Table 5, p. 393.

17 Oliver MacDonagh, *A Pattern of Government Growth 1800–60*, London, 1961.

18 Jacalyn Duffin, 'Census versus medical daybooks: a comparison of two sources on mortality in nineteenth-century Ontario', *Continuity and Change*, 12:2, 1997, p. 207.

19 MC Buer, *Health, Wealth, and Population in the Early Days of the Industrial Revolution*, London, 1926, 1968, p. 150.

20 Luckin and Mooney, 'Urban history and historical epidemiology', p. 40; Simon Szreter and Graham Mooney, 'Urbanization, mortality, and the standard of living debate: new estimates of the expectation of life at birth in nineteenth-century cities', *Economic History Review*, LI, 1, 1998, pp. 84–112.

21 Peter Razzell, 'The conundrum of eighteenth-century English population growth', *Social History of Medicine*, 11, 1998, 469–500; idem, *Essays in English population history*, London, 1994, especially pp. 202–206.

22 Bell and Millward, 'Public health expenditures and mortality', p. 241; Simon Szreter, 'The importance of social intervention in Britain's mortality decline c1850–1914': a reinterpretation of the role of public health', *Social History of Medicine*, 2, 1988.

23 Bell and Millward, 'Public health expenditures and mortality', p. 241.

24 Stephen J Kunitz, 'Premises, premises: comments on the compatibility of classifications', *Journal of the History of Medicine and Allied Sciences*, 54:2, April 1999, p. 240; Jacalyn Duffin, 'Census versus medical daybooks'.

25 Günter B Risse, 'Cause of death as a historical problem', *Continuity and Change*, 12:2, 1997, p. 183.

26 George C Alter and Ann G Carmichael, 'Classifying the dead: towards a history of the registration of causes of death', *Journal of the History of Medicine and Allied Sciences*, 54:2, April 1999, p. 125; Anne Hardy, 'Diagnosis, death, and diet: the case of London, 1750–1909', *Journal of Interdisciplinary History*, XVIII:3, Winter 1988, p. 393.

27 Registrar-General William Henry Archer, *Nosological Index or Guide to the Classification and Tabulation of the Various Causes of Death*, Melbourne, 1863.

28 Before the 1840s, a nosological synopsis, based on Cullen's classification, adopted from the naval service, was used on government-emigrant ships. See, for example, the surgeon's journal on the *Bussorah Merchant*, 1839, PRO, ADM 101/76, AJCP Reel 3213.

29 Smith, *The People's Health*, p. 67; see also Mooney, 'Still-births and the measurement of urban infant mortality rates'.

30 Haines, "'Little Anne is very low'", Tables 6, 8.
31 John Fitch Clark, diary on the *Nepaul*, 20 July 1852, in Moore, Garwood and Lutton (eds), *The Voyage Out*, p. 69.
32 Cited in Woolcock, *Rights of Passage*, p. 83.
33 S Walcott, CO Memo No. 5208/Domestic 1031, PRO, CO 384/116.
34 Harrison, 'A life on the ocean wave', p. 264.
35 Woolock, *Rights of Passage*, p. 259.
36 S Walcott, CO Memo No. 5208/1877/Domestic 1031, PRO, CO 384/116.
37 Woolcock, *Rights of Passage*, p. 256. It is unclear whether these primigravidae infants were, in fact, the first live births of the mother concerned.
38 Shlomowitz and McDonald, 'Babies at risk', pp. 96–97.
39 McDonald and Shlomowitz, 'Mortality on immigrant voyages', pp. 88, 93.
40 Woolcock, *Rights of Passage*, pp. 260–69.
41 Haines, unpublished tables. 1436 births were recorded on the 323 voyages to SA between 1848 and 1885. Of those, 151 died, a loss rate of 10.5 per cent. See also Table 5.
42 Woolcock, *Rights of Passage*, p. 262.
43 Haines, unpublished tables.
44 Irvine Loudon, 'The measurement of maternal mortality', *Journal of the History of Medicine and Allied Sciences*, 54:2, April 1999, pp. 312–29; idem, 'Maternal mortality: Definition and secular trends in England and Wales, 1850–1970', in Kenneth Kiple (ed.), *The Cambridge World History of Human Disease*, Cambridge, 1993, p. 214.
45 Christine McCabe, 'Strife on the ocean waves', *Weekend Australian*, 2–3 November 2002, Travel Extra, p. 7.
46 Surgeon's report on the *Sir Edward Parry*, 25 March 1854, SRSA, GRG 35/48/1854/7.
47 Haines, "'Little Anne is very low'", Appendix V, Groups 6 and 21, pp. 3, 7.
48 Naomi Williams and Graham Mooney, 'Infant mortality in an "Age of Great Cities": London and the English provincial cities compared, c1840–1910', *Continuity and Change*, 9:2, 1994, p. 199.
49 Millward and Bell, 'Infant mortality in Victorian Britain', pp. 705, 714–24.
50 S Walcott to GS Walters, South Australia's Emigration Agent in London, 30 May, 1863, in 'Families of Emigrants', *SAPP* 1863, no. 103, pp. 1–2.
51 Walcott to Walters, 11 June 1863, ibid.
52 Evidence of TWC Murdoch to SC on Emigrant Ships, *BPP*, 1854 (163) vol. XIII, Q 482–520, pp. 31–36.
53 CLEC to Merivale, 16 July 1855, enc. in no. 10, 'Papers relating to emigration to the Australian colonies', *BPP*, 1857 (144) vol. X sess. I, p. 80.
54 Immigration Agent's Quarterly Report, *SAGG*, 25 January 1866, p. 99.
55 Seventh General Report of the Colonial Land and Emigration Commission, *BPP*, 1847 [809] vol. XXXIII, p. 2.
56 Eighth General Report of the Colonial Land and Emigration Commissioners, *BPP*, 1847–48 [961.II] vol. XXVI, p. 12.
57 See Haines, "'Little Anne is very low'", Tables 2, 3, 4, 9, 21. Of the 2 per cent of voyages recording over 20 deaths, three voyages recorded 21–25 deaths; four voyages recorded 26–30 deaths; and one voyage recorded over 31 deaths.

Life at Sea and at Home

1 Adults were allowed to take the tools of their trade, but total baggage was not to weigh more than half of one ton, or exceed 20 cubic or solid feet in measurement. Boxes were not to exceed ten cubic feet. The compulsory outfit need not be new, but was to be sufficiently robust to endure a long passage. Inspected for quantity and quality before

departure, it was to contain not less than the following items. For males: six shirts, six pairs each of stockings and shoes, and two complete suits of exterior clothing. Two or three serge shirts for men and extra flannel for women and children were also recommended. For females: six shifts, two flannel petticoats, six pairs of stockings, two pairs of shoes, and two gowns. Sheets, towels and soap were also to be included in the kit, 'the larger the stock of Clothing the better for health and comfort during the voyage', suitable for very hot and very cold climates. Emigrants with insufficient or poor quality clothing were obliged to purchase new items, or be refused permission to embark. For a full review of the kit and clothing regulations, see Haines, *Emigration and the Labouring Poor*, p. 26, infra.

2   *The Dictionary of Medical and Surgical Knowledge and Complete Practical Guide in Health and Disease for Families, Emigrants, and Colonists*, London, 1864, p. 277.

3   Simon's First Report as Medical Officer of Health, 1849, cited in Anthony Wohl, *Endangered Lives: Public Health in Victorian Britain*, Methuen, 1983, p. 89. This is an excellent text for comparison with life at sea, especially Chapter Four, 'The Valleys of the Shadow of Death'.

4   Wohl, *Endangered Lives*, pp. 83–86.

5   Wohl, *Endangered Lives*, p. 83.

The 1820s and 1830s

1   James Dixon, *Narrative of a voyage to New South Wales and Van Diemen's Land in the ship Skelton during the year 1820*, Edinburgh, 1822 (facsimile edition, Melanie Publications, Hobart, n.d.)

2   'Letter written on the voyage to South Australia of George and Sarah Norman Brunskill to her parents [William and Mary Apsey] in Ely, Cambridgeshire, 1838/39', typed transcript, MLSA, D5203(L); 'Port Adelaide Manifest Book, vol. 1, Feb. 1838–Sept. 1839, p. 177, in SRSA, GRG 41/18.

3   Jill Statton (ed.), *Biographical Index of South Australians, 1836–1839*, Adelaide, 1986.

4   George Burder, *Village Sermons*, London, 1798, 7 volumes, reprinted until 1849.

5   'Statement of the system adopted for the moral government of male and female Emigrants aboard the 'Sarah', on the voyage from London to Hobart Town, 1834–5', handwritten, and signed 24 February 1835, enclosed in William Ronald Papers, *La Trobe Collection*, MS 1847-97, Box 1811/5.

6   Letter from the London Emigration Commission to Dr William Ronald, 26 April 1836, in William Ronald Papers, ibid.

7   Ibid.

8   Letter from Ellen Moger to her parents, dated Gouger Street, Adelaide, 28 January 1840, MLSA, D6249(L). According to official records, the ship departed London on 26 August and arrived on 19 December 1839. The baby was named Emma. I wish to thank the family of Vernon M Cross, who donated his great-grandmother's letter to the Mortlock Library of South Australiana. See correspondence attached to the file. See also RL Sexton, *Shipping Arrivals and Departures: South Australia*, Adelaide, 1990; Port Adelaide Manifest Book, vol. 2, August 1839–August 1840, p. 88, in SRSA GRG 41/18.

9   The term 'vaccination' — is derived from the Latin *vacca* (the cow), owing to the introduction by Edward Jenner in the late eighteenth century of inoculation with matter from cowpox pustules, rather than the former practice of variolation, whereby matter collected from active smallpox pustules was used. Immunisation against other diseases, including tuberculosis, was still over half a century away.

10 J Patchill, *Medical Journal of Emigrant Ship Crescent* 3 October 1839–12 February 1840, Mitchell Library, A3633 (CY 1117).

11 This anonymous surgeon's diary is housed as 'Surgeon Superintendent's log on the *Warrior*, Plymouth to South Australia, 16 November 1839 to 18 April 1840', Mitchell Library, B824 (CY479). Although Sexton, *Shipping arrivals and departures*, records his name as 'Dr B.A. Kent', as does the *Adelaide Chronicle* and the *South Australian Register*, the diary makes clear that Dr Kent was the cabin passenger whom he consulted. See also SRSA, GRG 24/1, letters 428, 445, 451, for 1840, for records pertaining to the *Warrior's* cargo. The ship departed on 16 November 1839, arriving on 18 April 1840.

12 Hugh Watson to his parents, 9 September 1839, MLSA, D6075(L). Parsons, *Migrant ships for South Australia*, p. 67. Hugh Watson gives the number of assisted immigrants on board as 400, though Parsons records 512.

13 Judith Raftery, 'Keeping healthy in nineteenth century Australia', *Health and History*, 1:4, 1999, p. 281; Sandra Holton, 'Social Medicine in Nineteenth Century South Australia', *Community Health Studies*, VII:2, p. 983; Philip Woodruff, *Two Million South Australians*, Adelaide, 1984, Chapter Three; Rob Linn, *Frail Flesh & Blood*, Adelaide, 1993; Ian Forbes, *From Colonial surgeon to health commission: the Government provision of health services in South Australia 1836–1995*, Adelaide, 1996.

The 1840s

1 WA Wellstead, 'Notes and information on the ship *Manlius*, which sailed from Greenock 21 October 1841 and arrived at Port Phillip on 14 February 1842', *La Trobe Collection*, MS 11473, typescript, Surrey Hills, n.d.

2 *Port Phillip Patriot*, 28 February 1842, cited in Wellstead, 'Notes and information on the ship *Manlius*'. See also *Glasgow Constitutional*, ibid.

3 Colin Holt, 'Family, kinship and friendship ties in assisted emigration from Cambridgeshire to Port Phillip District and Victoria, 1840–1867', unpublished MA thesis, La Trobe University, Melbourne, 1987, p. 42. See also Lemon and Morgan, *Poor Souls They Perished*.

4 Reminiscences of Richard Reid on the *William Nichol*, 1840, Greenock to Adelaide, MLSA, D3230/2(L). The ship's voyage began at Greenock, Scotland, and it picked up more emigrants in Dublin on 31 March 1840, arriving in Holdfast Bay on 7 July 1840.

5 'Remarks on a voyage from London to South Australia, April 1840, by James Bowley' on the *Fairlie*. I wish to thank Joyce Bayly of Victor Harbor for giving me a typescript copy of her ancestor's diary.

6 Basil Greenhill and Ann Giffard (eds), *Women Under Sail*, Newton Abbot, 1970, p. 86.

7 JS Prout, *Voyage from Plymouth to Sydney, Australia on board the* Royal Sovereign, Smith Elder, London, 1844.

8 Mary Anne Roberts to her sister Elizabeth Griffiths of Bristol, 16 May 1844, Mitchell Library, Ag 87/1.

9 Wohl, *Endangered Lives*; Lionel Rose, *Massacre of the Innocents: Infanticide in Great Britain 1800–1939*, London, 1986.

10 Caroline Dorling to her parents and parents-in-law, 1 August 1848, in 'Sarah and William Norman series', MLSA, D6806(L)/ D4836 L), typescript. The 'long letter' to which she refers is her husband's voyage diary, which was, perhaps, sent earlier.

11 Greenhill and Giffard (eds), *Women Under Sail*, p. 60.

12 Adelaide McLean and Harold Baker (eds), *The Voyage of the Atalanta, Plymouth to Adelaide, 1866: A diary by Edward Allchurch*, privately printed, n.d. I wish to thank Kate Shepherd of Adelaide for allowing me access to this privately printed transcript. The two-volume original can also be found at MLSA, D6253(L).

13 Notes attached to the manuscript 'Miss McRitchie's original letter', La Trobe Collection, MS 10233/MSB 185.

14 Diary of James Menzies on the *William Money* to Adelaide, 1848, La Trobe Collection, MS 10633/MSB 281, typescript, also lodged in MLSA, D6594(L).
15 Diary of Hugh May Wilson, from Granton, Scotland to Australia on the barque *Sarah*, 15 August to 9 December 1849, Mitchell Library, B1535 (CY 1024).
16 On depots, see Haines, *Emigration and the Labouring Poor*.

The 1850s (pages 166–195)

1 Lucy Hart to her mother, Mrs Lewis, Upper High Street, West Gate, Winchester, 1852, La Trobe Collection, MS 8838/Box 1659/2. I wish to thank Ruth Hill for information related to the Hart family and the well-travelled letter.
2 The Isle of Trinidade, in the Atlantic north-east of Rio de Janeiro, was described by another passenger as a 'large and very picturesque rock … upwards of 1200 feet high, uninhabited but with fresh water and green trees on it' (Emily Welch to her mother, Journal on board the *Belmont*, 14 April to 7 August 1853, Mitchell Library, B1114, also published in Pat Roberts (ed.), *Emily's Journal: the Welch Letters*, Adelaide, 1986). Some vessels sailed close to South America in an attempt to catch a fair southerly to carry them in a south-easterly direction, past Gough Island, south-west of Capetown.
3 Letter from Mary and James Marshall to her sister and brother in Chipping Warden, Warwickshire, 21 February 1851, Warwickshire County Record Office, CR 229/8/2, manuscript. The following transcription is by the author.
4 Thomas Marshall was her husband's brother, who followed Mary and James to Melbourne.
5 That is, her brother-in-law's intended wife.
6 Mary is probably referring to a letter from relatives in the town of Halford, Warwickshire, which is about 15 miles from Chipping Warden.
7 This is likely to be Aston le Walls, which is also about 15 miles from Halford, and about two miles from Chipping Warden. This triangle of three towns, all to the north-east and north-west of Banbury, one of Warwickshire's major towns, appears to represent the Marshalls' wider kinship network. Warwickshire was well represented as a county of origin among Australia's assisted-emigrants.
8 Mary Anne, to 'my dear Mama', November 1853, from Yass, Merseyside Maritime Museum, Folder 2, Isabella Hercus file.
9 Surgeon's report on the *Pestonjee Bomanjee*, SRSA, GRG 35/48/1854/21.
10 Diary of Malen Rumbelow from England to Australia June 13th 1854 to October 9th 1854. I wish to thank Ruth Moffatt, a descendant, for giving me a typescript of this diary, which can also be found at MLSA, D4878(L).
11 Summary report by Surgeon Superintendent Motherall, SRSA, GRG 35/48a/54/21.
12 Michael Page, *Victor Harbor: From pioneer port to seaside resort*, Victor Harbor, 1987, pp. 53–54.
13 Diary of Eliza Whicker, 1854, *Pestonjee Bomanjee*, 17 June to 7 October 1854, MLSA, D5886(L).
14 See William H Archer, *Nosological Index*.
15 Immigration Agent's Quarterly Report, *SAGG*, 1 February 1855.
16 Shipboard diary by TB Atkinson, voyage to Australia on board the *Hornet* 1857, La Trobe Collection, MS 12599, Box 3421/3.
17 Diary of Thomas Lyons on the *Invincible*, 5 October to 25 December 1856, La Trobe Collection, MS 10573/MSB 256.
18 Mary Anne to her mother, November 1853, Merseyside Maritime Museum, Folder 2, Isabella Hercus file, no ref., typescript.
19 Built by Isambard Kingdom Brunel, the SS *Great Britain* was famous for its fast runs to New York before it made its maiden voyage to Australia in 1852, the first of 32 voyages carrying emigrants to Sydney and Melbourne until 1876. It was said to have brought the ancestors of 250 000 Australians from the UK. See also Chapter 7, below.

The 1850s (pages 196–229)

1 Joseph Metcalf to his wife, Mary, from the ship *Anne Holzberg*, Gulf of St Vincent, Adelaide, 15 August 1853. I am indebted to Esma Cardinal, of Adelaide, for giving me copies of this and other letters written by her great-grandfather. Joseph Metcalf's 'Passenger contract ticket' was preserved with his letters. The ship was ultimately bound for Sydney, having sailed from Liverpool on 25 April 1853.

2 Joseph Metcalf to his wife, Mary.

3 Mr Sherlock, to the Committee of the Emigrants School Fund, 13 March 1849.

4 Ibid., 19 March 1849.

5 Private correspondence with Christopher Colyer, a descendant of George and Elizabeth Payne.

6 Richard Murphy (schoolmaster on the 672 ton *Blonde* bound for NSW with 179 adults and 47 children on its 105-day passage between 13 September and 27 December 1849, with Dr J Plomley superintending, who reported the deaths of two adults and one child), to the Secretary of the Emigrants' School Fund, 19 February 1850, reproduced in *Emigrants' Letters: Being a Collection of Recent Communications*, p. 123.

7 Janet McCalman, *Sex and Suffering: Women's Health and a Women's Hospital 1856–1996*, Melbourne, 1998.

8 See Brian Dickey, 'Why were there no Poor Laws in Australia?', *Journal of Policy History*, 4:2, 1992, pp. 111–33; idem, *Rations, Residences, Resources — a history of social welfare in South Australia since 1836*, Adelaide, 1986; idem, *No Charity There: A short history of social welfare in Australia*, Sydney, 1987.

9 See, for example, Despatch from Governor Young to Grey, 27 November 1848, SRSA, GRG 2/5/10.

10 Diary of Thomas Lyons on the *Invincible*, 5 October to 25 December 1856, typescript, La Trobe Collection, MS 10573/MSB 256. This was not an assisted emigrant vessel, and it appears to have landed in Melbourne.

11 Joseph Metcalf to his wife Mary, 17 September 1853.

12 Julia Cross, letter-diary to her family from the *James Fernie* on a voyage from Southampton to Moreton Bay, 1855. The originals are held in the Ely Museum, and I thank the Trustees of Ely Museum and its curator, Zara Matthews, for providing me with copies of the original correspondence, and giving me permission to cite them. Copies can also be found at the Oxley Library, M 1550.

13 William Wingate to his brother, Joseph Wingate, July 1855, MLSA, D4496/1-4(L).

14 Rev. JE Lindfield, grandson of Joseph Wingate, to the Agent General for South Australia, 29 August 1962, included in MLSA, D4496/1-4(L).

15 William Wingate to his brother Joseph, 20 October 1862, MLSA, D4496/1-4(L).

16 Eliza Pederick to Joseph Wingate, 27 January 1882, MLSA, D4496(L).

17 For an account of the Wiltshire Emigration Society and its emigrants, see Haines, *Emigration and the Labouring Poor*, pp. 24–25, 96–97, infra; Mark Baker, 'Aspects of the life of the Wiltshire agricultural labourer, c1850', in *Wiltshire Archaeological Magazine*, 74/75, 1981, pp. 162–69; idem, 'Some early Wiltshire emigrants to Australia', *The Hatcher Review*, 2:17, 1984, pp. 328–34; idem, 'A migration of Wiltshire agricultural labourers to Australia', *Journal of the Historical Society of South Australia*, 14, 1986, pp. 67–82.

18 At the time of emigration, Jacob and Charlotte Baker's children were aged: Timothy, 23, Mary Jane, 20, Fred, 18, Ann, 16, James, 14, Job, 10, Esther, 8, William, 5, and Henry, an infant. See records of the Wiltshire Emigration Society in Wiltshire Record Office, Savernake 9.

19 Lines composed by Jacob Baker, copied from the original by Miss Elizabeth Richards of Angastown. Recopied by his grand-daughter, IF Edson, MLSA, D5351 (Misc.)

20 Haines, *Emigration and the Labouring Poor*, pp. 119–20.

21 Jacob Baker's speech to an anti-free trade gathering of protectionist Wiltshire farmers, enti-

tled 'Swindon Protection Meeting: A Poor Man's Speech', was published in the *Devizes and Wiltshire Gazette*, 14 February 1850, after he was prevented from speaking at the meeting.

22 Thomas Dyke to the Editor, *Devizes and Wiltshire Gazette*, 22 July 1852.

23 Letter from Jacob Baker to his friends and neighbours, *Devizes and Wiltshire Gazette*, 22 July 1852; also printed in the *Scotsman*, 15 September 1852.

The 1860s

1 Robin Haines, *Children at sea: epidemics, ships, and doctors in the age of sail* (in preparation) discusses differential pay scales and the surgeons' performance.

2 Appendix 9, 27th General Report of the Emigration Commissioners (1866), Appendix 9, and previous reports.

3 Woolcock, *Rights of Passage*, p. 277.

4 Diary of William Kirk, from Queenstown to Brisbane, 11 April to 5 September 1862, Oxley Library, OM 89/18-18.

5 Diary written by Mary Anne Bedford for the benefit of her father, while on the voyage from England on the *Champion of the Seas*, La Trobe Collection, MS 10362/MSB 205.

6 Surgeon's report of arrival on the *Atalanta*, 28 April 1866, SRSA, GRG 35/48/10.

7 On the wreck of the *Marion*, see the Immigration Agent's quarterly report, 11 October 1851, in enc. in no. 11, 'Correspondence relating to emigration to the Australian Colonies, BPP, 1852–53, vol. XXXIV [1489], p. 101. See also Despatches from Governor H.E.F. Young, nos. 116 and 123, 25 August and 24 September 1851, ibid. For further excellent details on the *Marion*, its aftermath, and family record linkage concerning the descendants of its immigrants, see John Keynes (ed.), '*Marion Family' Periodical*, Adelaide, 2002 (www.users.on.net/esmarion) and in hard copy.

8 Surgeon's report of arrival on the *Atalanta*, 28 April 1866, SRSA, GRG 35/48/10.

9 'Arrival of the Atalanta with 394 government immigrants', *Advertiser*, 16 April 1866, cited in Adelaide McLean and Harold Baker, *The Voyage of the 'Atalanta': Plymouth to Adelaide 1866: A diary by Edward Allchurch*, privately published by Janet Lumsden and Harold Baker, Lakemba, 1978. I thank Kate Shepherd for giving access to this privately published edition of her forebear's diary.

10 McLean and Baker (eds), *The Voyage of the 'Atalanta'*.

11 Haines, '"Little Anne is very low:', Appendix III.

12 William Hogarth (1697–1764), whose flamboyant caricatures recorded English eighteenth-century urban life, and George Cruikshank (1792–1878), his successor.

13 'Diary of Rosamund Amelia D'Ouseley', housed in the Oxley Library, M 00828. I wish to thank the family of Ian Simmonds, who donated the diary to the Oxley Library. I wish also to thank the Hocken Library, Dunedin, where it is housed as Sea 041, for providing me with a typescript.

14 The *South Australian Register*, 19 August 1853.

15 Nicholson, *Log of Logs*, pp. 106–107, 212–14; the SS *Great Britain's* tonnage is given there as 3443 tons.

The Closing Decades

1 Crowley, 'British Migration to Australia: 1860–1914', p. 227.

2 Crowley, 'British Migration to Australia', p. 227.

3 Fitchett, *The Long Haul*, p. 8.

4 Bremer, *Home and Back*; Cooke, *Emigrant Ships*.

5 Crowley, 'British Migration to Australia', p. 234. Of the remainder, about 4 per cent travelled in first class and 6 per cent in second.

6 Crowley, 'British Migration to Australia', pp. 230–34. See also McDonald and

Shlomowitz, 'Passenger fares on sailing vessels to Australia in the nineteenth century'.
7 Another four 'short ships' (cargo ships carrying a few immigrants) also arrived.
8 ME McCallum, *The Dodson* Story, Introduction to the diary of George Dodson, privately printed, n.d., pp. 1–2. I am grateful to George Dodson's descendant, Andrea Alexander, for providing me with a copy of a transcript of the fragmentary diary, and commentary compiled by his grand-daughter.
9 Personal communication, Dr Andy Stein.
10 Surgeon Superintendent's Report, SRSA, GRG 35/48/1874.
11 Diary of GF Fletcher on the *Essex*, 1877–78, typescript, Oxley Library, M794, transcribed by Shirley Fletcher and typed by Joyce Bryant.
12 Diary of Dr HM Lightoller, on the *Scottish Bard*, 1878, cited in Don Charlwood, *The Long Farewell*, Burgewood Books, Melbourne, 1998, first published 1981, pp. 265–83.
13 Notes by Margaret Johnson, Frances Macadam Thomson's daughter, attached to 'Diary of Frances Thomson on board the *Selkirkshire*, 1882, on a voyage with emigrants from Glasgow to Rockhampton, Queensland, National Library of Australia, MS 1025.
14 Diary of Reuben Percival on the SS *Duke of Buckingham*, 3 December 1884 to 15 March 1885, Oxley Library, OM 92-150.
15 J Dixon to her brother Walter, 25 February 1884, Oxley Library, OM 89-11.
16 Diary of Alan Aitken, on board the SS *Chyebassa*, 1889, Oxley Library, OM 82-71.
17 'Forfoughten' may have been Allan Aitken's phonetic spelling of a local dialect word.
18 An excellent summary of the eruption can be found at George Pararas-Carayannis, *The Tsunami Page: The great explosion of the Kragatau Volcano ("Krakatoa") of August 26, 1883, in Indonesia*, http://www.geocities.com/CapeCanaveral/Lab/1029/Vocano1883Krakatoa.html.

1900–1950

1 Diary of Isaac Tarbitt, from Britain to Brisbane, 3 July 1912 to 6 August, 1912, typescript, Oxley Library, M1269/2.
2 The Orient Line's SS *Orama* was a triple-screwed, triple-expansion engine driving the wing shafts with a low-pressure turbine on the centre shaft. For excellent and accessible technical explanations concerning the transition from sail to steam, see Fitchett, *The Long Haul*, pp. 6–10, passim. The SS *Orama* was torpedoed off the Irish coast in 1917 and her replacement, SS *Orama (2)*, commissioned in 1924, was sunk by German warships in 1940. See Bremer, *Home and Back*, p. 122.
3 Further diaries of Isaac Tarbitt, 1913, Oxley Library, M1269/4/5.
4 'Candid chronicle: a Diary of a Scot by James Cameron', MLSA, D6831(L). For more information on the Australian Commonwealth Line, established in 1921, see Fitchett, *The Long Haul*, pp. 52–53.
5 Fitchett, *The Long Haul*, pp. 53. The *Moreton Bay* was built in 1921 and the other 'Bay Boats' were all launched by the end of 1922.
6 Diary of Mildred Alice Howell, on SS *Largs Bay*, England to Australia, 24 May to 2 July 1947, typescript, transcribed by her son, Mr Henry Howell, Oxley Library, M786.
7 Fitchett, *The Long Haul*, p. 56; Cooke, *Emigrant Ships*, Chapter Two.
8 Personal communication, Mrs E Britton, who arrived on the SS *Ranchi* in 1948.
9 Elizabeth Britton, *Memoirs*, 24, privately published, 1996.
10 Britton, *Memoirs*, 24.
11 Dated menu cards, for 'Children's Breakfast' and 'Children's Tea' aboard the SS *Ranchi*, in the possession of the author.
12 Personal communication, Mr Henry Howell.
13 Later Sir David Longland, Queensland's second Ombudsman, who became a family friend. Personal communication, Mr Henry Howell.

Bibliography

Manuscript sources

Official

ADM 101/1-75, PRO	Surgeons' logs and journals, convict ships, 1819–1856 (AJCP Reels 3187–3213).
ADM 101/76-79, PRO	Surgeons' logs and journals, emigrant ships, 1837–1853 (AJCP Reels 3213–3216).
CO 384/116, PRO	S Walcott, Memo no. 5208/Domestic 1031, 1877.
CO 386/76, PRO	Correspondence of the Emigration Commission.
CO 386/170-172, PRO	'Register of deaths on emigrant ships', in three volumes, 1847–54; 1854–60 and 1861–69; also on PRO Microfilms 6887–8.
CO 386/184, PRO	Manuscript summary of births and deaths at sea, 1854–60.
GRG 24/1, *SRSA*	Ships' papers: letters 428, 445, 451, for 1840
GRG 35/48, *SRSA*	Summary Reports of the Surgeon Superintendents.
GRG 41/18, *SRSA*	Port Adelaide Manifest Book, vol. 1, Feb. 1838–Sept. 1839; vol. 2, August 1839–August 1840.
GRG 78/49, *SRSA*	Adelaide Hospital Admissions Register.
P89/MRY1/533	Minutes of the Marylebone Board of Guardians, Greater London County Record Office.

Private: letters and diaries

CROWTHER LIBRARY OF TASMANIANA, STATE LIBRARY OF TASMANIA, HOBART

Diary of William Fordham, PQ 910.45.

ELY MUSEUM, ELY, UK

Julia Cross: Diary letter written on the *James Fernie* from Southampton to Moreton Bay, 1855. A copy is also housed in the Oxley Library at M1550.

HOCKEN LIBRARY, DUNEDIN, NZ

Rosamund Amelia D'Ouseley, Diary on the SS *Great Britain*, 1869 from Liverpool to Melbourne, Sea 041. A copy is also housed in the Oxley Library at M00828.

LA TROBE COLLECTION, STATE LIBRARY OF VICTORIA, MELBOURNE

Anonymous account of a voyage to Australia on board the *Digby* from Liverpool to Melbourne 1852–53, MS 9033/MSB 450.

TB Atkinson: Shipboard diary on the voyage to Australia on board the *Hornet* 1857, MS 12599, Box 3421/3.

Mary Anne Bedford: Diary on *The Champion of the Seas*, 1864, MS 10362/MSB 205.

Lucy Hart to her mother, 1851, MS 8838/Box 1659/2.

Thomas Lyons: Diary on the *Invincible*, 5 October to 25 December 1856, MS 10573/MSB 256.

Notes and information on the ship *Manlius*, which sailed from Greenock 21 October 1841 and arrived at Port Phillip on 14 February 1842, MS 11473, typescript, WA Wellstead, Surrey Hills, n.d.

James Menzies: Diary on the *William Money* to Adelaide, 1848, MS 10633/MSB 281, typescript, also lodged in MLSA, D6594(L).

William Ronald Papers, Voyage diary and reports on the *Sarah* from London to Hobart Town, 1834–5, handwritten, 24 February 1835, MS 1847-97, Box 1811/5.

James Cooper Stewart: Voyage diary, 27 September 1857, MS 12507, Box 3395/1.

Thomas Jones Vallance: Diary of Surgeon Superintendent of the *Apolline* to Melbourne, 1 July to 28 October 1852, MS 12619 Box 3445/3, Typescript.

MERSEYSIDE MARITIME MUSEUM, LIVERPOOL, UK

Mary Anne, to 'my dear Mama', November 1853, from Yass, Isabella Hercus file, Folder 2.

MITCHELL LIBRARY: STATE LIBRARY OF NEW SOUTH WALES, SYDNEY

Anonymous Surgeon Superintendent's log on the *Warrior*, Plymouth to South Australia, 16 November 1839 to 18 April 1840', B824 (CY479).

Dr Neil Campbell: Journal on the *King William*, 1842–43, A3234/43-91 (CY 1388).

Miss McRitchie's original letter, MS 10233/MSB 185.

J Patchill, *Medical Journal of Emigrant Ship Crescent* 3 October 1839–12 February 1840, A3633 (CY 1117).

Mary Anne Roberts to her sister Elizabeth Griffiths of Bristol, 16 May 1844, Ag 87/1.

William Usherwood's journal on board the *Beejapore* from Liverpool to Sydney, 12 October 1852 to 5 January 1853, B784 (CY 1117)

Emily Welch to her mother: Journal on board the *Belmont*, 14 April to 7 August 1853, B1114.

Hugh May Wilson: Diary on the barque *Sarah* from Granton, Scotland to Australia, 15 August to 9 December 1849, B1535 (CY 1024).

MORTLOCK LIBRARY OF SOUTH AUSTRALIANA, STATE LIBRARY OF SOUTH AUSTRALIA, ADELAIDE

Lines composed by Jacob Baker, D5351 (Misc.)

George and Sarah Brunskill, 'Letter written on the Voyage to South Australia' to her parents in Ely, Cambridgeshire, 1838–39, 27 November 1838, D5203(L), typed transcript.

James Cameron: Candid chronicle, a Diary of a Scot, D6831(L).

Clark family memoirs, PRG 389/9.
Caroline Dorling to her parents and parents-in-law, 1 August 1848, in 'Sarah and William Norman series', D6806(L)/ D4836 (L), typescript.
Ellen Moger to her parents, 28 January 1840, D6129(L), typed transcript.
Richard Reid: Reminiscences on *William Nichol*, 1840, Greenock to Adelaide, D3230/2(L).
Hugh Watson to his parents, 9 September 1839, MLSA, D6075(L).
Eliza Whicker: Diary on the *Pestonjee Bomanjee* 18 June to 7 October 1854, D5886(L).
William Wingate correspondence, MLSA, D4496/1-4(L).

NATIONAL LIBRARY OF AUSTRALIA, CANBERRA

Frances Thomson: Diary on board the *Selkirkshire*, 1882, with emigrants from Glasgow to Rockhampton, Queensland, MS 1025.

OXLEY LIBRARY, STATE LIBRARY OF QUEENSLAND, BRISBANE

Anonymous diary, M1265.
Allen Aitken: Diary on the SS *Chyebassa*, 1887, OM 82-71.
J Dixon to her brother Walter, 25 February 1884, OM 89-11.
GF Fletcher: Diary on the *Essex*, 1877–78, typescript, M794.
Mildred Alice Howell: Diary on the SS *Largs Bay*, England to Australia, 24 May to 2 July 1947, M786.
William Kirk, Voyage diary from Queenstown to Brisbane, 11 April to 5 September 1862, OM 89/18-18.
Reuben Percival: Diary on the SS *Duke of Buckingham*, 3 December 1884 to 15 March 1885, OM 92-150.
Isaac Tarbitt: Diary from Britain to Brisbane, 3 July 1912 to 6 August 1912, typescript, M1269/2.
———: Further diaries of 1913, M1269/4/5

PRIVATE HANDS

Edward Allchurch: *The Voyage of the Atalanta, Plymouth to Adelaide, 1866: A diary by Edward Allchurch*, transcribed and edited by Adelaide McLean & Harold Baker (eds), privately printed, n.d.
James Bowley: Remarks on a voyage from London to South Australia on the *Fairlie*, April 1840.
Elizabeth Britton: *Memoirs*, privately printed, 1996.
George Dodson: Diary on the *Lady Jocelyn*, 1875, transcribed by ME McCallum (ed.), *The Dodson Story*, privately printed, n.d.
Joseph Metcalf to his wife, Mary, from the ship *Anne Holzberg*, Gulf of St Vincent, Adelaide, 15 August 1853.
Malen Rumbelow: Diary of from England to Australia June 13th 1854 to October 9th 1854.

WARWICKSHIRE COUNTY RECORD OFFICE, WARWICK, UK

Mary and James Marshall: Letter to her sister and brother in Chipping Warden, Warwickshire, 21 February 1851, CR 229/8/2.

WILTSHIRE RECORD OFFICE, DEVIZES, UK

Wiltshire Emigration Society Records, Savernake 9.

Printed sources

Official

Board of Trade report on Emigrant Accommodation on board Atlantic steamships, *BPP*, 1881 [c2995], vol. LXXXII

Correspondence relating to emigration to the Australian colonies, *BPP*, various.

33 General Reports and appendices of the Colonial Land and Emigration Commission, *BPP*, various, 1840–72.

Historical Records of Australia.

Immigration Agents' Annual Reports, NSW, *Vic*, *SA*, *V&P*, various.

'Papers relative to emigration to the Australian Colonies', *BPP*, various.

Report from the Health Officer of Port Jackson for the Year 1853, 1 June 1854, *NSWPP*, 1854, vol. 2.

SC on Colonial Estimates, *SAPP*, 1855–56, no. 158.

SC on Colonization from Ireland, *BPP*, 1847 (737) vol. VI.

SC on Emigrant Ships, *BPP*, 1854 (163), vol. XIII.

SC of the House of Assembly on Immigration, *SAPP*, 1877, no. 102.

SC on Immigration, NSW, *NSWPP*, 1854, vol. 2.

SC on Transportation, *BPP*, 1812 (341), vol. II.

SC on Transportation, *BPP*, 1837 (15), vol. XIX.

South Australian Government Gazette.

Third Report of the Central Board of Health, *SAPP*, 1877, no. 88.

Contemporary books, articles and newspapers

Adelaide Chronicle.

Adelaide Observer.

Archer, WH, *Nosological Index or Guide to the classification and tabulation of the various causes of death; compiled principally for the use of the Registrar-General's Department; with Instructions to Deputy Registrars by the Registrar-General of Victoria*, 1862–63 (facsimile ed. Marjorie Morgan, 1987).

British Medical Journal.

Correspondence Relating to Her Majesty's Emigrant ship Hercules, Francis & John Rivington, London, c1854.

Devizes and Wiltshire Gazette.

The Dictionary of Medical and Surgical Knowledge and Complete Practical Guide in Health and Disease for Families, Emigrants, and Colonists, Houlston & Wright, London, 1864.

Dixon, James, *Narrative of a voyage to New South Wales and Van Diemen's Land in the ship Skelton during the year 1820*, Edinburgh, 1822 (Facsimile edition, Melanie Publications, Hobart, n.d.)

The Emigrant and Colonial Gazette, London.

Emigrant Tracts, vols 1 and II, SPCK, London, 1850–51.

The Emigrants' Guide containing practical and authentic information, and copies of original and unpublished letters from emigrants, to their friends in the counties of Mayo, Galway and Roscommon, John Hoban, Westport, 1832.

Emigrants' Letters: Being a collection of recent communications from settlers in the British Colonies, Committee of the Emigrants' School Fund, London, 1850.

Emigrants' Letters from the British Colonies: Letters from Schoolmasters on Board Emigrant Ships, Trelawney Saunders, London, 1850.

Emigration from the Highlands and Islands, Trelawney Saunders, London, 1852.

KE F[erguson], *Hints to Matrons*, Emigrant Tract 3, SPCK, London, 1850.

——, *Parting Words for Emigrant Parents: Emigrant Tracts:* Tract no. 2, SPCK, London, 1850.

Kingston, WHG, *How to Emigrate; or, The British Colonists: a Tale for all classes with an appendix, forming a complete manual for intending colonists and for those who may wish to assist them,* Groombridge & Sons, London, 1850.

——, *The Emigrant Voyagers' Manual: Preparations for the Voyage,* Trelawney Saunders, London, 1850.

Prout, JS, *Voyage from Plymouth to Sydney, Australia on board the* Royal Sovereign, Smith Elder, London, 1844.

The *Scotsman*

Scrope, Poulett, *Extracts from letters from Poor Persons (ex Corsley, Wilts),* London, 1832.

Sockett, T, *Emigration. A Letter to a Member of Parliament Containing a Statement of the Methods Pursued by the Petworth Committee,* Petworth, 1834.

South Australian Register

Books, articles, newspapers and theses, 1900–2003

Adams, Annmarie, *Architecture in the Family Way: Doctors, Houses, and Women, 1870–1900,* McGill-Queen's University Press, Montreal, 1996.

Alter, George C & Carmichael, Ann G, 'Classifying the dead: towards a history of the registration of causes of death', *Journal of the History of Medicine and Allied Sciences,* 54:2, April 1999, pp. 114–32.

——, 'Reflections on the causes of death', *Continuity and Change,* 12:2, 1997, pp. 169–74.

Alter, George & Carmichael, Ann, 'Studying causes of death in the past: Problems and models', *Historical Methods,* 29:2, Spring 1997, pp. 44–48.

Arrizabalaga, Jon, 'Medical causes of death in preindustrial Europe: Some historiographical considerations', *Journal of the History of Medicine and Allied Sciences,* 54:2, April 1999, pp. 241–60.

Atkins, P, 'Sophistication detected: or, the adulteration of the milk supply, 1850–1914', *Social History,* 16, 1991, pp. 317–39.

——, 'White poison? The social consequences of milk consumption in London, 1850–1839', *Social History of Medicine,* 5, 1992, pp. 207–28.

Baker, Mark, 'A migration of Wiltshire agricultural labourers to Australia', *Journal of the Historical Society of South Australia,* 14, 1986, pp. 67–82.

——, 'Aspects of the life of the Wiltshire agricultural labourer, c1850', in *Wiltshire Archaeological Magazine,* 74/75, 1981, pp. 162–69; idem, 'Some early Wiltshire emigrants to Australia', *The Hatcher Review,* 2:17, 1984, pp. 328–34.

Barritt, Emma Rose, '"Strong in health and spirits?": European morbidity in colonial Adelaide (1836–1846)', BA (Hons) Thesis, Flinders University, 2002.

Beaver, MW, 'Population, infant mortality and milk', *Population Studies,* 27, 1973, pp. 243–54.

Bell, Frances & Millward, Robert, 'Public health expenditures and mortality in England and Wales, 1870–1914', *Continuity and Change,* 13:2, 1998, pp. 221–49.

Braydon, Simon & Songhurst, Robert (eds), *The Diary of Joseph Sam: An emigrant in the "Northumberland" 1874,* HMSO, London, 1982.

Bremer, Stuart, *Home and Back: Australia's golden era of passenger ships,* Dreamweaver Books, Sydney, 1984.

Broeze, FJA, 'The Cost of Distance: Shipping and the Early Australian Economy, 1788–1850', *Economic History Review,* 28, 1975, pp. 582–97.

Bryder, Linda, *Below the Magic Mountain: A social history of tuberculosis in Britain,* Oxford University Press, 1988.

Buchanan, Ian, 'Infant feeding, sanitation and diarrhoea in colliery communities, 1880–1911', in DJ Oddy & DS Miller (eds), *Diet and Health in Modern Britain*, Croom Helm, London, 1985, pp. 148–77.

Buer, MC, *Health, Wealth, and Population in the Early Days of the Industrial Revolution* (1926, reprinted Routledge & Kegan Paul, London, 1968).

Burnett, John, *Plenty and Want: A social history of food in England from 1815 to the Present Day*, London, 1985.

Bushman, Richard L & Bushman, Claudia L, 'The Early History of Cleanliness in America', *Journal of American History*, 74, March 1988, pp. 1213–38.

Cannon, Michael, *Perilous Voyages to the New Land: Experiences of Australian pioneer families on the high seas*, Loch Haven Books, Mornington, 1996.

Carter, K Codell, 'Causes of disease and causes of death', *Continuity and Change*, 12:2, 1997, pp. 189–98.

Cartwright, FF, *A Social History of Medicine*, Longman, London, 1977.

Charlwood, Don, *The Long Farewell*, Allen Lane, Ringwood, 1981 (reprinted by Burgewood Books, Warrandyte, 1998).

——, *Settlers Under Sail*, Department of the Premier, Melbourne, 1978.

Cole, Rosemary & Corner, Gwen, *The Hamlyn Family; the Kay Family*, Lutheran Publishing House, Adelaide, 1977.

Coleman, Terry, *Passage to America: A History of Emigrants from Great Britain and Ireland to America in the Mid-Nineteenth Century*, London, 1972.

Condran, Gretchen A & Cheney, Rose A, 'Mortality trends in Philadelphia: Age- And Cause-Specific death rates 1870–1930', *Demography*, 19:1, February 1982, pp. 97–123.

——, 'What *Fatal Years* tells us that we did not already know', *Bulletin of the History of Medicine*, 68, pp. 95–104.

——, Henry Williams, & Cheney, Rose A, 'The decline of mortality in Philadelphia from 1870–1930: The role of municipal services', *The Pennsylvania Magazine*, CVIII:2, April 1984, pp. 153–77.

Connors, Libby, 'The politics of ethnicity: Irish orphan girls at Moreton Bay, in Rebecca Pelan (ed.), *Irish Australian Studies*, 7, Crossing Press, Sydney, 1994.

Cooke, Anthony, *Emigrant Ships: The vessels which carried migrants across the world, 1946–1972*, Carmania Press, London, n.d.

Crowley, FK, 'British migration to Australia: 1860–1914: A descriptive, analytical and statistical account of the immigration from the United Kingdom' unpublished D. Phil. thesis, Oxford University, 1951.

——, 'The British contribution to the Australian Population: 1860–1919', *University Studies in History and Economics*, July, 1954, pp. 55–88.

——, 'The British contribution to the Australian population: 1860–1919, *University Studies in History and Economics*, July 1954, pp. 55–88.

Cumpston, JHL & McCallum, F, *The History of the Intestinal Infections (and Typhus Fever) in Australia 1788–1923*, Commonwealth of Australia, Melbourne, 1927.

Curtin, PD, *Death by Migration: Europe's Encounter with the tropical world in the nineteenth century*, Cambridge University Press, Cambridge, 1989.

DeLacy, Margaret, 'Nosology, mortality, and disease theory in the eighteenth century', *Journal of the History of Medicine and Allied Sciences*, 54:2, April 1999, pp. 261–84.

Dickey, Brian, 'Why were there no Poor Laws in Australia?', *Journal of Policy History*, 4:2, 1992, pp. 111–33.

——, *No Charity There: A short history of social welfare in Australia*, Allen & Unwin, Sydney, 1987.

——, *Rations, Residences, Resources — a history of social welfare in South Australia since 1836*, Wakefield Press, Adelaide, 1986.

Dobson, MJ, *Contours of Death and Disease in Early Modern England*, Cambridge University Press, Cambridge, 1996.

Duffin, Jacalyn, 'Census versus medical daybooks: a comparison of two sources on mortality in nineteenth-century Ontario', *Continuity and Change*, 12:2, 1997, pp. 199–219.

Dwork, D, *War is good for babies and other young children: a history of the infant and child welfare movement in England, 1898–1918*, London, 1987.

Erickson, Charlotte, *Invisible Immigrants: the adaptation of English and Scottish immigrants in nineteenth-century America*, Weidenfeld & Nicolson, London, 1972.

Fildes, Valerie, *Breasts, Bottles, and Babies: A history of infant feeding*, Edinburgh University Press, 1986.

Fitchett, TK, *The Long Haul: Ships on the England-Australia run*, Rigby, Adelaide, 1980.

Fitzpatrick, David, *Oceans of Consolation: Personal Accounts of Irish Migration to Australia*, Cork University Press, 1994.

Floud, R, Wachter K & Gregory, A, *Height, Health and History: nutritional status in the United Kingdom, 1750–1980*, Cambridge University Press, Cambridge, 1990.

Foley, Jean Duncan, *In Quarantine: A History of Sydney's Quarantine Station 1828–1984*, Kangaroo Press, Sydney, 1995.

Forbes, Ian, *From Colonial surgeon to health commission: the Government provision of health services in South Australia 1836–1995*, Openbook, Adelaide, 1996.

Frost, Lucy, *No Place for a Nervous Lady: voices from the Australian Bush*, McPhee Gribble, Melbourne, 1984.

George, Dorothy, *London Life in the Eighteenth Century*, London, 1925.

Greenhill, Basil & Giffard, Ann (eds), *Women Under Sail*, David & Charles, Newton Abbot, 1970.

Haines, Robin, *Emigration and the Labouring Poor: Australian recruitment in Britain and Ireland 1831–1860*, Macmillan, London, 1997.

——, '"It is with plasure I take my pen in hand": Opportunity, skill, and colonial Australia's immigrant workers', in David Palmer, Ross Shanahan & Martin Shanahan (eds), *Australian Labour History Reconsidered*, Australian Academic Press, Adelaide, 1999, pp. 176–90.

——, '"Little Anne is very low, Harry is in a parlous way, a great many children has death on their faces": mortality and its causes on voyages to colonial South Australia, 1848–1855', Flinders University Working Paper, 2001.

——, '"Parrot pie is very good": immigrant diets in nineteenth century Australia', *Proceedings of the Nutrition Society of Australia*, vol. 22, December 1998, pp. 7–15.

——, '"The idle and the drunken won't do there": Poverty, the new poor law and nineteenth century government-assisted emigration to Australia from the United Kingdom', *Australian Historical Studies*, 28:108, April 1997, pp. 1–21.

——, 'Indigent misfits or shrewd operators? Government-assisted emigrants from the United Kingdom to Australia, 1831–1860', *Population Studies*, 48, 1994, pp. 223–47.

——, 'Maritime surgeons and the health of emigrants on government-assisted voyages to South Australia in the nineteenth century', in Judith Raftery (ed.), *Then and Now: Collected Papers of the Seventh Biennial Conference of the Australian Society for the History of Medicine*, ASHM, Melbourne, 2002, CD-ROM.

——, 'Medical superintendence and child health on voyages to South Australia in the nineteenth century', *Health and History*, 3:2, 2001, pp. 1–29.

——, 'Nineteenth century government assisted immigrants from the United Kingdom to Australia: Schemes, regulations and arrivals, 1831–1900 and some vital statistics 1834–1860, *Flinders University Occasional Papers in Economic History*, 1995.

——, '"The priest made a bother about it": the travails of "that unhappy sisterhood" bound for colonial Australia', in Trevor McClaughlin (ed.), *Irish Women in Colonial Australia*, Allen & Unwin, Sydney, 1998, pp. 22–42.

——, 'Therapeutic emigration: some South Australian and Victorian experiences', *Journal of Australian Studies*, 33, June 1992, pp. 76–90.

——, 'Workhouse to gangplank: mobilising Irish pauper women and girls bound for Australia in the mid-nineteenth century', in Richard Davis, et al. (eds), *Irish Australian Studies*, 8, Crossing Press, Sydney, 1996.

Haines, Robin & McDonald, John, 'Skills, origins and literacy: a comparison of bounty immigrants into New South Wales in 1841 with the convicts resident in the colony', *Australian Economic History Review*, 42:2, 2002, pp. 132–59.

Haines, Robin & Shlomowitz, Ralph, 'Causes of death and their time-patterning over voyages carrying British emigrants to South Australia, 1848–1885', *Social History of Medicine* 16:2, August 2003.

——, 'Explaining the decline in mortality in the eighteenth-century British slave trade', *Economic History Review*, LIII:2, 2000, pp. 262–83.

——, 'Explaining the modern mortality decline: What can we learn from sea voyages?', *Social History of Medicine*, 11:1, April 1998, pp. 15–48.

——, 'Immigration from the United Kingdom to Colonial Australia: A statistical analysis', *Journal of Australian Studies*, 34, September 1992, pp. 43–52.

——, 'Maritime mortality revisited', *International Journal of Maritime History*, June, 1996, pp. 133–72.

——, 'Mortality and the Transatlantic Slave trade: a re-evaluation', unpublished paper, Flinders University, 2000.

——, 'Nineteenth-century government-assisted and total immigration from the United Kingdom to Australia: Quinquennial estimates by colony', *Journal of the Australian Population Association*, 8:1, 1991, pp. 50–61.

Haines, Robin, Ralph Shlomowitz & McDonald, John, 'Mortality and voyage length in the middle passage revisited', *Explorations in Economic History*, 38:4, October 2001, pp. 503–33.

Hammerton, James, *Emigrant Gentlewomen: Genteel poverty and female emigration 1830–1914*, Croom Helm, London, 1979.

Hardy, Anne, '"Death is the cure of all diseases": Using the General Register Office Cause of Death statistics for 1837–1920', *Social History of Medicine*, 7:3, 1994, pp. 472–92.

——, 'Diagnosis, death, and diet: the case of London, 1750–1909', *Journal of Interdisciplinary History*, XVIII:3, Winter 1988, pp. 387–401.

——, *The Epidemic Streets: Infectious disease and the rise of preventive medicine, 1856–1900*, Clarendon Press, Oxford, 1993.

——, 'Rickets and Rest: Child-care, Diet and the Infectious Children's Diseases, 1850–1914', *Social History of Medicine*, 5:3, December 1992, pp. 389–412.

Hargreaves, RP & Hearn, TJ (eds), *Letters from Otago 1848–1849*, Hocken Library, Dunedin, 1978.

Harrison, Jennifer, 'A life on the ocean wave: children on immigrant ships to colonial Queensland 1866–1900', *Journal of the Royal Historical Society of Queensland*, 16:6, May 1997, pp. 259–71.

Hassam, Andrew, *No Privacy for Writing: Shipboard diaries 1852–1879*, Melbourne University Press, 1995.

——, *Sailing to Australia: Shipboard diaries by nineteenth-century British immigrants*, Melbourne University Press, 1995.

Hennock, EP, 'Vaccination policy against smallpox, 1835–1914: a comparison of England with Prussia and Imperial Germany', *Social History of Medicine*, 11:1, April 1998, pp. 49–71.

Hollett, David, *Passage to the New World: Packet ships and Irish famine emigrants 1845–1851*, PM Heaton Publishing, Abergavenny, 1995.

Holt, Colin, 'Family, kinship and friendship ties in assisted emigration from Cambridgeshire to Port Phillip District and Victoria, 1840–1867', unpublished MA thesis, La Trobe University, Melbourne, 1987.

Holton, Sandra, 'Social Medicine in Nineteenth Century South Australia', *Community Health Studies*, VII:2, 983, pp. 121–35.

Hoy, Suellen, *Chasing Dirt: The American Pursuit of Cleanliness*, Oxford University Press, New York, 1995.

Jalland, Pat, *Australian Ways of Death: A social and cultural history 1840–1918*, Oxford University Press, Melbourne, 2001.

Kennedy, Líam, Ell, Paul S, Crawford, EM & Clarkson, LA, *Mapping the Great Irish Famine: a survey of the Famine decades*, Four Courts Press, Dublin, 1999.

Keynes, John (ed.), '*Marion Family' Periodical*, Adelaide, 2002.

Kiple, Kenneth F, (ed.), *The Cambridge World History of Human Disease*, Cambridge University Press, 1993.

Klein, Herbert S, Engerman, Stanley, Haines, Robin & Shlomowitz, Ralph, 'Transoceanic mortality: The slave trade in comparative perspective', *William and Mary Quarterly*, 3rd series, LVIII, 2001, pp. 93–117.

Kunitz, Stephen J, 'Premises, premises: comments on the compatibility of classifications', *Journal of the History of Medicine and Allied Sciences*, 54:2, April 1999, pp. 226–40.

Landers, John, *Death and the Metropolis: studies in the demographic history of London, 1670–1830*, Cambridge University Press, Cambridge, 1993.

Lemon, Andrew & Morgan, Marjorie, *Poor Souls They Perished: The Cataraqui — Australia's Worst Shipwreck*, Melbourne, 1986.

Linn, Rob, *Frail Flesh & Blood: The health of South Australians since earliest times*, The Queen Elizabeth Hospital Research Foundation, Woodville, 1993.

Lord, Richard, *Impression Bay: Convict probation station to civilian quarantine station, being the story of the fever immigrant ship "Persian" … in 1857*, Richard Lord & Partners, Taroona, 1992.

Loudon, Irvine, 'Maternal mortality: Definition and secular trends in England and Wales, 1850–1970', in Kenneth Kiple (ed.), *The Cambridge World History of Human Disease*, Cambridge University Press, 1993.

——, 'The measurement of maternal mortality', *Journal of the History of Medicine and Allied Sciences*, 54:2, April 1999, pp. 312–29.

Lubbock, Basil, *The Best of Sail*, Patrick Stephens, Cambridge, 1975.

Luckin, Bill, 'Death and survival in the city: approaches to the history of disease', *Urban History Yearbook*, 1980, pp. 53–61.

——, 'Evaluating the sanitary revolution: typhus and typhoid in London, 1851–1900', in Robert Woods & John Woodward (eds), *Urban Disease and Mortality in Nineteenth-Century England*, Batsford Academic Press, London, 1984.

—— & Mooney, Graham, 'Urban history and historical epidemiology: the case of London, 1860–1920', *Urban History*, 24:2, 1997, pp. 37–55.

Ludlow, Peter, 'Quarantine as incarceration', in John Pearn & Peggy Carter (eds), *Islands of Incarceration*, Brisbane, 1995, pp. 93–109.

MacDonagh, Oliver, *Early Victorian Government, 1830–70*, Weidenfeld & Nicolson, London, 1977.

——, 'The nineteenth-century revolution in government: a reappraisal', *Historical Journal*, 1:1, 1958, pp. 52–67.

——, *A Pattern of Government Growth 1800–60*, MacGibbon Kee, London, 1961.

McCalman, Janet, *Sex and Suffering: Women's Health and a Women's Hospital 1856–1996*, Melbourne University Press, Melbourne, 1998.

McClaughlin, Trevor, *Barefoot and Pregnant? Irish famine orphans in Australia*, vols 1 and 2, Genealogical Society of Victoria, 1991 and 2001.

——, 'Exploited and abused: Irish orphan girls', in Rebecca Pelan (ed.), *Irish Australian Studies*, 7, Crossing Press, Sydney, 1994.

——, 'Vulnerable Irish Women in mid-to-late nineteenth century Australia', in Trevor McClaughlin (ed.), *Irish Women in Colonial Australia*, Allen & Unwin, Sydney, 1998.

McDonald, John & Richards, Eric, 'Workers for Australia: A profile of British and Irish migrants assisted to New South Wales in 1841', *Journal of the Australian Population Association*, 15, 1998, pp. 1–33;

McDonald, John & Shlomowitz, Ralph, 'Mortality on convict voyages to Australia, 1788–1868', *Social Science History*, 13:3, pp. 285–313.

——, 'Mortality on immigrant voyages to Australia in the 19th century', *Explorations in Economic History*, 27, 1990, pp. 84–113.

——, 'Passenger fares on sailing vessels to Australia in the Nineteenth Century', *Explorations in Economic History*, 28, 1991, pp. 192–207.

Meckel, Richard A, 'Judging Progressive-Era Infant Welfare in Light of *Fatal Years* — and Vice Versa', *Bulletin of the History of Medicine*, 68, 1994, pp. 105–12.

Mein Smith, Philippa, *Mothers and King Baby: Infant mortality, survival and welfare in an Imperial world — Australia 1880–1950*, London, Macmillan, 1997.

——, Philippa & Frost, Lionel, 'Suburbia and Infant death in late nineteenth- and early twentieth-century Adelaide', *Urban History*, 21:2, October 1994, pp. 252–72.

Millward, Robert & Bell, Frances, 'Infant mortality in Victorian Britain: the mother as medium', *Economic History Review*, LIV:4, November 2001, pp. 699–733.

Mooney, Graham, 'Did London pass the "sanitary test"? Seasonal infant mortality in London, 1870–1914', *Journal of Historical Geography*, 20:2, 1994, pp. 157–74.

Moore, Bryce, Garwood, Helen & Lutton, Nancy (eds), *The Voyage Out: 100 years of sea travel to Australia*, Fremantle Arts Press, 1991.

Nicholson, Ian, *Log of Logs*, Roebuck, n.d.

Oxley, Deborah *Convict Maids: the forced migration of convict women to Australia*, Cambridge University Press, Melbourne, 1996.

——, & Richards, Eric, 'Convict women and assisted female immigrants compared: 1841 — a turning point?', in E Richards (ed.), *Visible Women: Female Immigrants to Colonial Australia*, Highland Press, Canberra, 1995.

Pararas-Carayannis, George, *The Tsunami Page: The great explosion of the Krakatau Volcano ("Krakatoa") of August 26, 1883, in Indonesia*, http://www.geocities.com/CapeCanaveral/Lab/1029/Vocano1883Krakatoa.html

Parsons, Ronald, *Migrant Ships for South Australia 1836–1860*, Gould Books, Gumeracha, 1988.

Porter, Roy, 'Cleaning up the great wen: public health in eighteenth-century London', *Medical History Supplement*, 11, 1991, pp. 61–75.

Preston, Samuel & Haines, Michael, *Fatal Years: Child Mortality in Late Nineteenth-Century America*, Princeton University Press, NJ, 1991.

Raftery, Judith, 'Keeping healthy in nineteenth century Australia', *Health and History*, 1:4, 1999, pp. 274–97.

Razzell, Peter, *The Conquest of Smallpox*, Caliban Books, London, 1977.

——, 'The conundrum of eighteenth-century English population growth', *Social History of Medicine*, 11, 1998, pp. 469–500.

——, *Essays in English population history*, Caliban Books, London, 1994.

Richards, Eric, 'A voice from below: Benjamin Boyce in South Australia, 1839–1846', *Labour History*, November 1974, pp. 61–72.

Risse, Günter B, 'Cause of death as a historical problem', *Continuity and Change*, 12:2, 1997, pp. 175–88.

Roberts, Pat (ed.), *Emily's Journal: the Welch Letters*, Lutheran Publishing House, Adelaide, 1986.

Rose, Lionel, *Massacre of the Innocents: Infanticide in Great Britain 1800–1939*, Routledge, London, 1986.

Rosenberg, Harry M, 'Cause of Death as a Contemporary Problem', in *Journal of the History of Medicine and Allied Sciences*, 54:2, April 1999, pp. 133–53.

Ryan Johansson, S, 'Putting Death in Its Place: A Review Essay', *Historical Methods*, 32:4, Fall 1999, pp. 189–92.

Scally, Robert, 'Liverpool and Irish emigrants in the age of sail', *Journal of Social History*, XVII, 1983, pp. 5–30.

Shlomowitz, Ralph, 'Infant mortality and Fiji's Indian Migrants, 1879–1919', *Indian Economic and Social History Review*, 23, 1986, pp. 289–302.

——, *Mortality and Migration in the Modern World*, Variorum, London, 1996.

Sigsworth, Michael & Worboys, Michael, 'The public's view of public health in mid-Victorian Britain, *Urban History*, 21:2, October 1994, pp. 237–50.

Smith, FB, 'Comprehending Diphtheria', *Health and History*, 1:2&3, 1999, pp. 138–61.

——, *The People's Health 1830–1910*, Croom Helm, London, 1979.

——, *The Retreat of Tuberculosis, 1850–1950*, Croom Helm, London, 1988.

Smith, VS, 'Cleanliness, idea and practice in Britain, 1770–1850', unpublished PhD Thesis, University of London, 1985.

Staniforth, Mark, 'Care and control: Female convict transportation voyages to Van Diemen's Land, 1818–1853', *The Great Circle*, 16:1, 1994, pp. 23–42

——, 'Dangerous voyages? Aspects of the emigrant experience on the voyage to Australia 1837–1839', unpublished MA thesis, University of Sydney, 1993.

——, 'Deficiency disorder: Evidence of the occurrence of scurvy on convict and emigrant ships to Australia 1837–1839', *The Great Circle*, 13:2, pp. 119–32.

——, 'Diet, disease and death at sea on the voyage to Australia, 1837–1839', *International Journal of Maritime History*, VIII:2, December 1996, pp. 119–56.

Statton, Jill (ed.), *Biographical Index of South Australians, 1836–1839*, Genealogical and Heraldry Society, Adelaide, 1986.

Sundin, Jan, 'Child mortality and causes of death in a Swedish city, 1750–1860', *Historical Methods*, 29:3, Summer 1996, pp. 93–106.

Szreter, Simon, *Fertility, class and gender in Britain, 1860–1940*, Cambridge University Press, 1998.

——, 'Economic growth, disruption, deprivation, disease, and death: On the importance of the politics of public health for development', *Population and Development Review*, 23:4, December 1997, pp. 693–728.

——, 'The importance of social intervention in Britain's mortality decline c1850–1914: a re-interpretation of the role of public health', *Social History of Medicine*, 2, 1988, pp. 1–37.

——, 'Rapid population growth and security: urbanisation and economic growth in Britain in the Nineteenth Century', *Common Security Forum: Centre for History and Economics*, unpublished paper, June 1995.

—— & Mooney, Graham, 'Urbanization, mortality, and the standard of living debate: new estimates of the expectation of life at birth in nineteenth-century cities', *Economic History Review*, LI:1, 1998, pp. 84–112.

Thomas, Neil (ed.), *And the dog came too: Being an Account of a voyage from London to South Australia on the ship Templar in 1845 by Eliza Randall*, Libraries Board of South Australia, Adelaide, 2001.

Tomes, Nancy, *The Gospel of Germs: Men, Women, and the Microbe in American Life*, Harvard University Press, Harvard, 1998.

——, 'The Private Side of Public Health: Sanitary Science, Domestic Hygiene, and the Germ Theory, 1870–1900', *Bulletin of the History of Medicine*, 64, 1990, pp. 509–39.

Williams, Naomi, 'The reporting and classification of causes of death in mid-nineteenth century England', *Historical Methods*, Spring 1996, 29:2, pp. 58–70.

—— 'Death in its season: class, environment and the mortality of infants in nineteenth-century Sheffield', *Social History of Medicine*, 5, 1992, pp. 71–94.

—— & Mooney, Graham, 'Infant mortality in an "Age of Great Cities": London and the English provincial cities compared, c1840–1910', *Continuity and Change*, 9:2, 1994, pp. 185–212.

Wohl, Anthony S, *Endangered Lives: Public Health in Victorian Britain*, Methuen, London, 1983.

Woodruff, Philip, *Two Million South Australians*, Peacock Publications, Adelaide, 1984.

Woods, Robert & Shelton, Nicola, *An Atlas of Victorian Mortality*, Liverpool University Press, 1997.

Woods, RI, Watterson, PA & Woodward, JH, 'The causes of rapid infant mortality decline in England and Wales, 1861–1921' Part 1, *Population Studies*, 42, 1988, pp. 343–66.

——, 'The causes of rapid infant mortality decline in England and Wales, 1861–1921. Part II, *Population Studies*, 43, 1989, pp. 113–32.

Woolcock, Helen, 'Medical supervision on nineteenth century emigrant ships: The voyage of the 'Clifton', 1861–1862', in John Pearn (ed.), *Pioneer Medicine in Australia*, Amphion Press, Brisbane, 1988.

——, *Rights of Passage: Emigration to Australia in the Nineteenth Century*, Tavistock Press, London, 1986.

Index